The American Founding: Core Documents

The American Founding: Core Documents

Selected and Introduced by

Gordon Lloyd

Ashbrook Press

Library of Congress Cataloging-in-Publication Data

The American Founding: Core Documents;
Selected and Introduced by Gordon Lloyd

p. cm.
Includes Index
1. United States – Politics and government.

ISBN 978-1-878802-33-0
(pbk.)

Ashbrook Center at Ashland University
401 College Avenue
Ashland, Ohio 44805
www.ashbrook.org

First edition
2 3 4 5 6 7 8 9 10

ABOUT THE ASHBROOK CENTER

The Ashbrook Center restores and strengthens the capacities of the American people for constitutional self-government. Ashbrook teaches students and teachers across our country what America is and what she represents in the long history of the world. Offering a variety of resources and programs, Ashbrook is the largest university-based educator in the enduring principles and practice of free government. Dedicated in 1983 by President Ronald Reagan, the Ashbrook Center is governed by its own board and responsible for raising all of the funds necessary for its many programs.

BRING THE DOCUMENTS AND DEBATES OF THE NATION'S PAST INTO THE PRESENT

Readers of this volume may be particularly interested in Ashbrook's Teaching American History programs which provide an opportunity for secondary educators to explore themes in American history and self-government through the study of original historical documents. Designed especially for teachers, our seminar-style programs are offered online and on location, both on our campus and at sites around the country. We use discussions, not lectures and texts, not textbooks, so that each seminar is a conversation among peers in which each attendee is an active participant in learning.

For more information, please visit us online at Ashbrook.org, TeachingAmericanHistory.org, and ReligionInAmerica.org.

Contents

General Editor's Introduction

This collection of documents on the founding of the United States inaugurates a new series of document collections from the Ashbrook Center that will cover major periods, themes, and institutions in American history and government. When complete, the series will be comprehensive, and also authoritative, because it will present America's story in the words of those who wrote it — America's presidents, labor leaders, farmers, philosophers, industrialists, politicians, workers, explorers, religious leaders, judges, soldiers; its slaveholders and abolitionists; its expansionists and isolationists; its reformers and stand-patters; its strict and broad constructionists; its hard-eyed realists and visionary utopians — all united in their commitment to equality and liberty, yet all also divided often by their different understandings of these most fundamental American ideas. The documents are about all this — the still unfinished American experiment with self-government. There is no better place to begin to understand that experiment than with these documents from the American founding.

As this volume does, each of the volumes in the series will contain key documents on its period, theme, or institution, selected by an expert and reviewed by an editorial board. Each volume will have an introduction highlighting key documents and themes. In an appendix to each volume, there will also be a thematic table of contents, showing the connections between various documents. Another appendix will provide study questions for each document, as well as questions that refer to other documents in the collection, tying them together as the thematic table of contents does. Each volume may have, as this volume does, additional material in appendices to aid in understanding the documents. Each document will be checked against an authoritative original source and have an introduction outlining its significance. We will provide notes to each document to identify people, events, movements, or ideas that may be unfamiliar to non-specialist readers and to improve understanding of the document's historical context.

In sum, our intent is that the documents and their supporting material provide reliable and unique access to the richness of the American story.

Gordon Lloyd, Senior Fellow at the Ashbrook Center, selected the documents and wrote the introductions. Ellen Tucker and Josh Distel edited the collection. Lisa Ormiston of the Ashbrook Center oversaw production. Chris Burkett of Ashland University and Christopher Flannery of Azusa Pacific University answered questions and offered advice.

David Tucker
Senior Fellow
Ashbrook Center

Introduction

This volume presents some of the documents necessary to understand the essential ideas and debates that shaped the founding of the American civic order. All reflection upon and action within that civic order, if they are to do any good, must rest on an understanding of these debates and ideas.

The volume opens with four documents that set the stage for the central drama of the Founding, the debates in the Constitutional Convention. The Virginia Declaration of Rights and the Virginia Constitution (1776) express some of the central ideas that justified the Revolution. These ideas appear in one form or another throughout the documents of the Founding period. They appear in Jefferson's Draft of the Declaration of Independence (Document 2), written less than a month after Virginia adopted its Bill of Rights and Constitution. Jefferson's Draft of the Declaration also raised the issue of slavery, an issue that would prove to be both central and problematic in the debates at the Constitutional Convention (Documents 6, 11, 13, and 14). Document 3 is the Articles of Confederation, the system of government under which the states fought for their independence, but which proved defective in the eyes of many Americans. James Madison summarized these defects in his 1787 memorandum, "Vices of the Political System of the United States" (Document 4).

Madison's memorandum, written in preparation for the convention, best shows how the mood of the Revolutionary generation had shifted from hope to concern in the decade following the writing of the Declaration. For most of those years, the revolutionary struggle itself overshadowed realization of the political challenges that would face the new republic of federated states. After peace was declared, disagreements and discontents relating to unpaid war debts, protectionist trade measures unilaterally imposed by individual states, and other matters threatened the unity of the nation and effectiveness of its central government. Madison suggested a special meeting, to be held outside of the Continental Congress, to resolve the interstate trade issues. The meeting occurred in Annapolis, Maryland in 1786. Only five states sent delegates, however, and the Annapolis meeting ended with a call for a Constitutional Convention. Anticipating this convention, George Washington wrote to Madison expressing his wish that "the Convention may adopt no temporizing expedient, but probe the defects of the Constitution to the bottom, and provide radical cures, whether they are agreed to or not." This was the prompt Madison needed to write his memo. It became, in effect, the first draft of his famous defense of the extended republic in *Federalist* 10 (Document 20), one of a series of essays that Madison, Alexander Hamilton and John Jay wrote to defend the Constitution and secure its ratification.

Madison, Washington, and Hamilton, among others, had grasped that a fundamental ambiguity lay at the heart of the Articles of Confederation. Article III stated that the union of the states was to be "a firm league of friendship," and Article XIII declared that "the union shall be perpetual." Yet, according to Article II, each state retained every power that was not "expressly delegated" to the Congress. Madison criticized the Articles because they lacked "the great vital principles of a Political Constitution," namely, "sanction" and "coercion." The "evil" that alarmed him the most was that individual rights were being violated by unjust majorities in the state legislatures. Focusing on this problem, Madison redirected the long-standing American conversation about rights. Instead of securing the rights of the people against the unrestrained conduct of monarchs and aristocrats, the new challenge was to secure the rights of minorities against omnipotent majorities in the legislative branch. He challenged "the efficacy" of such traditional republican solutions as "a prudent regard" for the common good, "respect for character," and the restraints provided by religion. Instead, he argued, "a modification of the Sovereignty" was needed. The solution was to create an extended republic in which a multiplicity of opinions, passions, and interests "check each other."

Before Madison and others could defend the proposed constitution, it had to be drafted. Documents 5 through 15 are excerpted from Madison's account of the debate in the Constitutional Convention that met from May 25 to September 17, 1787, in Philadelphia. We are under no illusion that a reader's favorite exchanges or speeches at the Constitutional Convention will necessarily be included in this collection. The June 6, 1787 exchange between Madison and Sherman as well as Franklin's "More Perfect Union" speech on September 17, 1787 come to mind; both illuminate the essential issues at stake at the Convention. (The former is actually anticipated in Madison's *Vices* and most fully articulated in *Federalist* 10, both of which are included in this collection.) But to supply these absences, we are publishing a separate collection of documents on the Convention. We will also publish a separate collection of documents on the ratification debate, a volume that includes documents from selected state ratifying conventions as well as a greater selection of writings by those who supported and opposed ratification.

Yet we do include in this volume some writings from the debate over ratification (Documents 16 through 23). The most fundamental question these writings discuss is what a republic is, and therefore what kind of republican government is best. All the disputants agreed that, as the Declaration declared, all men are equal and thus must be governed only with their consent. But how must a republic and its government be structured so that self-government does not become tyranny or anarchy?

Document 24 is an exchange of letters between Madison and Thomas Jefferson, who was serving in Paris as America's Ambassador to France during the Constitutional Convention and ratification process. Among other things, the two men discussed the need to add a bill of rights to the new Constitution. The lack of such a bill was a principal reason Antifederalists opposed the work of the convention. In their correspondence, Madison explained to Jefferson that the extended republic would secure the civil and religious rights of individuals from the danger of majority faction. Jefferson responded favorably two months later. He was troubled, however, by claims that a bill of rights was unnecessary. He reminded Madison that "a bill of rights is what the people are entitled to against every government on earth, general or particular; and what no just government should refuse, or rest on inference." He listed six essential rights that should be declared: "freedom of religion, freedom of the press, protection against standing armies, restriction of monopolies, the eternal and unremitting force of the habeas corpus laws, and trials by jury in all matters." Upon being informed by Madison that the Constitution had been adopted, he reiterated his list of six rights.

George Washington mentioned the need for a bill of rights in his First Inaugural address (Document 25) and Madison, persuaded by Jefferson, argued forcefully for a guarantee of these rights in a speech to the new House of Representatives on June 8, 1789 (Document 26). These final two documents also show the new experiment in self-government at work, and thus bring to a fitting close the story of the American Founding.

Taken as a whole, the documents in this volume express six important themes in the American Founding. 1) How should a Constitution distribute the powers of government between the national government and the states? Should it follow the Articles of Confederation, in enumerating these powers, as the New Jersey Plan does? Or should it leave them largely unspecified, like the Virginia Plan? 2) How should a Constitution allow for representation of the various participants—or interests—in the "scheme" to be devised? 3) Does a small territorial size, along with the virtue and homogeneity of the citizenry, matter for the well-being of a republic? Or should we move toward an extended commercial republic? 4) How might bicameralism and the separation of powers contribute toward effective government that still honors citizens' freedoms? And how separate do the powers need to be to ensure that one branch of government does not encroach on another? 5) What are the sources of faction, and do we eliminate its cause or control its effects? 6) How important is a bill of rights to preserving federal decentralization and republican liberty?

The framers who met in the Constitutional Convention, the citizens who debated whether the resulting Constitution should be ratified, and the legislators who hammered out the first 10 amendments to it — the Bill of Rights — answered these questions. Yet in one form or another they continue to animate American political life.

To enhance the clarity of the documents for today's readers, we have sometimes modernized spelling, capitalization or punctuation (although we refrained from doing so in the case of iconic documents such as the Declaration and Constitution, since in those cases a long publication history has preserved the original usage). We have footnoted individuals and events that might not be known to the modern reader. In addition, we have provided several appendices to give further context for the documents. One of these is a thematic table of contents that highlights the stages in the deliberations during the Founding.

A Note on Usage:

In recording the debates at the Convention, Madison uses the terms "house" and "branch" interchangeably with reference to what would become the House of Representatives and the Senate. To modern ears, "branch" connotes the three divisions of our government (legislative, executive, and judicial). However, to respect the language used by Madison and the delegates, we generally use the term "legislative branches" when speaking of the two houses of Congress.

While a few delegates, following the British way of thinking, used the terms "upper" and "lower" to distinguish between what we call the House and the Senate, most delegates preferred to speak of the House of Representatives as the "first" branch of the legislature and of the Senate as the "second" branch.

The terms "upper" and "lower" carried an aristocratic connotation. Madison and many other delegates preferred the more democratic terminology of "first" and "second."

The American Founding: Core Documents

Document 1

Virginia Declaration of Rights and Constitution

June 12 and 29, 1776

The Virginia Declaration of Rights was adopted by the House of Burgesses in June, 1776. Among the delegates were George Mason, the most important contributor, and twenty-five-year-old James Madison, who drafted the section on the "free exercise of religion." Also present at the creation of the Virginia Declaration and Constitution were John Blair and Edmund Randolph. Eleven years later, these four delegates were chosen to the seven-member Virginia delegation to the Constitutional Convention.

The "rights" listed in the first five sections might strike the contemporary reader as odd; it is important to remember, however, that among the most fundamental rights articulated by the revolutionary generation was the right of the people to choose their form of government. Note the articulation of the separation of powers doctrine. Sections six through fourteen cover familiar ground. Most of the civil rights and criminal procedures listed were part of the Americanized version of the "rights of Englishmen" tradition. Section fifteen reflects the traditional republican argument that free government could survive only if the people were virtuous. Because colonial America turned to religion to perform this important political function, there was a presumption that religion had an "established" status. In 1776, the Anglican Church was the established church of Virginia, and there is nothing in the Virginia Declaration of Rights that challenges this establishment. On the other hand, Madison incorporated into Section sixteen an argument for the free exercise of religion, claiming that "the duty which we owe to our CREATOR, and the manner of discharging it, can be directed only by reason and conviction, not by force or violence." This assertion challenges the establishment of any particular sect, even for the purpose of inculcating the morality that Madison himself elsewhere argued was essential to republican government.

The same Convention also framed and adopted the Virginia Constitution. The first, and longest, section anticipates the Declaration of Independence: Twenty-one separate indictments are listed against King George. Section two provides the authorization for establishing a new foundation. Sections three through eight and ten through twelve pertain to the bicameral legislature; and most of the remaining sections focus on the election, appointment, or removal of executive and judicial officers. Section twenty-one lays the foundation for the Northwest Ordinance, by ceding western lands disputed between Virginia and other states to the latter, and by anticipating the creation of new states in the western territory Virginia still held title to. (The ordinance, which laid the plan for settling the western territory and admitting sections of it as new states, would be passed by the Confederation Congress in 1787.)

The Arabic numerals identifying the separate sections of the Declaration of Rights *are in the original. We have followed W. W. Hening,* Statutes at Large *(Richmond: George Cochran, 1823 [IX: 109-119]) and added section numbers to the Virginia Constitution. These sections are identified by Roman numerals.*

A DECLARATION OF RIGHTS made by the representatives of the good people of Virginia, assembled in full and free Convention; which rights do pertain to them and their posterity, as the basis and foundation of government.

1. THAT all men are by nature equally free and independent, and have certain inherent rights, of which, when they enter into a state of society, they cannot, by any compact, deprive or divest their posterity; namely, the enjoyment of life and liberty, with the means of acquiring and possessing property, and pursuing and obtaining happiness and safety.

2. That all power is vested in, and consequently derived from, the people; that magistrates are their trustees and servants, and at all times amenable to them.

3. That government is, or ought to be, instituted for the common benefit, protection, and security of the people, nation, or community; of all the various modes and forms of government, that is best, which is capable of producing the greatest degree of happiness and safety, and is most effectually secured against the danger of maladministration; and that whenever any government shall be found inadequate or contrary to these purposes, a majority of the community hath an indubitable, unalienable, and indefeasible right, to reform, alter, or abolish it, in such manner as shall be judged most conducive to the public weal.[1]

4. That no man, or set of men, are entitled to exclusive or separate emoluments and privileges from the community, but in consideration of public

---

[1] welfare

services; which, not being descendible,[2] neither ought the offices of magistrate, legislator, or judge to be hereditary.

5. That the legislative and executive powers of the State should be separate and distinct from the judiciary; and that the members of the two first may be restrained from oppression, by feeling and participating the burthens[3] of the people, they should, at fixed periods, be reduced to a private station, return into that body from which they were originally taken, and the vacancies be supplied by frequent, certain, and regular elections, in which all, or any part of the former members, to be again eligible, or ineligible, as the laws shall direct.

6. That elections of members to serve as representatives of the people, in assembly, ought to be free; and that all men, having sufficient evidence of permanent common interest with, and attachment to, the community, have the right of suffrage, and cannot be taxed or deprived of their property for public uses without their own consent, or that of their representative so elected, nor bound by any law to which they have not, in like manner, assented, for the public good.

7. That all power of suspending laws, or the execution of laws, by any authority, without consent of the representatives of the people, is injurious to their rights, and ought not to be exercised.

8. That in all capital or criminal prosecutions a man hath a right to demand the cause and nature of his accusation, to be confronted with the accusers and witnesses, to call for evidence in his favor, and to a speedy trial by an impartial jury of twelve men of his vicinage,[4] without whose unanimous consent he cannot be found guilty, nor can he be compelled to give evidence against himself; that no man be deprived of his liberty, except by the law of the land or the judgment of his peers.

9. That excessive bail ought not to be required, nor excessive fines imposed, nor cruel and unusual punishments inflicted.

10. That general warrants, whereby any officer or messenger may be commanded to search suspected places without evidence of a fact committed, or to seize any person or persons not named, or whose offence is not particularly described and supported by evidence, are grievous and oppressive, and ought not to be granted.

---

[2] able to descend to an heir

[3] burdens

[4] living in the same area or neighborhood

11. That in controversies respecting property, and in suits between man and man, the ancient trial by jury is preferable to any other, and ought to be held sacred.

12. That the freedom of the press is one of the great bulwarks of liberty, and can never be restrained but by despotic governments.

13. That a well regulated militia, composed of the body of the people, trained to arms, is the proper, natural, and safe defense of a free state; that standing armies, in time of peace, should be avoided, as dangerous to liberty; and that, in all cases, the military should be under strict subordination to, and governed by, the civil power.

14. That the people have a right to uniform government; and therefore, that no government separate from, or independent of, the government of Virginia, ought to be erected or established within the limits thereof.

15. That no free government, or the blessing of liberty, can be preserved to any people, but by a firm adherence to justice, moderation, temperance, frugality, and virtue, and by frequent recurrence to fundamental principles.

16. That religion, or the duty which we owe to our CREATOR, and the manner of discharging it, can be directed only by reason and conviction, not by force or violence, and therefore all men are equally entitled to the free exercise of religion, according to the dictates of conscience; and that it is the mutual duty of all to practice Christian forbearance, love, and charity, towards each other.

Virginia Constitution

The CONSTITUTION or FORM of GOVERNMENT, agreed to and resolved upon by the Delegates and Representatives of the several counties and corporations of Virginia.

I. WHEREAS George the third, King of Great Britain and Ireland, and elector of Hanover, heretofore entrusted with the exercise of the kingly office in this government, hath endeavored to pervert the same into a detestable and insupportable tyranny, by putting his negative on laws the most wholesome and necessary for the public good:

By denying his governors permission to pass laws of immediate and pressing importance, unless suspended in their operation for his assent, and, when so suspended, neglecting to attend to them for many years:

By refusing to pass certain other laws, unless the persons to be benefitted by them would relinquish the inestimable right of representation in the legislature:

By dissolving legislative Assemblies repeatedly and continually, for opposing with manly firmness his invasions of the rights of the people:

When dissolved, by refusing to call others for a long space of time, thereby leaving the political system without any legislative head:

By endeavoring to prevent the population of our country, and, for that purpose, obstructing the laws for the naturalization of foreigners:

By keeping among us, in times of peace, standing armies and ships of war:

By affecting to render the military independent of, and superior to, the civil power:

By combining with others to subject us to a foreign jurisdiction, giving his assent to their pretended acts of legislation:

For quartering large bodies of armed troops among us:

For cutting off our trade with all parts of the world:

For imposing taxes on us, without our consent:

For depriving us of the benefits of trial by jury:

For transporting us beyond seas, to be tried for pretended offences:

For suspending our own legislatures, and declaring themselves invested with power to legislate for us in all cases whatsoever:

By plundering our seas, ravaging our coasts, burning our towns, and destroying the lives of our people:

By inciting insurrections of our fellow subjects, with the allurements of forfeiture and confiscation:

By prompting our negroes to rise in arms among us, those very negroes whom, by an inhuman use of his negative, he hath refused us permission to exclude by law:

By endeavoring to bring on the inhabitants of our frontiers the merciless Indian savages, whose known rule of warfare is an undistinguished destruction of all ages, sexes, and conditions of existence:

By transporting, at this time, a large army of foreign mercenaries, to complete the works of death, desolation, and tyranny, already begun with circumstances of cruelty and perfidy unworthy the head of a civilized nation:

By answering our repeated petitions for redress with a repetition of injuries:

And finally, by abandoning the helm of government, and declaring us out of his allegiance and protection.

By which several acts of misrule, the government of this country, as formerly exercised under the crown of Great Britain, is TOTALLY DISSOLVED.

II. We therefore, the delegates and representatives of the good people of Virginia, having maturely considered the premises, and viewing with great concern the deplorable condition to which this once happy country must be reduced, unless some regular, adequate mode of civil polity is speedily adopted, and in compliance with a recommendation of the General Congress, do ordain and declare the future form of government of Virginia to be as follows:

III. The legislative, executive, and judiciary departments, shall be separate and distinct, so that neither exercise the powers properly belonging to the other; nor shall any person exercise the powers of more than one of them at the same time, except that the justices of the county courts shall be eligible to either House of Assembly.

IV. The legislative shall be formed of two distinct branches, who, together, shall be a complete legislature. They shall meet once, or oftener, every year, and shall be called the GENERAL ASSEMBLY OF VIRGINIA.

V. One of these shall be called the HOUSE OF DELEGATES, and consist of two representatives to be chosen for each county, and for the District of West-Augusta, annually, of such men as actually reside in, and are freeholders of the same, or duly qualified according to law, and also of one delegate or representative to be chosen annually for the city of Williamsburg, and one for the borough of Norfolk, and a representative for each of such other cities and boroughs as may hereafter be allowed particular representation by the legislature; but when any city or borough shall so decrease as that the number of persons having right of suffrage therein shall have been for the space of seven years successively less than half the number of voters in some one county in Virginia, such city or borough thenceforward shall cease to send a delegate or representative to the Assembly.

VI. The other shall be called the SENATE, and consist of twenty four members, of whom thirteen shall constitute a House to proceed on business, for whose election the different counties shall be divided into twenty four districts, and each county of the respective district, at the time of the election of its delegates, shall vote for one Senator, who is actually a resident and freeholder within the district, or duly qualified according to law, and is upwards of twenty five years of age; and the sheriffs of each county within five days at farthest after the last county election in the district, shall meet at some convenient place, and from the poll so taken in their respective counties return as a Senator the man who shall have the greatest number of votes in the whole district. To keep up this Assembly by rotation, the districts shall be equally divided into four classes, and numbered by lot. At the end of one year after the general election, the six members elected by the first division shall be displaced, and the vacancies thereby occasioned supplied from such class or division, by new election, in the manner aforesaid. This rotation shall be applied to each division, according to its number, and continued in due order annually.

VII. The right of suffrage in the election of members for both Houses shall remain as exercised at present, and each House shall choose its own speaker, appoint its own officers, settle its own rules of proceeding, and direct writs of election for supplying intermediate vacancies.

VIII. All laws shall originate in the House of Delegates, to be approved or rejected by the Senate, or to be amended with the consent of the House of Delegates; except money bills, which in no instance shall be altered by the Senate, but wholly approved or rejected.

IX. A Governor, or chief magistrate, shall be chosen annually, by joint ballot of both Houses, to be taken in each House respectively, deposited in the conference room, the boxes examined jointly by a committee of each house, and the numbers severally reported to them, that the appointments may be entered (which shall be the mode of taking the joint ballot of both Houses in all cases) who shall not continue in that office longer than three years successively, nor be eligible until the expiration of four years after he shall have been out of that office. An adequate, but moderate salary, shall be settled on him during his continuance in office; and he shall, with the advice of a Council of State, exercise the executive powers of government according to the laws of this commonwealth; and shall not, under any pretense, exercise any power or prerogative by virtue of any law, statute, or custom, of England: But he shall, with the advice of the Council of State, have the power of granting reprieves or pardons, except where the prosecution shall have been carried on by the House of Delegates, or the law shall otherwise particularly direct; in which cases, no reprieve or pardon shall be granted, but by resolve of the House of Delegates.

X. Either House of the General Assembly may adjourn themselves respectively. The Governor shall not prorogue[5] or adjourn the Assembly during their sitting, nor dissolve them at any time; but he shall, if necessary, either by advice of the Council of State, or on application of a majority of the House of Delegates, call them before the time to which they shall stand prorogued or adjourned.

---

[5] discontinue or postpone the meetings of

XI. A Privy Council, or Council of State, consisting of eight members, shall be chosen by joint ballot of both Houses of Assembly, either from their own members or the people at large, to assist in the administration of government. They shall annually choose out of their own members a president, who, in case of the death, inability, or necessary absence of the Governor from the government, shall act as Lieutenant Governor. Four members shall be sufficient to act, and their advice and proceedings shall be entered on record; and signed by the members present (to any part whereof any member may enter his dissent) to be laid before the General Assembly, when called for by them. This Council may appoint their own clerk, who shall have a salary settled by law, and take an oath of secrecy in such matters as he shall be directed by the board to conceal. A sum of money appropriated to that purpose shall be divided annually among the members, in proportion to their attendance; and they shall be incapable, during their continuance in office, of sitting in either House of Assembly. Two members shall be removed by joint ballot of both Houses of Assembly at the end of every three years, and be ineligible for the three next years. These vacancies, as well as those occasioned by death or incapacity, shall be supplied by new elections, in the same manner.

XII. The delegates for Virginia to the Continental Congress shall be chosen annually, or superseded in the mean time by joint ballot of both Houses of Assembly.

XIII. The present militia officers shall be continued, and vacancies supplied by appointment of the Governor, with the advice of the Privy Council, or recommendations from the respective county courts; but the Governor and Council shall have a power of suspending any officer, and ordering a court-martial on complaint for misbehavior or inability, or to supply vacancies of officers happening when in actual service. The Governor may embody the militia, with the advice of the Privy Council; and, when embodied, shall alone have the direction of the militia under the laws of the country.

XIV. The two Houses of Assembly shall, by joint ballot, appoint Judges of the Supreme Court of Appeals, and General Court, Judges in Chancery, Judges of Admiralty, Secretary, and the Attorney-General, to be commissioned by the Governor, and continue in office during good behavior. In case of death, incapacity, or resignation, the Governor, with the advice of the Privy Council, shall appoint persons to succeed in office, to be approved or displaced by both Houses. These officers shall have fixed and adequate salaries, and, together with all others holding lucrative offices, and all ministers of the Gospel of every denomination, be incapable of being elected members of either House of assembly, or the Privy Council.

XV. The Governor, with the advice of the Privy Council, shall appoint Justices of the Peace for the counties; and in case of vacancies, or a necessity of increasing the number hereafter, such appointments to be made upon the recommendation of the respective county courts. The present acting Secretary in Virginia, and Clerks of all the County Courts, shall continue in office. In case of vacancies, either by death, incapacity, or resignation, a Secretary shall be appointed as before directed, and the Clerks by the respective courts. The present and future Clerks shall hold their offices during good behavior, to be judged of and determined in the General Court. The Sheriffs and Coroners shall be nominated by the respective courts, approved by the Governor, with the advice of the Privy Council, and commissioned by the Governor. The Justices shall appoint Constables, and all fees of the aforesaid officers be regulated by law.

XVI. The Governor, when he is out of office, and others offending against the state, either by maladministration, corruption, or other means by which the safety of the state may be endangered, shall be impeachable by the House of Delegates. Such impeachment to be prosecuted by the Attorney-General, or such other person or persons as the House may appoint in the General Court, according to the laws of the land. If found guilty, he or they shall be either for ever disabled to hold any office under government, or removed from such Office *pro tempore*,[6] or subjected to such pains or penalties as the laws shall direct.

XVII. If all, or any of the Judges of the General Court, shall, on good grounds (to be judged of by the House of Delegates) be accused of any of the crimes or offences before-mentioned, such House of Delegates may, in like manner, impeach the Judge or Judges so accused, to be prosecuted in the Court of Appeals; and he or they, if found guilty, shall be punished in the same manner as is prescribed in the preceding clause.

XVIII. Commissions and grants shall run, *In the name of the COMMONWEALTH of VIRGINIA*, and bear test by the Governor with the seal of the commonwealth annexed. Writs shall run in the same manner, and bear test by the clerks of the several courts. Indictments shall conclude, *Against the peace and dignity of the commonwealth.*

XIX. A treasurer shall be appointed annually, by joint ballot of both Houses.

---

[6] temporarily

XX. All escheats,[7] penalties, and forfeitures, heretofore going to the king, shall go to the commonwealth, save only such as the legislature may abolish, or otherwise provide for.

XXI. The territories contained within the charters erecting the colonies of Maryland, Pennsylvania, North and South Carolina, are hereby ceded, released, and for ever confirmed to the people of those colonies respectively, with all the rights of property, jurisdiction, and government, and all other rights whatsoever which might at any time heretofore have been claimed by Virginia, except the free navigation and use of the rivers Potowmack[8] and Pohomoke[9], with the property of the Virginia shores or strands bordering on either of the said rivers, and all improvements which have been or shall be made thereon. The western and northern extent of Virginia shall in all other respects stand as fixed by the Charter of King James the first, in the year one thousand six hundred and nine, and by the public treaty of peace between the courts of Great Britain and France in the year one thousand seven hundred and sixty three; unless by act of legislature, one or more territories shall hereafter be laid off, and governments established westward of the Allegheny mountains. And no purchase of land shall be made of the Indian natives but on behalf of the public, by authority of the General Assembly.

XXII. In order to introduce this government, the representatives of the people met in Convention shall choose a Governor and Privy Council, also such other officers directed to be chosen by both Houses as may be judged necessary to be immediately appointed. The Senate to be first chosen by the people, to continue until the last day of March next, and the other officers until the end of the succeeding session of Assembly. In case of vacancies, the speaker of either House shall issue writs for new elections.

---

[7] reversions of property in absence of a legal heir

[8] Potomac River.

[9] Pocomoke River.

Document 2

Draft of The Declaration of Independence

Thomas Jefferson

July 2 - 4, 1776

Nowhere were the novel, and transcendental, implications of the Declaration so visible as in Jefferson's attempt to include a denunciation of slavery. The Second Continental Congress received a draft of the Declaration from Jefferson that made the British rejection of the petition submitted by the First Continental Congress to end the slave trade one of the grounds for severing ties. However, in order not to offend the sensibilities of the delegates from Georgia and South Carolina, the Congress elected to omit Jefferson's denunciation of slavery from the final declaration. As Jefferson's notes (below) report, northern delegates also smarted under the censure of slavery because "tho' their people have very few slaves themselves yet they had been pretty considerable carriers of them to others." We suggest that the inclusion of such an indictment would have had a profound impact on the continuing American conversation about rights.

In Jefferson's notes on the debate in Congress over the Declaration, he gives a short account of how his draft of the Declaration was amended, afterwards recopying that first draft to show what he originally proposed. This memoir is found in the nine-volume collection, The Writings of Thomas Jefferson, *edited by H. A. Washington (New York: John C. Riker, 1853), which was authorized for publication in 1853 by Congress. We have relied on that edition here, including Jefferson's explanatory note, and underlining, as Jefferson did, the parts of the Declaration deleted by Congress. While Jefferson's original draft relegated the parts inserted by Congress to the margin, we italicize them and place them within brackets in the body of the text.*

Congress proceeded the same day to consider the Declaration of Independence, which had been reported and lain on the table the Friday preceding, and on Monday referred to a committee of the whole. The pusillanimous idea that we had friends in England worth keeping terms with, still haunted the minds of many. For this reason, those passages which conveyed censures on the people of England were struck out, lest they should give them offence. The clause too, reprobating the enslaving the inhabitants of Africa, was struck out in complaisance to[1] South Carolina and Georgia, who had never attempted to restrain the importation of slaves, and who, on the contrary, still wished to continue it. Our northern brethren also, I believe, felt a little tender under those censures; for though their people have very few slaves themselves, yet they had been pretty considerable carriers of them to others. The debates, having taken up the greater parts of the 2d, 3d, and 4th days of July, were, in the evening of the last, closed; the Declaration was reported by the committee, agreed to by the House, and signed by every member present, except Mr. Dickinson.[2] As the sentiments of men are known not only by what they receive, but what they reject also, I will state the form of the Declaration as originally reported. The parts struck out by Congress shall be distinguished by a black line drawn under them; and those inserted by them shall be placed in the margin or in a concurrent column(s).

A Declaration by the Representatives of the United States of America, in General Congress assembled

When, in the course of human events, it becomes necessary for one people to dissolve the political bands which have connected them with another, and to assume among the powers of the earth the separate and equal station to which the laws of nature and of nature's God entitle them, a decent respect to the opinions of mankind requires that they should declare the causes which impel them to the separation.

We hold these truths to be self evident: that all men are created equal; that they are endowed by their creator with {*certain*} <u>inherent and</u> inalienable rights; that among these are life, liberty and the pursuit of happiness; that to secure these rights, governments are instituted among men, deriving their just powers from the consent of the governed; that whenever any form of government becomes destructive of these ends, it is the right of the people to alter or to abolish it, and to institute new government, laying its foundation on

---

[1] in order to respect the feelings of

[2] John Dickinson, at the time a delegate to the Continental Congress from Pennsylvania, refused to sign in part because he still hoped to win a redress of grievances against Britain without resorting to war, and in part because he thought the colonists should draft a governing document prior to declaring independence. He would go on to write the first draft of the Articles of Confederation.

such principles, and organizing its powers in such form, as to them shall seem most likely to effect their safety and happiness. Prudence, indeed, will dictate that governments long established should not be changed for light and transient causes; and accordingly all experience hath shown that mankind are more disposed to suffer while evils are sufferable, than to right themselves by abolishing the forms to which they are accustomed. But when a long train of abuses and usurpations, begun at a distinguished period and pursuing invariably the same object, evinces a design to reduce them under absolute despotism, it is their right, it is their duty to throw off such government, and to provide new guards for their future security. Such has been the patient sufferance of these colonies; and such is now the necessity which constrains them to {*alter*} expunge their former systems of government. The history of the present king of Great Britain is a history of [*repeated*] unremitting injuries and usurpations, among which appears no solitary fact to contradict the uniform tenor of the rest but all have [*all having*] in direct object the establishment of an absolute tyranny over these states. To prove this let facts be submitted to a candid world for the truth of which we pledge a faith yet unsullied by falsehood.

He has refused his assent to laws the most wholesome and necessary for the public good.

He has forbidden his governors to pass laws of immediate and pressing importance, unless suspended in their operation till his assent should be obtained; and, when so suspended, he has utterly neglected to attend to them.

He has refused to pass other laws for the accommodation of large districts of people, unless those people would relinquish the right of representation in the legislature, a right inestimable to them and formidable to the tyrants only.

He has called together legislative bodies at places unusual, uncomfortable, and distant from the depository of their public records, for the sole purpose of fatiguing them into compliance with his measures.

He has dissolved representative houses repeatedly and continually for opposing with manly firmness his invasions on the rights of the people.

He has refused for a long time after such dissolutions to cause others to be elected, whereby the legislative powers, incapable of annihilation, have returned to the people at large for their exercise, the state remaining, in the meantime, exposed to all the dangers of invasion from without and convulsions within.

He has endeavored to prevent the population of these states; for that purpose obstructing the laws for naturalization of foreigners, refusing to pass others to encourage their migrations hither, and raising the conditions of new appropriations of lands.

He has {*obstructed*} suffered the administration of justice totally to cease in some of these states {*by*} refusing his assent to laws for establishing judiciary powers.

He has made *our* judges dependent on his will alone for the tenure of their offices, and the amount and payment of their salaries.

He has erected a multitude of new offices by a self assumed power and sent hither swarms of new officers to harass our people and eat our their substance.

He has kept among us in times of peace standing armies and ships of war without the consent of our legislatures.

He has affected to render the military independent of, and superior to, the civil power.

He has combined with others to subject us to a jurisdiction foreign to our constitutions and unacknowledged by our laws, giving his assent to their acts of pretended legislation for quartering large bodies of armed troops among us; for protecting them by a mock trial from punishment for any murders which they should commit on the inhabitants of these states; for cutting off our trade with all parts of the world; for imposing taxes on us without our consent; for depriving us [*in many cases*] of the benefits of trial by jury; for transporting us beyond seas to be tried for pretended offences; for abolishing the free system of English laws in a neighboring province,[3] establishing therein an arbitrary government, and enlarging its boundaries, so as to render it at once an example and fit instrument for introducing the same absolute rule into these [*colonies*] states; for taking away our charters, abolishing our most valuable laws, and altering fundamentally the forms of our governments; for suspending our own legislatures, and declaring themselves invested with power to legislate for us in all cases whatsoever.

He has abdicated government here {*by declaring us out of his protection and waging war against us.*} withdrawing his governors, and declaring us our of his allegiance and protection.

He has plundered our seas, ravaged our coasts, burnt our towns, and destroyed the lives of our people.

He is at this time transporting large armies of foreign mercenaries to complete the works of death, desolation and tyranny already begun with

---

[3] Canada

circumstances of cruelty and perfidy {*scarcely paralleled in the most barbarous ages, and totally*} unworthy the head of a civilized nation.

He has constrained our fellow citizens taken captive on the high seas, to bear arms against their country, to become the executioners of their friends and brethren, or to fall themselves by their hands.

He has {*excited domestic insurrections among us, and has*} endeavored to bring on the inhabitants of our frontiers the merciless Indian savages, whose known rule of warfare is an undistinguished destruction of all ages, sexes, and conditions of existence.

He has incited treasonable insurrections of our fellow citizens, with the allurements of forfeiture and confiscation of our property.

He has waged cruel war against human nature itself, violating its most sacred rights of life and liberty in the persons of a distant people who never offended him, captivating and carrying them into slavery in another hemisphere or to incur miserable death in their transportation thither. This piratical warfare, the opprobrium of INFIDEL powers, is the warfare of the CHRISTIAN king of Great Britain. Determined to keep open a market where MEN should be bought and sold, he has prostituted his negative for suppressing every legislative attempt to prohibit or to restrain this execrable commerce. And that this assemblage of horrors might want no fact of distinguished die,[4] he is now exciting those very people to rise in arms among us, and to purchase that liberty of which he has deprived them, by murdering the people on whom he also obtruded them: thus paying off former crimes committed against the LIBERTIES of one people, with crimes which he urges them to commit against the LIVES of another.

In every stage of these oppressions we have petitioned for redress in the most humble terms: our repeated petitions have been answered only by repeated injuries. A prince whose character is thus marked by every act which may define a tyrant is unfit to be the ruler of a [*free*] people who mean to be free. Future ages will scarcely believe that the hardiness of one man adventured, within the short compass of twelve years only, to lay a foundation so broad and so undisguised for tyranny over a people fostered and fixed in principle of freedom.

Nor have we been wanting in attentions to our British brethren. We have warned them from time to time of attempts by their legislature to extend {*an*

---

[4] The stamp used to certify documents as authentic pronouncements of the governing authority is sometimes called a "die." By "want no fact of distinguished die," Jefferson may mean "not be lacking an official stamp."

unwarrantable} a jurisdiction over {*us*} these our states. We have reminded them of the circumstances of our emigration and settlement here, no one of which could warrant so strange a pretension: that these were effected at the expense of our own blood and treasure, unassisted by the wealth or the strength of Great Britain: that in constituting indeed our several forms of government, we had adopted one common king, thereby laying a foundation for perpetual league and amity with them: but that submission to their parliament was no part of our constitution, nor ever in idea, if history may be credited: and, we {*have*} appealed to their native justice and magnanimity and {*we have conjured them by*} as well as to the ties of our common kindred to disavow these usurpations which {*would inevitably*} were likely to interrupt our connection and correspondence. They too have been deaf to the voice of justice and of consanguinity, and when occasions have been given them, by the regular course of their laws, of removing from their councils the disturbers of our harmony, they have, by their free election, re-established them in power. At this very time too, they are permitting their chief magistrate to send over not only soldiers of our common blood, but Scotch and foreign mercenaries to invade and destroy us. These facts have given the last stab to agonizing affection, and manly spirit bids us to renounce for ever these unfeeling brethren. We must endeavor to forget our former love for them, and to hold them as we hold the rest of mankind, enemies in war, in peace friends. We might have been a free and a great people together; but a communication of grandeur and of freedom, it seems, is below their dignity. Be it so, since they will have it. The road to happiness and to glory is open to us too. We will tread it apart from them, and {*We must therefore*} acquiesce in the necessity which denounces our eternal separation {*and hold them as we hold the rest of mankind, enemies in war, in peace friends.*}!

Editor: The two final paragraphs, in their original and amended forms, were placed next to each other in H. A. Washington's edition: the original draft appeared in a left hand column, and the amended and final version were placed in a right hand column.

Jefferson's Original draft:

We, therefore, the representatives of the United States of America in General Congress assembled, do in the name, and by the authority of the good people of these states reject and renounce all allegiance and subjection to the kings of Great Britain and all others who may hereafter claim by, through or under them; we utterly dissolve all political connection which may heretofore have subsisted between us and the people or parliament of Great Britain: and finally we do assert and declare these colonies to be free and independent states, and that as free and independent states, they have full power to levy war, conclude peace, contract alliances, establish commerce, and to do all other acts and things which independent states may of right do.

And for the support of this declaration, we mutually pledge to each other our lives, our fortunes, and our sacred honor.

The Amended and Final Version:

We, therefore, the representatives of the United States of America in General Congress assembled, appealing to the supreme judge of the world for the rectitude of our intentions, do in the name, and by the authority of the good people of these colonies, solemnly publish and declare, that these united colonies are, and of right ought to be free and independent states; that they are absolved from all allegiance to the British crown, and that all political connection between them and the state of Great Britain is, and ought to be, totally dissolved; and that as free and independent states, they have full power to levy war, conclude peace, contract alliances, establish commerce and to do all other acts and things which independent states may of right do.

And for the support of this declaration, with a firm reliance on the protection of divine providence, we mutually pledge to each other our lives, our fortunes, and our sacred honor.

Document 3

The Articles of Confederation

1781

The Second Continental Congress not only issued a directive to the colonial legislatures to create new state constitutions; they also initiated the adoption of the first governmental system for the United States. On May 15, 1776, the Second Continental Congress, meeting in Independence Hall, Philadelphia, issued a "Resolve" to the thirteen colonies. And the Second Continental Congress created the first continental system of governance: the Articles of Confederation. The Articles created an "assemblage" of pre-existing states, as opposed to a government over, of, and by individuals. The states received equal representation in the confederation regardless of the size of population. The Articles created a single Congress exercising legislative, executive, and judicial powers, and the powers of this Continental Congress were limited to those expressly enumerated in the Articles. To act, Congress required a super majority of the thirteen states. Only amendments could endow the confederation with powers not expressly granted, and amendments required the approval of all thirteen state legislatures. Because of territorial disputes between two states, the Articles did not come into operation until March 1781.

Representatives Samuel Adams of Massachusetts, John Dickinson of Delaware, Richard Henry Lee of Virginia, and Roger Sherman of Connecticut helped draft the Articles of Confederation. Signers of the Articles included Daniel Carroll of Maryland, John Dickinson, Gouverneur Morris and Robert Morris, both of Pennsylvania, and Roger Sherman, all of whom would later sign the Constitution.

Source: Charles Tansill, ed., Documents Illustrative of the Formation of the Union of the United States *(Washington, DC: Government Printing Office, 1927), 27-37. The Roman numerals identifying each of the thirteen articles are in the original.*

Articles of Confederation and perpetual Union between the states of New Hampshire, Massachusetts-bay, Rhode Island and Providence Plantations, Connecticut, New York, New Jersey, Pennsylvania, Delaware, Maryland, Virginia, North Carolina, South Carolina and Georgia.

Article I. The Stile of this Confederacy shall be "The United States of America".

Article II. Each state retains its sovereignty, freedom, and independence, and every power, jurisdiction, and right, which is not by this Confederation expressly delegated to the United States, in Congress assembled.

Article III. The said States hereby severally enter into a firm league of friendship with each other, for their common defense, the security of their liberties, and their mutual and general welfare, binding themselves to assist each other, against all force offered to, or attacks made upon them, or any of them, on account of religion, sovereignty, trade, or any other pretense whatever. . . .

Article V. For the most convenient management of the general interests of the United States, delegates shall be annually appointed in such manner as the legislatures of each State shall direct, to meet in Congress on the first Monday in November, in every year, with a power reserved to each State to recall its delegates, or any of them, at any time within the year, and to send others in their stead for the remainder of the year.

No State shall be represented in Congress by less than two, nor more than seven members; and no person shall be capable of being a delegate for more than three years in any term of six years; nor shall any person, being a delegate, be capable of holding any office under the United States, for which he, or another for his benefit, receives any salary, fees or emolument of any kind.

Each State shall maintain its own delegates in a meeting of the States, and while they act as members of the committee of the States.

In determining questions in the United States in Congress assembled, each State shall have one vote. . . .

Article VI. No State, without the consent of the United States in Congress assembled, shall send any embassy to, or receive any embassy from, or enter into any conference, agreement, alliance or treaty with any King, Prince or State; nor shall any person holding any office of profit or trust under the United States, or any of them, accept any present, emolument, office or title of any kind whatever from any King, Prince or foreign State; nor shall the United States in Congress assembled, or any of them, grant any title of nobility.

No two or more States shall enter into any treaty, confederation or alliance whatever between them, without the consent of the United States in Congress assembled, specifying accurately the purposes for which the same is to be entered into, and how long it shall continue. . . .

No vessel of war shall be kept up in time of peace by any State, except such number only, as shall be deemed necessary by the United States in Congress assembled, for the defense of such State, or its trade; nor shall any body of forces be kept up by any State in time of peace, except such number only, as in the judgment of the United States in Congress assembled, shall be deemed requisite to garrison the forts necessary for the defense of such State; but every State shall always keep up a well-regulated and disciplined militia, sufficiently armed and accoutered,[1] and shall provide and constantly have ready for use, in public stores, a due number of field pieces and tents, and a proper quantity of arms, ammunition and camp equipage.

No State shall engage in any war without the consent of the United States in Congress assembled, unless such State be actually invaded by enemies . . . .

Article VIII. All charges of war, and all other expenses that shall be incurred for the common defense or general welfare, and allowed by the United States in Congress assembled, shall be defrayed out of a common treasury, which shall be supplied by the several States in proportion to the value of all land within each State, granted or surveyed for any person, as such land and the buildings and improvements thereon shall be estimated according to such mode as the United States in Congress assembled, shall from time to time direct and appoint.

The taxes for paying that proportion shall be laid and levied by the authority and direction of the legislatures of the several States within the time agreed upon by the United States in Congress assembled.

Article IX. The United States, in Congress assembled, shall have the sole and exclusive right and power of determining on peace and war, except in the cases mentioned in the sixth article—of sending and receiving ambassadors—entering into treaties and alliances . . . .

The United States, in Congress assembled, shall have authority to . . . . ascertain the necessary sums of money to be raised for the service of the United States, and to appropriate and apply the same for defraying the public expenses—to borrow money, or emit bills on the credit of the United States, transmitting every half-year to the respective States an account of the sums of money so borrowed or emitted—to build and equip a navy—to agree upon the number of land forces, and to make requisitions from each State for its quota, in proportion to the number of white inhabitants in such State; which requisition shall be binding, and thereupon the legislature of each State shall

---

[1] provided with the appropriate attire and equipment

appoint the regimental officers, raise the men and cloath, arm and equip them in a solid-like manner, at the expense of the United States....

The United States, in Congress assembled, shall never engage in a war, nor grant letters of marque[2] or reprisal in time of peace, nor enter into any treaties or alliances, nor coin money, nor regulate the value thereof, nor ascertain the sums and expenses necessary for the defense and welfare of the United States, or any of them, nor emit bills, nor borrow money on the credit of the United States, nor appropriate money, nor agree upon the number of vessels of war, to be built or purchased, or the number of land or sea forces to be raised, nor appoint a commander in chief of the army or navy, unless nine States assent to the same: nor shall a question on any other point, except for adjourning from day to day be determined, unless by the votes of the majority of the United States in Congress assembled....

Article XIII. Every State shall abide by the determination of the United States in Congress assembled, on all questions which by this confederation are submitted to them. And the Articles of this Confederation shall be inviolably observed by every State, and the Union shall be perpetual; nor shall any alteration at any time hereafter be made in any of them; unless such alteration be agreed to in a Congress of the United States, and be afterwards confirmed by the legislatures of every State....

---

[2] license to capture the ships of another nation—that is, to commit piracy.

Document 4

"Vices of the Political System of the United States"

James Madison

April 1787

George Washington wrote to Madison expressing his wish that "the Convention may adopt no temporizing expedient, but probe the defects of the Constitution to the bottom, and provide radical cures, whether they are agreed to or not." Madison's "Vices" is, in effect, the first draft of his famous defense of the extended republic in Federalist *10. Madison criticized the Articles because they lacked "the great vital principles of a Political Constitution," namely, "sanction," and "coercion." The "evil" that alarmed him the most was that individual rights were being violated by unjust majorities in the state legislatures. Madison shifted the ground of the conversation over rights away from securing the rights of the people against the unrestrained conduct of monarchs and aristocrats to the then unfamiliar ground of securing the rights of minorities from omnipotent majorities. In the process, he questioned the efficacy of such traditional republican solutions as "a prudent regard" for the common good, "respect for character," and the restraints provided by religion. Madison's argument was that rights would not be secure until the constitutional protection the Articles gave to the state legislatures against federal intervention were removed. Madison felt the federal government needed this power to check factious or unjust laws. "A modification of the Sovereignty" was needed. The solution, said Madison, was to create an extended republic in which a multiplicity of opinions, passions, and interests "check each other."*

For the complete original version, including the location of Madison's headings and inserts, see Hunt Gaillard, ed., The Writings of James Madison *(New York: G. P. Putnam's Sons, 1900-1910, I: 319-328). We have followed Philip B. Kurland and Ralph Lerner, eds.,* The Founders' Constitution *(Chicago: University of Chicago Press, 1987), 1:166-169, and placed Madison's section headings in the main body of the text rather than in the margin. We have, however, put the headings in upper case in order to distinguish them clearly from Madison's commentary.*

---

1. FAILURE OF THE STATES TO COMPLY WITH THE CONSTITUTIONAL REQUISITIONS.[1]

This evil has been so fully experienced both during the war and since the peace, results so naturally from the number and independent authority of the States, and has been so uniformly exemplified in every similar Confederacy, that it may be considered as not less radically and permanently inherent in, than it is fatal to the object of, the present System.

2. ENCROACHMENTS BY THE STATES ON THE FEDERAL AUTHORITY.

Examples of this are numerous and repetitions may be foreseen in almost every case where any favorite object of a State shall present a temptation. Among these examples are the wars and Treaties of Georgia with the Indians, the unlicensed compacts between Virginia and Maryland, and between Pennsylvania and New Jersey, the troops raised and to be kept up by Massachusetts.

3. VIOLATIONS OF THE LAW OF NATIONS AND OF TREATIES.

From the number of Legislatures, the sphere of life from which most of their members are taken, and the circumstances under which their legislative business is carried on, irregularities of this kind must frequently happen. Accordingly, not a year has passed without instances of them in some one or other of the States. The Treaty of peace, the treaty with France, the treaty with Holland, have each been violated.[2] The causes of these irregularities must necessarily produce frequent violations of the law of nations in other respects.

As yet foreign powers have not been rigorous in animadverting[3] on us. This moderation, however, cannot be mistaken for a permanent partiality to our faults, or a permanent security against those disputes with other nations, which, being among the greatest of public calamities, it ought to be least in the power of any part of the community to bring on the whole.

4. TRESPASSES OF THE STATES ON THE RIGHTS OF EACH OTHER.

These are alarming symptoms, and may be daily apprehended, as we are admonished by daily experience. See the law of Virginia restricting foreign

---

[1] Under the Articles of Confederation, Congress requested money from the states, which often failed to meet their obligations for the reasons Madison gives in his essay.

[2] Madison refers, apparently, to the Treaty of Paris (1783) that ended the Revolutionary War, the Treaty of Alliance (1778) between the United States and France, and the Treaty of Amity and Commerce (1782) with the Dutch Republic.

[3] taking notice of this and censuring us for it

vessels to certain ports; of Maryland in favor of vessels belonging to her own citizens; of New York in favor of the same.

Paper money, instalments of debts, occlusion of courts,[4] making property a legal tender, may likewise be deemed aggressions on the rights of other States. As the citizens of every State, aggregately taken, stand more or less in the relation of creditors or debtors to the citizens of every other State, acts of the debtor State in favor of debtors affect the creditor State in the same manner, as they do its own citizens, who are, relatively, creditors towards other citizens. This remark may be extended to foreign nations. If the exclusive regulation of the value and alloy of coin was properly delegated to the federal authority, the policy of it equally requires a control on the States in the cases above mentioned. It must have been meant — 1. To preserve uniformity in the circulating medium throughout the nation. 2. To prevent those frauds on the citizens of other States, and the subjects of foreign powers, which might disturb the tranquility at home, or involve the Union in foreign contests.

The practice of many States in restricting the commercial intercourse with other States, and putting their productions and manufactures on the same footing with those of foreign nations, though not contrary to the federal articles, is certainly adverse to the spirit of the Union, and tends to beget retaliating regulations, not less expensive and vexatious in themselves than they are destructive of the general harmony.

5. WANT OF CONCERT IN MATTERS WHERE COMMON INTEREST REQUIRES IT.

This defect is strongly illustrated in the state of our commercial affairs. How much has the national dignity, interest, and revenue, suffered from this cause? Instances of inferior moments are the want of uniformity in the laws concerning naturalization and literary property; of provision for national seminaries;[5] for grants of incorporation for national purposes, for canals and other works of general utility; which may at present be defeated by the perverseness of particular States whose concurrence is necessary.

6. WANT OF GUARANTY TO THE STATES OF THEIR CONSTITUTIONS AND LAWS AGAINST INTERNAL VIOLENCE.

The Confederation is silent on this point, and therefore by the second article the hands of the federal authority are tied. According to Republican Theory, Right and power being both vested in the majority, are held to be synonymous. According to fact and experience, a minority may, in an appeal to

---

[4] closing courts to prevent legal proceedings to recover debts

[5] schools

force, be an overmatch for the majority. 1. If the minority happen to include all such as possess the skill and habits of military life, and such as possess the great pecuniary resources, one third only may conquer the remaining two thirds. 2. One third of those who participate in the choice of the rulers, may be rendered a majority by the accession[6] of those whose poverty excludes them from a right of suffrage, and who for obvious reasons will be more likely to join the standard of sedition than that of the established Government. 3. Where slavery exists, the republican Theory becomes still more fallacious.

7. WANT OF SANCTION TO THE LAWS, AND OF COERCION IN THE GOVERNMENT OF THE CONFEDERACY.

A sanction is essential to the idea of law, as coercion is to that of Government. The federal system being destitute of both, wants the great vital principles of a Political Constitution. Under the form of such a Constitution, it is in fact nothing more than a treaty of amity, of commerce, and of alliance, between independent and Sovereign States. From what cause could so fatal an omission have happened in the articles of Confederation? From a mistaken confidence that the justice, the good faith, the honor, the sound policy of the several legislative assemblies would render superfluous any appeal to the ordinary motives by which the laws secure the obedience of individuals; a confidence which does honor to the enthusiastic virtue of the compilers, as much as the inexperience of the crisis apologizes for their errors. The time which has since elapsed has had the double effect of increasing the light and tempering the warmth with which the arduous work may be revised. It is no longer doubted that a unanimous and punctual obedience of 13 independent bodies to the acts of the federal Government ought not to be calculated on. Even during the war, when external danger supplied in some degree the defect of legal and coercive sanctions, how imperfectly did the States fulfill their obligations to the Union? In time of peace we see already what is to be expected. How, indeed, could it be otherwise? In the first place, every general act of the Union must necessarily bear unequally hard on some particular member or members of it; secondly, the partiality of the members to their own interests and rights, a partiality which will be fostered by the courtiers of popularity, will naturally exaggerate the inequality where it exists, and even suspect it where it has no existence; thirdly, a distrust of the voluntary compliance of each other may prevent the compliance of any, although it should be the latent disposition of all. Here are causes and pretexts which will never fail to render federal measures abortive. If the laws of the States were

---

[6] consent

merely recommendatory to their citizens, or if they were to be rejudged by county authorities, what security, what probability would exist that they would be carried into execution? Is the security or probability greater in favor of the acts of Congress, which, depending for their execution on the will of the State legislatures, which are tho' nominally authoritative, in fact recommendatory only?

8. WANT OF RATIFICATION BY THE PEOPLE OF THE ARTICLES OF CONFEDERATION.

In some of the States the Confederation is recognized by and forms a part of the Constitution. In others, however, it has received no other sanction than that of the Legislative authority. From this defect two evils result: 1. Whenever a law of a State happens to be repugnant to an act of Congress, particularly when the latter is of posterior date to the former, it will be at least questionable whether the latter must not prevail; and as the question must be decided by the Tribunals of the State, they will be most likely to lean on the side of the State. 2. As far as the Union of the States is to be regarded as a league of sovereign powers, and not as a political Constitution, by virtue of which they are become one sovereign power, so far it seems to follow from the doctrine of compacts, that a breach of any of the articles of the confederation by any of the parties to it absolves the other parties from their respective obligations, and gives them a right if they choose to exert it, of dissolving the Union altogether.

9. MULTIPLICITY OF LAWS IN THE SEVERAL STATES.

In developing the evils which viciate the political system of the United States, it is proper to include those which are found within the States individually, as well as those which directly affect the States collectively, since the former class have an indirect influence on the general malady, and must not be overlooked in forming a complete remedy. Among the evils, then, of our situation, may well be ranked the multiplicity of laws, from which no State is exempt. As far as laws are necessary to mark with precision the duties of those who are to obey them, and to take from those who are to administer them a discretion which might be abused, their number is the price of liberty. As far as the laws exceed this limit they are a nuisance; a nuisance of the most pestilent kind. Try the Codes of the several States by this test, and what a luxuriancy[7] of legislation do they present. The short period of independency has filled as many pages as the century which preceded it. Every year, almost every session, adds a new volume. This may be the effect in part, but it can only be in part, of the situation in which the revolution has placed us. A review of the several

[7] an overgrowth

Codes will show that every necessary and useful part of the least voluminous of them might be compressed into one tenth of the compass, and at the same time be rendered tenfold as perspicuous.[8]

10. MUTABILITY OF THE LAWS OF THE STATES.

This evil is intimately connected with the former, yet deserves a distinct notice, as it emphatically denotes a vicious legislation. We daily see laws repealed or superseded before any trial can have been made of their merit, and even before a knowledge of them can have reached the remoter districts within which they were to operate. In the regulations of trade this instability becomes a snare not only to our citizens but to foreigners also.

11. INJUSTICE OF THE LAWS OF STATES.

If the multiplicity and mutability of laws prove a want of wisdom, their injustice betrays a defect still more alarming; more alarming, not merely because it is a greater evil in itself, but because it brings more into question the fundamental principle of republican Government, that the majority who rule in such Governments are the safest guardians both of public good and of private rights. To what causes is this evil to be ascribed?

These causes lie —1. in the Representative bodies. 2. in the people themselves.

1. Representative appointments are sought from 3 motives: 1. Ambition 2. Personal interest. 3. Public good.

Unhappily, the two first are proved by experience to be most prevalent. Hence, the candidates who feel them, particularly, the second, are most industrious, and most successful in pursuing their object; and forming often a majority in the legislative Councils, with interested views, contrary to the interest and views of their constituents, join in a perfidious sacrifice of the latter to the former. A succeeding election, it might be supposed, would displace the offenders, and repair the mischief. But how easily are base and selfish measures masked by pretexts of public good and apparent expediency? How frequently will a repetition of the same arts and industry which succeeded in the first instance again prevail on the unwary to misplace their confidence?

How frequently, too, will the honest but unenlightened representative be the dupe of a favorite leader, veiling his selfish views under the professions of public good, and varnishing his sophistical arguments with the glowing colors of popular eloquence?

2. A still more fatal, if not more frequent cause, lies among the people themselves. All civilized societies are divided into different interests and

[8] easily understood

factions, as they happen to be creditors or debtors, rich or poor, husbandmen, merchants, or manufacturers, members of different religious sects, followers of different political leaders, inhabitants of different districts, owners of different kinds of property and &c, &c. In republican Government, the majority, however composed, ultimately give the law. Whenever, therefore, an apparent interest or common passion unites a majority, what is to restrain them from unjust violations of the rights and interests of the minority, or of individuals? Three motives only: 1. A prudent regard to their own good, as involved in the general and permanent good of the community. This consideration, although of decisive weight in itself, is found by experience to be too often unheeded. It is too often forgotten, by nations as well as by individuals, that honesty is the best policy. 2dly. Respect for character. However strong this motive may be in individuals, it is considered as very insufficient to restrain them from injustice. In a multitude its efficacy is diminished in proportion to the number which is to share the praise or the blame. Besides, as it has reference to public opinion, which within a particular society, is the opinion of the majority, the standard is fixed by those whose conduct is to be measured by it. The public opinion without the society will be little respected by the people at large of any Country. Individuals of extended views and of national pride may bring the public proceedings to this standard, but the example will never be followed by the multitude. Is it to be imagined that an ordinary citizen or even an Assemblyman of R[hode] Island, in estimating the policy of paper money, ever considered or cared in what light the measure would be viewed in France or Holland; or even in Massachusetts or Connecticut? It was a sufficient temptation to both that it was for their interest; it was a sufficient sanction to the latter that it was popular in the State; to the former that it was so in the neighborhood. 3dly. Will Religion, the only remaining motive be a sufficient restraint? It is not pretended to be such, on men individually considered. Will its effect be greater on them considered in an aggregate view? Quite the reverse. The conduct of every popular assembly acting on oath, the strongest of religious ties, proves that individuals join without remorse in acts against which their consciences would revolt if proposed to them under the like sanction, separately, in their closets. When, indeed, Religion is kindled into enthusiasm, its force, like that of other passions, is increased by the sympathy of a multitude. But enthusiasm is only a temporary state of religion, and, while it lasts, will hardly be seen with pleasure at the helm of Government. Besides, as religion in its coolest state, is not infallible, it may become a motive to oppression as well as a restraint from injustice. Place three individuals in a situation wherein the interest of each depends on the voice of the others, and give to two of them an interest opposed to the rights of the third: Will the latter be secure? The prudence of every man would shun the danger. The rules and forms of justice suppose and guard against it. Will two thousand in a like situation be less likely to encroach on the rights of one thousand? The contrary is witnessed by the notorious factions and oppressions which take place in corporate towns, limited as the opportunities are, and in little republics, when uncontrolled by apprehensions of external danger. If an enlargement of the sphere is found to lessen the insecurity of private rights, it is not because the impulse of a common interest or passion is less predominant in this case with the majority; but because a common interest or passion is less apt to be felt, and the requisite combinations less easy to be formed, by a great than by a small number. The society becomes broken into a greater variety of interests and pursuits of passions, which check each other, whilst those who may feel a common sentiment have less opportunity of communication and concert. It may be inferred that the inconveniences of popular States contrary to the prevailing Theory, are in proportion not to the extent, but to the narrowness of their limits.

The great desideratum[9] in Government is such a modification of the sovereignty as will render it sufficiently neutral between the different interests and factions to control one part of the Society from invading the rights of another, and, at the same time, sufficiently controlled itself from setting up an interest adverse to that of the whole society. In absolute Monarchies the prince is sufficiently neutral towards his subjects, but frequently sacrifices their happiness to his ambition or his avarice. In small Republics, the sovereign will is sufficiently controlled from such a Sacrifice of the entire Society, but is not sufficiently neutral towards the parts composing it. As a limited monarchy tempers the evils of an absolute one, so an extensive Republic meliorates the administration of a small Republic.

An auxiliary desideratum for the melioration of the Republican form is such a process of elections as will most certainly extract from the mass of the society the purest and noblest characters which it contains; such as will at once feel most strongly the proper motives to pursue the end of their appointment, and be most capable to devise the proper means of attaining it.

---

[9] thing that is desired

Document 5

The Virginia Plan

May 29, 1787

Edmund Randolph introduced the Virginia Plan as an answer to five specific defects of the Articles of Confederation that he enumerated near the beginning of his speech: 1) that it provided "no security against foreign invasion;" 2) did not empower Congress to resolve disputes between states; 3) did not empower Congress to enact beneficial commercial legislation; 4) did not protect the power of the federal government "against encroachments from the states;" and (5) that it was not regarded as the "paramount" authority, superior to the states' own constitutions.

Randolph proposed a remedy that, he said, conformed to "the republican principle." Five provisions for the legislative branch distinguish the Virginia Plan from the Articles of Confederation: 1) the people of each State ought to elect the First Branch of the National Legislature; 2) the Second Branch of the National Legislature ought to be elected by the first, out of a pool of candidates nominated by the state legislatures, and 3) states would send representatives to Congress according to some rule of proportion, rather than each state having an equal number of representatives; 4) the National Legislature would have power "to legislate in all cases to which the separate States are incompetent," and would also have power (5) "to negative all laws passed by the States, contravening, in the opinion of the National Legislature, the articles of Union."

Our best source for the Virginia Plan is that provided by James Madison, who throughout the convention took notes which he nightly elaborated in a journal. These notes were first published in 1840, in an edition edited by Henry Gilpin. The version of the Virginia Plan reprinted here is taken from Gordon Lloyd, ed., Debates in the Federal Convention of 1787 by James Madison, a Member *(Ashland, Ohio: Ashbrook Center, 2014), 6-10.*

Mr. Randolph expressed his regret, that it should fall to him, rather than those who were of longer standing in life and political experience, to open the great subject of their mission. But as the Convention had originated from Virginia, and his colleagues supposed that some proposition was expected from them, they had imposed this task on him.

He then commented on the difficulty of the crisis, and the necessity of preventing the fulfilment of the prophecies of the American downfall.

He observed, that, in revising the federal system we ought to inquire, first, into the properties which such a government ought to possess; secondly, the defects of the Confederation; thirdly, the danger of our situation; and fourthly, the remedy.

1. The character of such a government ought to secure, first, against foreign invasion; secondly, against dissensions between members of the Union, or seditions in particular States; thirdly, to procure to the several States various blessings of which an isolated situation was incapable; fourthly, it should be able to defend itself against encroachment; and fifthly, to be paramount to the State Constitutions.

2. In speaking of the defects of the Confederation, he professed a high respect for its authors, and considered them as having done all that patriots could do, in the then infancy of the science of constitutions, and of confederacies; when the inefficiency of requisitions was unknown — no commercial discord had arisen among any States — no rebellion had appeared, as in Massachusetts — foreign debts had not become urgent — the havoc of paper-money had not been foreseen — treaties had not been violated — and perhaps nothing better could be obtained, from the jealousy of the States with regard to their sovereignty.

He then proceeded to enumerate the defects:

First, that the Confederation produced no security against foreign invasion; Congress not being permitted to prevent a war, nor to support it by their own authority. Of this he cited many examples; most of which tended to show, that they could not cause infractions of treaties, or of the law of nations, to be punished; that particular States might by their conduct provoke war without control; and that, neither militia nor drafts being fit for defense on such occasions, enlistments only could be successful, and these could not be executed without money.

Secondly, that the Federal Government could not check the quarrel between States, nor a rebellion in any, not having constitutional power nor means to interpose according to the exigency.

Thirdly, that there were many advantages which the United States might acquire, which were not attainable under the Confederation — such as a productive impost — counteraction of the commercial regulations of other nations — pushing of commerce *ad libitum,*[1] &c. &c.

---

[1] according to Congress's own will

Fourthly, that the Federal Government could not defend itself against encroachments from the States.

Fifthly, that it was not even paramount to the State Constitutions, ratified as it was in many of the States.

3. He next reviewed the danger of our situation; and appealed to the sense of the best friends of the United States — to the prospect of anarchy from the laxity of government every where — and to other considerations.

4. He then proceeded to the remedy; the basis of which he said must be the republican principle.

He proposed, as conformable to his ideas, the following resolutions, which he explained one by one.

"1. Resolved, that the Articles of Confederation ought to be so corrected and enlarged as to accomplish the objects proposed by their institution; namely, "common defense, security of liberty, and general welfare."

"2. Resolved, therefore, that the rights of suffrage in the National Legislature ought to be proportioned to the quotas of contribution, or to the number of free inhabitants, as the one or the other rule may seem best in different cases.

"3. Resolved, that the National Legislature ought to consist of two branches.

"4. Resolved, that the members of the first branch of the National Legislature ought to be elected by the people of the several States every — for the term of —; to be of the age of — years at least; to receive liberal stipends by which they may be compensated for the devotion of their time to the public service; to be ineligible to any office established by a particular State, or under the authority of the United States, except those peculiarly belonging to the functions of the first branch, during the term of service, and for the space of — after its expiration; to be incapable of reelection for the space of — after the expiration of their term of service, and to be subject to recall.

"5. Resolved, that the members of the second branch of the National Legislature ought to be elected by those of the first, out of a proper number of persons nominated by the individual Legislatures, to be of the age of — years at least; to hold their offices for a term sufficient to insure their independency; to receive liberal stipends, by which they may be compensated for the devotion of their time to the public service; and to be ineligible to any office established by a particular State, or under the authority of the United States, except those peculiarly belonging to the functions of the second branch, during the term of service, and for the space of — after the expiration thereof.

"6. Resolved, that each branch ought to possess the right of originating acts; that the National Legislature ought to be empowered to enjoy the legislative rights vested in Congress by the Confederation, and moreover to legislate in all cases to which the separate States are incompetent, or in which the harmony of the United States may be interrupted by the exercise of individual legislation; to negative all laws passed by the several States contravening, in the opinion of the National Legislature, the Articles of Union, or any treaty subsisting under the authority of the Union; and to call forth the force of the Union against any member of the Union failing to fulfil its duty under the Articles thereof.

"7. Resolved, that a National Executive be instituted; to be chosen by the National Legislature for the term of —; to receive punctually, at stated times, a fixed compensation for the services rendered, in which no increase nor diminution shall be made, so as to affect the magistracy existing at the time of increase or diminution; and to be ineligible a second time; and that, besides a general authority to execute the national laws, it ought to enjoy the executive rights vested in Congress by the Confederation.

"8. Resolved, that the Executive, and a convenient number of the national Judiciary, ought to compose a Council of Revision, with authority to examine every act of the National Legislature, before it shall operate, and every act of a particular Legislature before a negative thereon shall be final; and that the dissent of the said council shall amount to a rejection, unless the act of the National Legislature be again passed, or that of a particular Legislature be again negatived by — of the members of each branch.

"9. Resolved, that a National Judiciary be established; to consist of one or more supreme tribunals, and of inferior tribunals to be chosen by the National Legislature; to hold their offices during good behavior, and to receive punctually, at stated times, fixed compensation for their services, in which no increase or diminution shall be made, so as to affect the persons actually in office at the time of such increase or diminution. That the jurisdiction of the inferior tribunals shall be to hear and determine, in the first instance, and of the supreme tribunal to hear and determine, in the dernier[2] resort, all piracies and felonies on the high seas; captures from an enemy; cases in which foreigners, or citizens of other States, applying to such jurisdictions, may be interested; or which respect the collection of the national revenue; impeachments of any national officers, and questions which may involve the national peace and harmony.

---

[2] last

"10. Resolved, that provision ought to be made for the admission of States lawfully arising within the limits of the United States, whether from a voluntary junction of government and territory, or otherwise, with the consent of a number of voices in the National Legislature less than the whole.

"11. Resolved, that a republican government, and the territory of each State, except in the instance of a voluntary junction of government and territory, ought to be guaranteed by the United States to each State.

"12. Resolved, that provision ought to be made for the continuance of Congress and their authorities and privileges, until a given day after the reform of the Articles of Union shall be adopted, and for the completion of all their engagements.

"13. Resolved, that provision ought to be made for the amendment of the Articles of Union, whensoever it shall seem necessary; and that the assent of the National Legislature ought not to be required thereto.

"14. Resolved, that the legislative, executive, and judiciary powers, within the several States ought to be bound by oath to support the Articles of Union.

"15. Resolved, that the amendments which shall be offered to the Confederation, by the Convention, ought, at a proper time or times, after the approbation of Congress, to be submitted to an assembly or assemblies of representatives, recommended by the several Legislatures, to be expressly chosen by the people to consider and decide thereon."

He concluded with an exhortation, not to suffer the present opportunity of establishing general peace, harmony, happiness and liberty in the United States to pass away unimproved.

It was then resolved, that the House will tomorrow resolve itself into a Committee of the Whole House, to consider of the state of the American Union; and that the propositions moved by Mr. Randolph be referred to the said committee. . . .

Document 6

Introducing a Fateful Compromise: A Debate on Property, and the Revised Virginia Plan

June 11 and 13, 1787

The June 6 vote on popular representation in the first branch was 8-3 in favor of the Virginia Plan (Connecticut, New Jersey, and South Carolina voted "no"). Madison (who authored the Virginia plan) had carried the day for popular election and representation in the first branch.

Yet the delegates voted against another resolution of the Virginia Plan that would have had the second branch elected by the first branch. With the question of how to constitute the second branch of the legislature remaining unsettled, the delegates examined other options. On June 7, the state delegations voted 10-0 in favor of a proposal that "the second branch of the national legislature be elected by the individual legislatures," an option that Madison wholly disapproved.

But a state-based election of the second branch was only one part of the equation. On June 11, Roger Sherman (a Connecticut delegate who would play a crucial role throughout the convention) asked for equal representation for each state in the second branch — a concession he thought reasonable in return for agreeing to proportional representation in the first branch. "Everything," he said, "depended on this." Sherman's motion was rejected — for now — by a vote of 5 ayes to 6 noes. Delegates from South Carolina also introduced a third dimension to the discussion concerning representation in both branches. "Money was power," said Pierce Butler. And, therefore, shouldn't wealth be represented as well as people and states? The result was the introduction of the 3/5 clause, which, for purposes of allocating representation, counted three-fifths of the slave population in the overall population count. That this was a strange maneuver, counting only "property" in human beings as a representation of wealth, did not go unnoticed. As Elbridge Gerry of Massachusetts asked, "Why . . . should the blacks, who were property in the South, be in the rule of representation more than the cattle and horses of the North?" Yet without recording further debate on the question, Madison recorded the vote on the proposed measure. Language counting "three fifths of all other persons" besides those described as "free" or "bound to servitude for a term of years" was adopted with reference to the first branch on a 9-2 vote, although only adopted in regard to the second branch (which at this point was still based on proportional representation) by a 6-5 vote.

On June 13, a committee presented an updated working draft of the Virginia Plan that preserved its original institutional structure but incorporated the two key changes decided by the Convention in the preceding days: that the members of the second legislative branch would be elected by the state legislatures (Resolution 4); and that when counting population for purposes of apportioning representatives to both branches, three-fifths of the slave population would be included (Resolutions 7 and 8).

The three-fifths clause was incorporated into both branches of the legislature for the moment in order to secure the principle of popular representation. Consequently, the Constitution would now incorporate into the balancing of regional powers an implicit recognition of slavery, an institution that many, including several slaveholders in the Virginia delegation, abhorred and wished to see abolished. During the debates that would follow, delegates would voice their discomfort. Nevertheless, anticipating an eventual end to the institution that discredited American ideals, Madison, Sherman and others would insist on excluding the actual words "slave" and "slavery" from the language of the Constitution and on amending language implying federal recognition of slavery as lawful (see Document 13 and Document 14, excerpt #6).

Source: Gordon Lloyd, ed., Debates in the Federal Convention of 1787 by James Madison, a Member *(Ashland, Ohio: Ashbrook Center, 2014), 77-86.*

June 11

Mr. SHERMAN[1] proposed, that the proportion of suffrage in the first branch should be according to the respective numbers of free inhabitants; and that in the second branch, or Senate, each State should have one vote and no more. He said, as the States would remain possessed of certain individual rights, each State ought to be able to protect itself; otherwise, a few large States will rule the rest. The House of Lords in England, he observed, had certain particular rights under the Constitution, and hence they have an equal vote with the House of Commons, that they may be able to defend their rights.

Mr. RUTLEDGE[2] proposed, that the proportion of suffrage in the first branch should be according to the quotas of contribution. The justice of this

[1] Roger Sherman of Connecticut

[2] John Rutledge of South Carolina

rule, he said, could not be contested. Mr. BUTLER urged the same idea; adding, that money was power; and that the States ought to have weight in the government in proportion to their wealth.

Mr. KING[3] and Mr. WILSON[4] moved, "that the right of suffrage in the first branch of the National Legislature ought not to be according to the rule established in the Articles of Confederation, but according to some equitable ratio of representation." The clause, so far as it related to suffrage in the first branch, was postponed, in order to consider this motion.

Mr. DICKINSON[5] contended for the *actual* contributions of the States, as the rule of their representation and suffrage in the first branch. By thus connecting the interests of the States with their duty, the latter would be sure to be performed.

Mr. KING remarked, that it was uncertain what mode might be used in levying a national revenue; but that it was probable, imposts would be one source of it. If the *actual* contributions were to be the rule, the non-importing States, as Connecticut and New Jersey, would be in a bad situation, indeed. It might so happen that they would have no representation. . . .

The question being about to be put, Doctor FRANKLIN[6] said, he had thrown his ideas of the matter on a paper, which Mr. WILSON read to the Committee in the words following:

"Mr. CHAIRMAN, — It has given me great pleasure to observe, that, till this point, the proportion of representation, came before us, our debates were carried on with great coolness and temper. If any thing of a contrary kind has on this occasion appeared, I hope it will not be repeated; for we are sent here to *consult*, not to *contend*, with each other; and declarations of a fixed opinion, and of determined resolution never to change it, neither enlighten nor convince us. Positiveness and warmth on one side naturally beget their like on the other, and tend to create and augment discord and division, in a great concern wherein harmony and union are extremely necessary to give weight to our councils, and render them effectual in promoting and securing the common good. . . .

"My learned colleague (Mr. WILSON) has already mentioned, that the present method of voting by States was submitted to originally by Congress under a conviction of its impropriety, inequality, and injustice. This appears in

---

[3] Rufus King of Massachusetts
[4] James Wilson of Pennsylvania
[5] John Dickinson of Delaware
[6] Benjamin Franklin of Pennsylvania

the words of their resolution. It is of the sixth of September, 1774. The words are:

"Resolved, that in determining questions in this Congress each Colony or Province shall have one vote; the Congress not being possessed of, or at present able to procure, materials for ascertaining the importance of each Colony."

On the question for agreeing to Mr. KING'S and Mr. WILSON'S motion, it passed in the affirmative, — Massachusetts, Connecticut, Pennsylvania, Virginia, North Carolina, South Carolina, Georgia, aye — 7; New York, New Jersey, Delaware, no — 3; Maryland, divided.

It was then moved by Mr. RUTLEDGE, seconded by Mr. BUTLER, to add to the words, "equitable ratio of representation," at the end of the motion just agreed to, the words "according to the quotas of contribution."

On motion of Mr. WILSON, seconded by Mr. PINCKNEY, [7] this was postponed; in order to add, after the words, "equitable ratio of representation," the words following: "in proportion to the whole number of white and other free citizens and inhabitants of every age, sex and condition, including those bound to servitude for a term of years, and three-fifths of all other persons not comprehended in the foregoing description, except Indians not paying taxes, in each State" — this being the rule in the act of Congress, agreed to by eleven States, for apportioning quotas of revenue on the States, and requiring a census only every five, seven, or ten years.

Mr. GERRY[8] thought property not the rule of representation. Why, then, should the blacks, who were property in the South, be in the rule of representation more than the cattle and horses of the North?

On the question, — Massachusetts, Connecticut, New York, Pennsylvania, Maryland, Virginia, North Carolina, South Carolina, Georgia, aye — 9; New Jersey, Delaware, no — 2.

Mr. SHERMAN moved, that a question be taken, whether each State shall have one vote in the second branch. Every thing, he said, depended on this. The smaller States would never agree to the plan on any other principle than an equality of suffrage in this branch. Mr. ELLSWORTH[9] seconded the motion.

On the question for allowing each State one vote in the second branch, — Connecticut, New York, New Jersey, Delaware, Maryland, aye — 5;

---

[7] Charles Pinckney of South Carolina

[8] Elbridge Gerry of Massachusetts

[9] Oliver Ellsworth of Connecticut

Massachusetts, Pennsylvania, Virginia, North Carolina, South Carolina, Georgia, no — 6.

Mr. WILSON and Mr. HAMILTON moved, that the right of suffrage in the second branch ought to be according to the same rule as in the first branch.

On this question for making the ratio of representation, the same in the second as in the first branch, it passed in the affirmative, — Massachusetts, Pennsylvania, Virginia, North Carolina, South Carolina, Georgia, aye — 6; Connecticut, New York, New Jersey, Delaware, Maryland, no — 5. . . .

The Revised Virginia Plan

June 13

The Committee rose, and Mr. GORHAM[10] made a report, which was postponed till to-morrow, to give an opportunity for other plans to be proposed — the Report was in the words following:

1. Resolved, that it is the opinion of this Committee, that a national Government ought to be established, consisting of a supreme Legislative, Executive and Judiciary.

2. Resolved, that the National Legislature ought to consist of two branches.

3. Resolved, that the members of the first branch of the National Legislature ought to be elected by the people of the several States for the term of three years; to receive fixed stipends by which they may be compensated for the devotion of their time to the public service, to be paid out of the National Treasury; to be ineligible to any office established by a particular State, or under the authority of the United States, (except those peculiarly belonging to the functions of the first branch,) during the term of service, and under the national Government for the space of one year after its expiration.

4. Resolved, that the members of the second branch of the National Legislature ought to be chosen by the individual Legislatures; to be of the age of thirty years at least; to hold their offices for a term sufficient to insure their independence, namely, seven years; to receive fixed stipends by which they may be compensated for the devotion of their time to the public service, to be paid out of the National Treasury; to be ineligible to any office established by a particular State, or under the authority of the United States, (except those peculiarly belonging to the functions of the second branch,) during the term of service, and under the national Government, for the space of one year after its expiration.

---

[10] Nathaniel Gorham of Massachusetts

5. Resolved, that each branch ought to possess the right of originating acts.

6. Resolved, that the National Legislature ought to be empowered to enjoy the legislative rights vested in Congress by the Confederation; and moreover to legislate in all cases to which the separate States are incompetent, or in which the harmony of the United States may be interrupted by the exercise of individual legislation; to negative all laws passed by the several States contravening, in the opinion of the National Legislature, the Articles of Union, or any treaties subsisting under the authority of the Union.

7. Resolved, that the rights of suffrage in the first branch of the National Legislature, ought not to be according to the rule established in the Articles of Confederation, but according to some equitable ratio of representation, namely, in proportion to the whole number of white and other free citizens and inhabitants, of every age, sex and condition, including those bound to servitude for a term of years, and three-fifths of all other persons, not comprehended in the foregoing description, except Indians not paying taxes, in each State.

8. Resolved, that the right of suffrage in the second branch of the National Legislature, ought to be according to the rule established for the first.

9. Resolved, that a National Executive be instituted, to consist of a single person; to be chosen by the National Legislature, for the term of seven years; with power to carry into execution the national laws; to appoint to offices in cases not otherwise provided for; to be ineligible a second time; and to be removable on impeachment and conviction of malpractices or neglect of duty; to receive a fixed stipend by which he may be compensated for the devotion of his time to the public service, to be paid out of the National Treasury.

10. Resolved, that the national Executive shall have a right to negative any legislative act which shall not be afterwards passed by two-thirds of each branch of the national Legislature.

11. Resolved, that a national Judiciary be established, to consist of one supreme tribunal, the Judges of which shall be appointed by the second branch of the national Legislature, to hold their offices during good behavior, and to receive punctually, at stated times, a fixed compensation for their services, in which no increase or diminution shall be made, so as to affect the persons actually in office at the time of such increase or diminution.

12. Resolved, that the national Legislature be empowered to appoint inferior tribunals.

13. Resolved, that the jurisdiction of the national Judiciary shall extend to all cases which respect the collection of the national revenue, impeachments of

any national officers, and questions which involve the national peace and harmony.

14. Resolved, that provision ought to be made for the admission of States lawfully arising within the limits of the United States, whether from a voluntary junction of government and territory, or otherwise, with the consent of a number of voices in the national Legislature less than the whole.

15. Resolved, that provision ought to be made for the continuance of Congress and their authorities and privileges, until a given day, after the reform of the Articles of Union shall be adopted, and for the completion of all their engagements.

16. Resolved, that a republican constitution, and its existing laws, ought to be guaranteed to each State, by the United States.

17. Resolved, that provision ought to be made for the amendment of the Articles of Union, when so ever it shall seem necessary.

18. Resolved, that the Legislative, Executive and Judiciary powers within the several States, ought to be bound by oath to support the Articles of Union.

19. Resolved, that the amendments which shall be offered to the Confederation by the Convention ought, at a proper time or times after the approbation of Congress, to be submitted to an assembly or assemblies recommended by the several Legislatures, to be expressly chosen by the people to consider and decide thereon.

Document 7

Return to Starting Point: The New Jersey Plan

June 15, 1787

Although on June 13 the delegates had seemed to endorse the Revised Virginia Plan, which preserved, with modifications, the new institutional structure proposed by the original Virginia Plan, not all were content. On June 15, William Patterson presented the alternative New Jersey Plan, which restored the structure of the Articles of Confederation but at the same time added to the powers of Congress. Why, after two weeks of negotiation concerning the representation of people, states, and property, would the New Jersey coalition insist on starting all over again?

Madison gives a clue in a footnote to his coverage of the debates: "This plan had been concerted among the Deputations, or members thereof, from Connecticut, New York, New Jersey, Delaware, and perhaps Mr. Martin, from Maryland, who made with them a common cause, though on different principles. Connecticut and New York were against a departure from the principle of the Confederation, wishing rather to add a few new powers to Congress than to substitute a National Government. The States of New Jersey and Delaware were opposed to a National Government, because its patrons considered a proportional representation of the States as the basis of it. The eagerness displayed by the members opposed to a National Government, from these different motives, began now to produce serious anxiety for the result of the Convention." At this point delegates had approved, in the working draft of the Virginia Plan, to proportional suffrage in both houses of Congress, although to a different mode of election in each (direct election in the first house and appointment by state legislatures in the second). In the same footnote to the June 15 debate, Madison comments that John Dickinson of Delaware turned to him and said, "You see the consequence of pushing things too far. Some of the members from the small States wish for two branches in the General Legislature, and are friends to a good National Government; but we would sooner submit to a foreign power, than submit to be deprived in both branches of an equality of suffrage, and thereby be thrown under the domination of the larger States."

The smaller states did not deny the weakness of the federal government under the Articles. But they opposed using the Constitution to make an end-run around the states by basing representation entirely on the people. The New Jersey plan did incorporate the three-fifths compromise into its Resolution 3, which stipulated that the amounts of "requisitions"—funds sent from the states to supply the needs of the federal government—would be calculated according each state's population.

Source: Gordon Lloyd, ed., Debates in the Federal Convention of 1787 by James Madison, a Member *(Ashland, Ohio: Ashbrook Center, 2014), 77-86.*

June 15

In Convention, — Mr. PATTERSON laid before the Convention the plan which he said several of the Deputations wished to be substituted in place of that proposed by Mr. RANDOLPH.[1]

After some little discussion of the most proper mode of giving it a fair deliberation, it was agreed, that it should be referred to a Committee of the Whole; and that, in order to place the two plans in due comparison, the other should be recommitted.

At the earnest request of Mr. LANSING[2] and some other gentleman, it was also agreed that the Convention should not go into Committee of the Whole on the subject till to-morrow; by which delay the friends of the plan proposed by Mr. PATTERSON would be better prepared to explain and support it, and all would have an opportunity of taking copies.

The propositions from New Jersey, moved by Mr. PATTERSON, were in the words following:

1. Resolved, that the Articles of Confederation ought to be so revised, corrected, and enlarged, as to render the Federal Constitution adequate to the exigencies of government, and the preservation of the Union.

2. Resolved, that, in addition to the powers vested in the United States in Congress, by the present existing Articles of Confederation, they be authorized to pass acts for raising a revenue, by levying a duty or duties on all goods or merchandizes of foreign growth or manufacture, imported into any part of the United States; by stamps on paper, vellum or parchment; and by a postage on all letters or packages passing through the general post-office; to be applied to such Federal purposes as they shall deem proper and expedient; to make rules and regulations for the collection thereof; and the same, from time to time, to alter and amend in such manner as they shall think proper; to pass acts for the regulation of trade and commerce, as well with foreign nations as with each other; provided that all punishments, fines, forfeitures and penalties, to be

---

[1] Edmund Randolph of Virginia, who had proposed the Virginia plan on May 29.

[2] John Lansing, Jr. of New York

incurred for contravening such acts, rules and regulations, shall be adjudged by the common law Judiciaries of the State in which any offence contrary to the true intent and meaning of such acts, rules, and regulations, shall have been committed or perpetrated, with liberty of commencing in the first instance all suits and prosecutions for that purpose in the Superior common law Judiciary in such State; subject, nevertheless, for the correction of all errors, both in law and fact, in rendering judgment, to an appeal to the Judiciary of the United States.

3. Resolved, that whenever requisitions shall be necessary, instead of the rule for making requisitions mentioned in the Articles of Confederation, the United States in Congress be authorized to make such requisitions in proportion to the whole number of white and other free citizens and inhabitants, of every age, sex, and condition, including those bound to servitude for a term of years, and three-fifths of all other persons not comprehended in the foregoing description, except Indians not paying taxes; that, if such requisitions be not complied with, in the time specified therein, to direct the collection thereof in the non-complying States; and for that purpose to devise and pass acts directing and authorizing the same; provided, that none of the powers hereby vested in the United States in Congress, shall be exercised without the consent of at least — States; and in that proportion, if the number of confederated States should hereafter be increased or diminished.

4. Resolved, that the United States in Congress be authorized to elect a Federal Executive, to consist of — persons, to continue in office for the term of — years; to receive punctually, at stated times, a fixed compensation for their services, in which no increase nor diminution shall be made so as to affect the persons composing the Executive at the time of such increase or diminution; to be paid out of the Federal treasury; to be incapable of holding any other office or appointment during their time of service, and for — years thereafter: to be ineligible a second time, and removable by Congress, on application by a majority of the Executives of the several States; that the Executive, besides their general authority to execute the Federal acts, ought to appoint all Federal officers not otherwise provided for, and to direct all military operations; provided, that none of the persons composing the Federal Executive shall, on any occasion, take command of any troops, so as personally to conduct any military enterprise, as General, or in any other capacity.

5. Resolved, that a Federal Judiciary be established, to consist of a supreme tribunal, the Judges of which to be appointed by the Executive, and to hold their offices during good behavior; to receive punctually, at stated times, a

fixed compensation for their services, in which no increase nor diminution shall be made so as to affect the persons actually in office at the time of such increase or diminution. That the Judiciary so established shall have authority to hear and determine, in the first instance, on all impeachments of Federal officers; and, by way of appeal, in the dernier[3] resort, in all cases touching the rights of ambassadors; in all cases of captures from an enemy; in all cases of piracies and felonies on the high seas; in all cases in which foreigners may be interested; in the construction of any treaty or treaties, or which may arise on any of the acts for the regulation of trade, or the collection of the Federal revenue: that none of the Judiciary shall, during the time they remain in office, be capable of receiving or holding any other office or appointment during their term of service, or for — thereafter.

6. Resolved, that all acts of the United States in Congress, made by virtue and in pursuance of the powers hereby, and by the Articles of Confederation, vested in them, and all treaties made and ratified under the authority of the United States, shall be the supreme law of the respective States, so far forth as those acts or treaties shall relate to the said States or their citizens; and that the Judiciary of the several States shall be bound thereby in their decisions, any thing in the respective laws of the individual States to the contrary notwithstanding: and that if any State, or any body of men in any State, shall oppose or prevent the carrying into execution such acts or treaties, the Federal Executive shall be authorized to call forth the power of the confederated States, or so much thereof as may be necessary, to enforce and compel an obedience to such acts, or an observance of such treaties.

7. Resolved, that provision be made for the admission of new States into the Union.

8. Resolved, that the rule for naturalization ought to be the same in every State.

9. Resolved, that a citizen of one State committing an offence in another State of the Union, shall be deemed guilty of the same offence as if it had been committed by a citizen of the State in which the offence was committed.

[3] last

Document 8

The Hamilton Plan

June 18, 1787

On June 18, Hamilton expressed his displeasure with both the Revised Virginia Plan and the New Jersey Plan. Then he proposed a plan of his own that did not, at the time, make much of an impact on the other delegates. They were interested in settling the issue of who or what should be represented in the new government. Hamilton thought the debate over sovereignty, whether the people or the states should be represented in the legislature, missed the critical issue: the problem of insuring what elsewhere he called "good government." He articulated what we might call national rather than federal principles. More than the balance of powers between the states, what interested Hamilton was the location of powers between the branches of a new national government. For Hamilton, "we ought to go as far, in order to attain stability and permanency, as republican principles will admit." This required Hamilton to challenge the traditional understanding of republicanism that where annual elections end, tyranny begins. He maintained that good government requires long terms in office. But don't these long terms put republican principles in danger? No, says Hamilton, as long as the representatives are chosen by and removable by the people. These ideas presented in the Hamilton Plan played a greater part in the August conversation than they did in June.

Source: Gordon Lloyd, ed., Debates in the Federal Convention of 1787 by James Madison, a Member *(Ashland, Ohio: Ashbrook Center, 2014), 92-101.*

Mr. HAMILTON had been hitherto silent on the business before the Convention, partly from respect to others whose superior abilities, age and experience, rendered him unwilling to bring forward ideas dissimilar to theirs; and partly from his delicate situation with respect to his own State, to whose sentiments, as expressed by his colleagues, he could by no means accede. The crisis, however, which now marked our affairs, was too serious to permit any scruples whatever to prevail over the duty imposed on every man to contribute his efforts for the public safety and happiness. He was obliged, therefore, to declare himself unfriendly to both plans.

He was particularly opposed to that from New Jersey, being fully convinced, that no amendment of the Confederation, leaving the States in possession of their sovereignty, could possibly answer the purpose. On the other hand, he confessed he was much discouraged by the amazing extent of country, in expecting the desired blessings from any general sovereignty that could be substituted.

As to the powers of the Convention, he thought the doubts started on that subject had arisen from distinctions and reasonings too subtle. A *federal* government he conceived to mean an association of independent communities into one. Different confederacies have different powers, and exercise them in different ways. In some instances, the powers are exercised over collective bodies, in others, over individuals, as in the German Diet; and among ourselves, in cases of piracy. Great latitude, therefore, must be given to the signification of the term.

The plan last proposed[1] departs, itself, from the *federal* idea, as understood by some, since it is to operate eventually on individuals. He agreed, moreover, with the Honorable gentleman from Virginia, (Mr. RANDOLPH[2]), that he owed it to our country, to do, on this emergency, whatever we should deem essential to its happiness. The States sent us here to provide for the exigencies of the Union. To rely on and propose any plan not adequate to these exigencies, merely because it was not clearly within our powers, would be to sacrifice the means to the end. It may be said, that the States cannot *ratify* a plan not within the purview of the Article of the Confederation providing for alterations and amendments. But may not the States themselves, in which no constitutional authority equal to this purpose exists in the Legislatures, have had in view a reference to the people at large? . . .

The great question is what provision shall we make for the happiness of our country? He would first make a comparative examination of the two plans — prove that there were essential defects in both — and point out such changes as might render a national one efficacious.

The great and essential principles necessary for the support of government are:

1. An active and constant interest in supporting it. This principle does not exist in the States, in favor of the Federal Government. They have evidently in a high degree, the *esprit de corps*.[3] They constantly pursue internal interests

---

[1] the New Jersey Plan

[2] Edmund Randolph

[3] a feeling of camaraderie within a group

adverse to those of the whole. They have their particular debts, their particular plans of finance, &c. All these, when opposed to, invariably prevail over, the requisitions and plans of Congress.

2. The love of power. Men love power. The same remarks are applicable to this principle. The States have constantly shown a disposition rather to regain the powers delegated by them, than to part with more, or to give effect to what they had parted with. The ambition of their demagogues is known to hate the control of the General Government. It may be remarked, too, that the citizens have not that anxiety to prevent a dissolution of the General Government as of the particular governments. A dissolution of the latter would be fatal; of the former, would still leave the purposes of government attainable to a considerable degree. Consider what such a State as Virginia will be in a few years, a few compared with the life of nations. How strongly will it feel its importance and self-sufficiency!

3. An habitual attachment of the people. The whole force of this tie is on the side of the State Government. Its sovereignty is immediately before the eyes of the people; its protection is immediately enjoyed by them. From its hand distributive justice, and all those acts which familiarize and endear a government to a people, are dispensed to them.

4. *Force,* by which may be understood a *coercion of laws,* or *coercion of arms.* Congress have not the former, except in few cases. In particular States, this coercion is nearly sufficient; though he held it, in most cases, not entirely so. A certain portion of military force is absolutely necessary in large communities. Massachusetts is now feeling this necessity, and making provision for it. But how can this force be exerted on the States collectively? It is impossible. It amounts to a war between the parties. Foreign powers also will not be idle spectators. They will interpose; the confusion will increase; and a dissolution of the Union will ensue.

5. *Influence,* — he did not mean corruption, but a dispensation of those regular honors and emoluments which produce an attachment to the government. Almost all the weight of these is on the side of the States; and must continue so as long as the States continue to exist. All the passions, then, we see, of avarice, ambition, interest, which govern most individuals, and all public bodies, fall into the current of the States, and do not flow into the stream of the General Government. The former, therefore, will generally be an overmatch for the General Government, and render any confederacy in its very nature precarious.

Theory is in this case fully confirmed by experience. . . . How then are all these evils to be avoided? Only by such a complete sovereignty in the General

Government as will turn all the strong principles and passions abovementioned on its side.

Does the scheme of New Jersey produce this effect? Does it afford any substantial remedy whatever? On the contrary, it labors under great defects, and the defect of some of its provisions will destroy the efficacy of others. It gives a direct revenue to Congress, but this will not be sufficient. The balance can only be supplied by requisitions; which experience proves cannot be relied on. If States are to deliberate on the mode, they will also deliberate on the object, of the supplies; and will grant or not grant, as they approve or disapprove of it. The delinquency of one will invite and countenance it in others. Quotas too, must, in the nature of things, be so unequal, as to produce the same evil. To what standard will you resort?

Land is a fallacious one. Compare Holland with Russia; France, or England, with other countries of Europe; Pennsylvania with North Carolina, — will the relative pecuniary abilities, in those instances, correspond with the relative value of land? Take numbers of inhabitants for the rule, and make like comparison of different countries, and you will find it to be equally unjust. The different degrees of industry and improvement in different countries render the first object a precarious measure of wealth. Much depends, too, on *situation*. Connecticut, New Jersey, and North Carolina, not being commercial States, and contributing to the wealth of the commercial ones, can never bear quotas assessed by the ordinary rules of proportion. They will, and must, fail in their duty. Their example will be followed, — and the union itself be dissolved. Whence, then, is the national revenue to be drawn? From commerce; even from exports, which, notwithstanding the common opinion, are fit objects of moderate taxation; from excise, &c., &c. — These, though not equal, are less unequal than quotas.

Another destructive ingredient in the plan is that equality of suffrage which is so much desired by the small States. It is not in human nature that Virginia and the large States should consent to it; or, if they did, that they should long abide by it. It shocks too much all ideas of justice, and every human feeling. Bad principles in a government, though slow, are sure in their operation, and will gradually destroy it. A doubt has been raised whether Congress at present have a right to keep ships or troops in time of peace. He leans to the negative.

Mr. PATTERSON'S[4] plan provides no remedy. If the powers proposed were adequate, the organization of Congress is such, that they could never be

[4] William Patterson of New Jersey

properly and effectually exercised. The members of Congress, being chosen by the States and subject to recall, represent all the local prejudices. Should the powers be found effectual, they will from time to time be heaped on them, till a tyrannic sway shall be established. The General power, whatever be its form, if it preserves itself, must swallow up the state powers. Otherwise, it will be swallowed up by them. It is against all the principles of a good government, to vest the requisite powers in such a body as Congress. Two sovereignties cannot co-exist within the same limits. Giving powers to Congress must eventuate in a bad government, or in no government. The plan of New Jersey, therefore, will not do.

What, then, is to be done? Here he was embarrassed. The extent of the country to be governed discouraged him. The expense of a General Government was also formidable; unless there were such a diminution of expense on the side of the State Governments, as the case would admit. If they were extinguished, he was persuaded that great economy might be obtained by substituting a General Government. He did not mean, however, to shock the public opinion by proposing such a measure.

On the other hand, he saw no *other* necessity for declining it. They are not necessary for any of the great purposes of commerce, revenue, or agriculture. Subordinate authorities, he was aware, would be necessary. There must be district tribunals; corporations for local purposes. But *cui bono*[5] the vast and expensive apparatus now appertaining to the States?

The only difficulty of a serious nature which occurred to him, was that of drawing representatives from the extremes to the center of the community. What inducements can be offered that will suffice? The moderate wages for the first branch could only be a bait to little demagogues. Three dollars, or thereabouts, he supposed, would be the utmost. The Senate, he feared, from a similar cause, would be filled by certain undertakers, who wish for particular offices under the government. This view of the subject almost led him to despair that a republican government could be established over so great an extent.

He was sensible, at the same time, that it would be unwise to propose one of any other form. In his private opinion, he had no scruple in declaring, supported as he was by the opinion of so many of the wise and good, that the British Government was the best in the world: and that he doubted much whether any thing short of it would do in America.

---

[5] who benefits from

He hoped gentlemen of different opinions would bear with him in this, and begged them to recollect the change of opinion on this subject which had taken place, and was still going on. It was once thought, that the power of Congress was amply sufficient to secure the end[6] of their institution. The error was now seen by every one. The members most tenacious of republicanism, he observed, were as loud as any in declaiming against the vices of democracy. This progress of the public mind led him to anticipate the time, when others as well as himself, would join in the praise bestowed by Mr. NECKAR[7] on the British Constitution, namely, that it is the only government in the world "which unites public strength with individual security."

In every community where industry is encouraged, there will be a division of it into the few and the many. Hence, separate interests will arise. There will be debtors and creditors, &c. Give all power to the many, they will oppress the few. Give all power to the few, they will oppress the many. Both, therefore, ought to have the power, that each may defend itself against the other. To the want of this check we owe our paper-money, instalment laws,[8] &c. To the proper adjustment of it the British owe the excellence of their constitution. Their House of Lords is a most noble institution. Having nothing to hope for by a change, and a sufficient interest, by means of their property, in being faithful to the national interest, they form a permanent barrier against every pernicious innovation, whether attempted on the part of the Crown or of the Commons. No temporary Senate will have firmness enough to answer the purpose.

The Senate of Maryland which seems to be so much appealed to, has not yet been sufficiently tried. Had the people been unanimous and eager in the late appeal to them on the subject of a paper emission,[9] they would have yielded to the torrent. Their acquiescing in such an appeal is a proof of it. Gentlemen differ in their opinions concerning the necessary checks, from the different estimates they form of the human passions. They suppose seven years a sufficient period to give the Senate an adequate firmness, from not duly considering the amazing violence and turbulence of the democratic spirit. When a great object of government is pursued, which seizes the popular

---

[6] Hamilton means that it was thought that the power of Congress under the Articles of Confederation would secure the purpose of the Congress.

[7] Jacques Necker, a Geneva banker, and finance minister under Louis XVI.

[8] laws that frustrated the collection of debts by allowing repayment in distant future installments.

[9] issuing paper money

passions, they spread like wild-fire and become irresistible. He appealed to the gentlemen from the New England States, whether experience had not there verified the remark.

As to the Executive, it seemed to be admitted that no good one could be established on republican principles. Was not this giving up the merits of the question; for can there be a good government without a good Executive? The English model was the only good one on this subject. The hereditary interest of the King was so interwoven with that of the nation, and his personal emolument so great, that he was placed above the danger of being corrupted from abroad; and at the same time was both sufficiently independent and sufficiently controlled, to answer the purpose of the institution at home. One of the weak sides of republics was their being liable to foreign influence and corruption. Men of little character, acquiring great power, become easily the tools of intermeddling neighbors. Sweden was a striking instance. The French and English had each their parties during the late revolution, which was effected by the predominant influence of the former.

What is the inference from all these observations? That we ought to go as far, in order to attain stability and permanency, as republican principles will admit. Let one branch of the Legislature hold their places for life, or at least during good behavior. Let the Executive also, be for life. He appealed to the feelings of the members present, whether a term of seven years would induce the sacrifices of private affairs which an acceptance of public trust would require, so as to insure the services of the best citizens. On this plan, we should have in the Senate a permanent will, a weighty interest, which would answer essential purposes. But is this a republican government, it will be asked. Yes, if all the magistrates are appointed and vacancies are filled by the people, or a process of election originating with the people.

He was sensible that an Executive, constituted as he proposed, would have in fact but little of the power and independence that might be necessary. On the other plan, of appointing him for seven years, he thought the Executive ought to have but little power. He would be ambitious, with the means of making creatures; and as the object of his ambition would be to *prolong* his power, it is probable that, in case of war he would avail himself of the emergency, to evade or refuse a degradation from his place. An Executive for life has not this motive for forgetting his fidelity, and will therefore be a safer depository of power.

It will be objected, probably, that such an Executive will be an *elective monarch*, and will give birth to the tumults which characterize that form of government. He would reply, that *monarch* is an indefinite term. It marks not either the degree or duration of power. If this Executive magistrate would be a monarch for life, the other proposed by the Report from the Committee of the Whole would be a monarch for seven years. The circumstance of being elective was also applicable to both.

It had been observed, by judicious writers, that elective monarchies would be the best if they could be guarded against the tumults excited by the ambition and intrigues of competitors. He was not sure that *tumults* were an inseparable evil. He thought this character of elective monarchies had been taken rather from particular cases, than from general principles. The election of Roman Emperors was made by the *army*. In *Poland* the election is made by great rival *princes,* with independent power, and ample means of raising commotions. In the German Empire, the appointment is made by the Electors and Princes, who have equal motives and means for exciting cabals and parties. Might not such a mode of election be devised among ourselves, as will defend the community against these effects in any dangerous degree?

Having made these observations, he would read to the Committee a sketch of a plan which he should prefer to either of those under consideration. He was aware that it went beyond the ideas of most members. But will such a plan be adopted out of doors?[10] In return he would ask, will the people adopt the other plan? At present they will adopt neither. But he sees the Union dissolving, or already dissolved — he sees evils operating in the States which must soon cure the people of their fondness for democracies — he sees that a great progress has been already made, and is still going on, in the public mind. He thinks, therefore, that the people will in time be unshackled from their prejudices; and whenever that happens, they will themselves not be satisfied at stopping where the plan of Mr. RANDOLPH would place them, but be ready to go as far at least as he proposes. He did not mean to offer the paper he had sketched as a proposition to that Committee. It was meant only to give a more correct view of his ideas, and to suggest the amendments which he should probably propose to the plan of Mr. RANDOLPH, in the proper stages of its future discussion. He reads his sketch in the words following: to wit.

"I. The supreme Legislative power of the United States of America to be vested in two different bodies of men; the one to be called the Assembly, the other the Senate; who together shall form the Legislature of the United States, with power to pass all laws whatsoever, subject to the negative hereafter mentioned.

[10] outside the Convention

"II. The Assembly to consist of persons elected by the people to serve for three years.

"III. The Senate to consist of persons elected to serve during good behavior; their election to be made by electors chosen for that purpose by the people. In order to this, the States to be divided into election districts. On the death, removal or resignation of any Senator, his place to be filled out of the district from which he came.

"IV. The supreme Executive authority of the United States to be vested in a Governor, to be elected to serve during good behavior; the election to be made by Electors chosen by the people in the Election Districts aforesaid. The authorities and functions of the Executive to be as follows: to have a negative on all laws about to be passed, and the execution of all laws passed; to have the direction of war when authorized or begun; to have, with the advice and approbation of the Senate, the power of making all treaties; to have the sole appointment of the heads or chief officers of the Departments of Finance, War, and Foreign Affairs; to have the nomination of all other officers, (ambassadors to foreign nations included,) subject to the approbation or rejection of the Senate; to have the power of pardoning all offences except treason, which he shall not pardon without the approbation of the Senate.

"V. On the death, resignation, or removal of the Governor, his authorities to be exercised by the President of the Senate till a successor be appointed.

"VI. The Senate to have the sole power of declaring war; the power of advising and approving all treaties; the power of approving or rejecting all appointments of officers, except the heads or chiefs of the Departments of Finance, War, and Foreign Affairs.

"VII. The supreme Judicial authority to be vested in Judges, to hold their offices during good behavior, with adequate and permanent salaries. This court to have original jurisdiction in all causes of capture, and an appellative jurisdiction in all causes in which the revenues of the General Government, or the citizens of foreign nations, are concerned.

"VIII. The Legislature of the United States to have power to institute courts in each State for the determination of all matters of general concern.

"IX. The Governor, Senators, and all officers of the United States, to be liable to impeachment for mal- and corrupt conduct; and upon conviction to be removed from office, and disqualified for holding any place of trust or profit: all impeachments to be tried by a Court to consist of the Chief —, or Judge of the Superior Court of Law of each State, provided such Judge shall hold his place during good behavior and have a permanent salary.

"X. All laws of the particular States contrary to the Constitution or laws of the United States to be utterly void; and the better to prevent such laws being passed, the Governor or President of each State shall be appointed by the General Government, and shall have a negative upon the laws about to be passed in the State of which he is the Governor or President.

"XI. No State to have any forces land or naval; and the militia of all the States to be under the sole and exclusive direction of the United States, the officers of which to be appointed and commissioned by them."

On these several articles he entered into explanatory observations corresponding with the principles of his introductory reasoning. The Committee rose, and the House adjourned.

Document 9

Partly National, Partly Federal

June 29 - 30, 1787

On June 29, the delegates approved (6 in favor, 4 opposed, and 1 state divided) proportional representation in the House. The delegates then turned to Resolution 8 of the revised Virginia plan on representation in the second branch (Document 6). Oliver Ellsworth introduced the "Connecticut Compromise": equal representation of states in the second branch in exchange for proportional representation of population in the first branch.

As early as June 6, John Dickinson of Delaware had expressed a willingness to entertain popular election of the first branch of government as long as the states elected the second branch. On June 11, Roger Sherman of Connecticut bluntly stated that each state should have equal representation in the Senate "to protect itself; otherwise, a few large States will rule the rest." This evoked a rare but gently worded protest from Pennsylvania delegate Benjamin Franklin, who offered a careful demonstration that "it is equally in the power of the lesser States to swallow up the greater." A combination of Senators from smaller states could easily thwart the proposals of the three largest states.

Sherman replied to these arguments on June 28, noting that equal representation in the second branch would protect the rights of the minority. "The question is, not what rights naturally belong to man, but how they may be most equally and effectually guarded in society. And if some give up more than others, in order to obtain this end, there can be no room for complaint. To do otherwise, to require an equal concession from all, if it would create danger to the rights of some, would be sacrificing the end to the means." Yet Madison "entreated the gentlemen representing the small States to renounce a principle which was confessedly unjust, which could never be admitted, and if admitted must infuse mortality into a Constitution which we wished to last forever."

Division over the issue of representation brought the Convention to "a full stop" by the end of June. The impatient Alexander Hamilton left the Convention and returned to New York on June 29th, not to return until early September. Yet this day also saw the restoration of the New Jersey coalition. It would vote with Connecticut, New York, Delaware, and Mr. Luther Martin from Maryland in yet another effort to resist proportional representation in both branches.

Oliver Ellsworth of Connecticut claimed that a substantive principle and not a mere compromise was involved. He announced the discovery of a new principle of dual representation: "We were partly national; partly federal." He trusted "that on this middle ground a compromise would take place. He did not see that it could take place on any other. And if no compromise should take place, our meeting would not only be in vain but worse than in vain."

The "great division" in America, responded Madison on June 30, is NOT "between the large and small States; it lay between the Northern and Southern" over "their having or not having slaves." Accordingly, if we are interested in the balance of interests doctrine, we should be talking about balancing North and South rather than large and small States in the Senate.

On June 30, William Davie of North Carolina threw his weight behind Ellsworth's newly discovered partly national, partly federal concept. He would lead the North Carolina delegation from the wholly national position it held in early June to a strong partly national, partly federal position by July 16. Benjamin Franklin's papers indicate that on June 30 he too was attracted to the notion.

Loose talk of division and disunion came from Gunning Bedford of Delaware, who remained unconvinced that there was a third or middle way "between a perfect consolidation and a mere confederacy of the States." He thought the attempt to compromise on the structure of the federal government was an illusion. He held out for adding powers to the government and leaving its structure alone.

Nevertheless, Bedford was elected on Monday July 2 to the Gerry Committee to work out the very compromise that he found so objectionable on Saturday. He accepted the committee assignment.

Source: Gordon Lloyd, ed., Debates in the Federal Convention of 1787 by James Madison, a Member *(Ashland, Ohio: Ashbrook Center, 2014), 65-72, 159-177.*

June 29

In Convention. — Doctor JOHNSON.[1] The controversy must be endless whilst gentlemen differ in the grounds of their arguments; those on one side considering the States as districts of people composing one political society: those on the other, considering them as so many political societies. The fact is, that the States do exist as political societies, and a government is to be formed for them in their political capacity, as well as for the individuals composing them. . . .

---

[1] William Samuel Johnson of Connecticut

Mr. MADISON agreed with Doctor JOHNSON, that the mixed nature of the Government ought to be kept in view; but thought too much stress was laid on the rank of the States as political societies. There was a gradation, he observed, from the smallest corporation, with the most limited powers, to the largest empire, with the most perfect sovereignty. . . .

He entreated the gentlemen representing the small States to renounce a principle which was confessedly unjust; which could never be admitted; and which, if admitted, must infuse mortality into a Constitution which we wished to last forever. He prayed them to ponder well the consequences of suffering the Confederacy to go to pieces. . . .

Mr. ELLSWORTH moved, "that the rule of suffrage in the second branch be the same with that established by the Articles of Confederation." [*Representation was by states, rather than by population.*] He was not sorry, on the whole, he said, that the vote just passed [*representation in the first branch, which became the House of Representatives, would not be representation by states*] had determined against this rule in the first branch. He hoped it would become a ground of compromise with regard to the second branch. We were partly national, partly federal. The proportional representation in the first branch was conformable to the national principle, and would secure the large States against the small. An equality of voices [*among the states*] was conformable to the federal principle, and was necessary to secure the small States against the large. He trusted that on this middle ground a compromise would take place. He did not see that it could on any other, and if no compromise should take place, our meeting would not only be in vain, but worse than in vain. To the eastward, he was sure Massachusetts was the only State that would listen to a proposition for excluding the States, as equal political societies, from an equal voice in both branches. The others would risk every consequence rather than part with so dear a right. An attempt to deprive them of it was at once cutting the body of America in two, . . . The large States he conceived would, notwithstanding the equality of votes, have an influence that would maintain their superiority. Holland, as had been admitted (by Mr. MADISON), had, notwithstanding a like equality in the Dutch confederacy, a prevailing influence in the public measures. The power of self-defense was essential to the small States. Nature had given it to the smallest insect of the creation. He could never admit that there was no danger of combinations among the large States. They will like individuals find out and avail themselves of the advantage to be gained by it. It was true the danger would be greater if they were contiguous, and had a more immediate and common interest. A defensive combination of the small States was rendered more difficult by their greater number. He would mention another consideration of great weight. The existing Confederation was founded on the equality of the States in the article of suffrage, — was it meant to pay no regard to this antecedent plighted faith? Let a strong Executive, a Judiciary, and Legislative power, be created, but let not too much be attempted, by which all may be lost. He was not in general a half-way man, yet he preferred doing half the good we could, rather than do nothing at all. The other half may be added when the necessity shall be more fully experienced.

Mr. BALDWIN[2] could have wished that the powers of the general Legislature had been defined, before the mode of constituting it had been agitated. He should vote against the motion of Mr. ELLSWORTH, though he did not like the Resolution as it stood in the Report of the Committee of the Whole. He thought the second branch ought to be the representation of property, and that, in forming it, therefore, some reference ought to be had to the relative wealth of their constituents, and to the principles on which the Senate of Massachusetts was constituted. He concurred with those who thought it would be impossible for the General Legislature to extend its cares to the local matters of the States.

June 30

Mr. WILSON[3] did not expect such a motion after the establishment of the contrary principle in the first branch; and considering the reasons which would oppose it, even if an equal vote had been allowed in the first branch. The gentleman from Connecticut (Mr. ELLSWORTH) had pronounced, that if the motion should not be acceded to, of all the States north of Pennsylvania one only would agree to any General Government. He entertained more favorable hopes of Connecticut and of the other Northern States. He hoped the alarms exceeded their cause, and that they would not abandon a country to which they were bound by so many strong and endearing ties. But should the deplored event happen, it would neither stagger his sentiments nor his duty. If the minority of the people of America refuse to coalesce with the majority on just and proper principles; if a separation must take place, it could never happen on better grounds. The votes of yesterday against the just principle of representation, were as twenty-two to ninety of the people of America. Taking the opinions to be the same on this point — and he was sure, if there was any room for change, it could not be on the side of the majority — the question

[2] Abraham Baldwin of Georgia

[3] James Wilson of Pennsylvania

will be, shall less than one-fourth of the United States withdraw themselves from the Union, or shall more than three-fourths renounce the inherent, indisputable and unalienable rights of men, in favor of the artificial system of States? If issue must be joined, it was on this point he would choose to join it. The gentleman from Connecticut, in supposing that the preponderance secured to the majority in the first branch had removed the objections to an equality of votes [*among the states*] in the second branch for the security of the minority, narrowed the case extremely. Such an equality will enable the minority to control, in all cases whatsoever, the sentiments and interests of the majority. Seven States will control six: seven States, according to the estimates that had been used, composed twenty-four ninetieths of the whole people. It would be in the power, then, of less than one third to overrule two thirds, whenever a question should happen to divide the States in that manner. Can we forget for whom we are forming a Government? Is it for *men*, or for the imaginary beings called *States*? Will our honest constituents be satisfied with metaphysical distinctions? Will they, ought they to, be satisfied with being told, that the one third compose the greater number of States? The rule of suffrage ought on every principle to be the same in the second as in the first branch. If the Government be not laid on this foundation, it can be neither solid nor lasting. Any other principle will be local, confined and temporary. . . . We talk of States, till we forget what they are composed of. Is a real and fair majority the natural hot-bed of aristocracy? It is a part of the definition of this species of government, or rather of tyranny, that the smaller number governs the greater. It is true that a majority of States in the second branch cannot carry a law against a majority of the people in the first. But this removes half only of the objection. Bad governments are of two sorts, — first, that which does too little; secondly, that which does too much; that which fails through weakness, and that which destroys through oppression. Under which of these evils do the United States at present groan? Under the weakness and inefficiency of its government. To remedy this weakness we have been sent to this Convention. If the motion should be agreed to, we shall leave the United States fettered precisely as heretofore; with the additional mortification of seeing the good purpose of the fair representation of the people in the first branch, defeated in the second. Twenty-four will still control sixty-six. He lamented that such a disagreement should prevail on the point of representation; as he did not foresee that it would happen on the other point most contested, the boundary between the general and the local authorities. He thought the States necessary and valuable parts of a good system.

Mr. ELLSWORTH. The capital objection of Mr. WILSON, "that the minority will rule the majority," is not true. The power is given to the few to save them from being destroyed by the many. If an equality of votes had been given to them in both branches, the objection might have had weight. Is it a novel thing that the few should have a check on the many? Is it not the case in the British Constitution, the wisdom of which so many gentlemen have united in applauding? Have not the House of Lords, who form so small a proportion of the nation, a negative on the laws, as a necessary defense of their peculiar rights against the encroachments of the Commons? No instance of a confederacy has existed in which an equality of voices has not been exercised by the members of it. We are running from one extreme to another. We are razing the foundations of the building, when we need only repair the roof. No salutary measure has been lost for want of a *majority of the States* to favor it. If security be all that the great States wish for, the first branch secures them. The danger of combinations among them is not imaginary. Although no particular abuses could be foreseen by him, the possibility of them would be sufficient to alarm him. But he could easily conceive cases in which they might result from such combinations. Suppose, that, in pursuance of some commercial treaty or arrangement, three or four free ports and no more were to be established, would not combinations be formed in favor of Boston, Philadelphia, and some port of the Chesapeake? A like concert might be formed in the appointment of the great offices. He appealed again to the obligations of the Federal pact, which was still in force, and which had been entered into with so much solemnity; persuading himself that some regard would still be paid to the plighted faith under which each State, small as well as great, held an equal right of suffrage in the general councils. His remarks were not the result of partial or local views. The State he represented (Connecticut) held a middle rank.

Mr. MADISON. It was urged, he said, continually, that an equality of votes in the second branch was not only necessary to secure the small, but would be perfectly safe to the large ones; whose majority in the first branch was an effectual bulwark. But notwithstanding this apparent defense, the majority of States might still injure the majority of the people. . . . He admitted that every peculiar interest, whether in any class of citizens, or any description of States, ought to be secured as far as possible. Wherever there is danger of attack, there ought to be given a constitutional power of defense. But he contended that the States were divided into different interests, not by their difference of size, but by other circumstances; the most material of which resulted partly from climate, but principally from the effects of their having or not having slaves. These two causes concurred in forming the great division of interests in the United States. It did not lie between the large and small States. It lay between the Northern and Southern; and if any defensive power were necessary, it ought to be mutually given to these two interests....

Mr. DAVIE was much embarrassed,[4] and wished for explanations. The Report of the Committee, allowing the Legislatures to choose the Senate, and establishing a proportional representation in it, seemed to be impracticable. There will, according to this rule, be ninety members in the outset, and the number will increase as new States are added. It was impossible that so numerous a body could possess the activity and other qualities required in it. Were he to vote on the comparative merits of the Report, as it stood, and the amendment, he should be constrained to prefer the latter. The appointment of the Senate by electors, chosen by the people for that purpose, was, he conceived, liable to an insuperable difficulty. The larger counties or districts, thrown into a general district, would certainly prevail over the smaller counties or districts, and merit in the latter would be excluded altogether. The Report, therefore, seemed to be right in referring the appointment to the Legislatures, whose agency in the general system did not appear to him objectionable, as it did to some others. The fact was, that the local prejudices and interests which could not be denied to exist, would find their way into the national councils, whether the Representatives should be chosen by the Legislatures, or by the people themselves. On the other hand, if a proportional representation was attended with insuperable difficulties, the making the Senate the representative of the States looked like bringing us back to Congress again, and shutting out all the advantages expected from it. Under this view of the subject, he could not vote for any plan for the Senate yet proposed. He thought that, in general, there were extremes on both sides. We were partly federal, partly national, in our union; and he did not see why the Government might not in some respects operate on the States, in others on the people....

Doctor FRANKLIN. The diversity of opinions turns on two points. If a proportional representation takes place, the small States contend that their liberties will be in danger. If an equality of votes is to be put in its place, the large States say their money will be in danger. When a broad table is to be made, and the edges of planks do not fit, the artist takes a little from both, and makes a good joint. In like manner, here, both sides must part with some of their demands, in order that they may join in some accommodating proposition....

---

[4] thrown into a state of confusion

Mr. KING observed, that . . . he was . . . filled with astonishment, that, if we were convinced that every man in America was secured in all his rights, we should be ready to sacrifice this substantial good to the phantom of *State* sovereignty. That his feelings were more harrowed and his fears more agitated for his country than he could express; that he conceived this to be the last opportunity of providing for its liberty and happiness: that he could not, therefore, but repeat his amazement, that when a just government, founded on a fair representation of the *people* of America, was within our reach, we should renounce the blessing, from an attachment to the ideal freedom and importance of *States*. That should this wonderful illusion continue to prevail, his mind was prepared for every event, rather than sit down under a Government founded on a vicious principle of representation, and which must be as short-lived as it would be unjust. . . .

Mr. BEDFORD,[5] contended, that there was no middle way between a perfect consolidation, and a mere confederacy of the States. The first is out of the question; and in the latter they must continue, if not perfectly, yet equally, sovereign. If political societies possess ambition, avarice, and all the other passions which render them formidable to each other, ought we not to view them in this light here? Will not the same motives operate in America as elsewhere? If any gentleman doubts it, let him look at the votes. Have they not been dictated by interest, by ambition? Are not the large States evidently seeking to aggrandize themselves at the expense of the small? . . . The three large States have a common interest to bind them together in commerce. But whether a combination, as we supposed, or a competition, as others supposed, shall take place among them, in either case the small States must be ruined. We must, like Solon,[6] make such a government as the people will approve. Will the smaller States ever agree to the proposed degradation of them? It is not true that the people will not agree to enlarge the powers of the present Congress. The language of the people has been, that Congress ought to have the power of collecting an impost, and of coercing the States where it may be necessary. On the first point they have been explicit, and, in a manner, unanimous in their declarations. And must they not agree to this, and similar measures, if they ever mean to discharge their engagements? The little States are willing to observe their engagements, but will meet the large ones on no ground but that of the Confederation. We have been told, with a dictatorial air, that this is the last moment for a fair trial in favor of a good government. It will be the last, indeed,

---

[5] Gunning Bedford, Jr. of Delaware

[6] ancient Athenian lawmaker and statesman

if the propositions reported from the Committee go forth to the people. He was under no apprehensions. The large States dare not dissolve the Confederation. If they do, the small ones will find some foreign ally, of more honor and good faith, who will take them by the hand, and do them justice. He did not mean, by this, to intimidate or alarm. It was a natural consequence, which ought to be avoided by enlarging the Federal powers, not annihilating the Federal system. This is what the people expect. All agree in the necessity of a more efficient government, and why not make such an one as they desire?

Mr. ELLSWORTH. Under a National Government, he should participate in the national security . . . but that was all. What he wanted was domestic happiness. The National Government could not descend to the local objects on which this depended. It could only embrace objects of a general nature. He turned his eyes, therefore, for the preservation of his rights, to the State Governments. From these alone he could derive the greatest happiness he expects in this life. His happiness depends on their existence, as much as a new-born infant on its mother for nourishment. If this reasoning was not satisfactory, he had nothing to add that could be so. . . .

Document 10

The Gerry Committee Report

July 2 and 5, 1787

On July 2, there was a tie vote, 5-5-,1 on the motion of Connecticut delegate Oliver Ellsworth giving each State one vote in the second branch and proportional representation in the first branch.

It was time to compromise and move forward or admit deadlock and go home. The vote was 10-1 to commit to a committee of one member from each state. Only Pennsylvania voted "no." Madison, firmly committed to proportional representation in both houses and skeptical that a committee would resolve the dispute, could not persuade his home state to vote "no."

Despite the intransigence of Madison and the decided opinions of certain others, the overall mood of the Convention had shifted. Some of the former advocates for proportional representation were now willing to refer the problem to committee. Each state delegation selected its committee member. The composition of the committee tilted toward the federal principle of equal state representation in the second branch. Six were supporters of it in at least the second branch throughout June: Elbridge Gerry, who was chosen from Massachusetts over Rufus King and Nathaniel Gorham; Oliver Ellsworth, who would represent Connecticut; Robert Yates, who was chosen from New York; William Patterson, representing New Jersey; and Gunning Bedford, Jr., representing Delaware. Others on the committee had not yet declared a particular stance. The independent-minded Luther Martin was chosen over Daniel of St. Thomas Jennifer to represent Maryland, and Abraham Baldwin was chosen over William Houstoun for Georgia. The self-deprecating William Davie was chosen to represent North Carolina and the ever prudent Benjamin Franklin was chosen over Gouverner Morris and James Wilson to represent Pennsylvania. John Rutledge was elected from South Carolina. And George Mason, rather than Madison or John Blair or Edmund Randolph, was elected to represent Virginia.

On July 5, the Gerry Committee presented its report, which offered a compromise: if the second branch of the legislature had representation by states, the other would be given sole authority to originate all bills "raising or appropriating money." This provision also became a subject of debate.

Source: Gordon Lloyd, ed., Debates in the Federal Convention of 1787 by James Madison, a Member *(Ashland, Ohio: Ashbrook Center, 2014), 177-190.*

July 2

In Convention, — On the question for allowing each State one vote in the second branch, as moved by Mr. ELLSWORTH, it was lost, by an equal division of votes, — Connecticut, New York, New Jersey, Delaware, Maryland, aye — 5; Massachusetts, Pennsylvania, Virginia, North Carolina, South Carolina, no — 5; Georgia, divided (Mr. Baldwin aye, Mr. Houston, no),

Mr. PINCKNEY[1] thought an equality of votes in the second branch inadmissible. At the same time he was extremely anxious that something should be done, considering this as the last appeal to a regular experiment. Congress have failed in almost every effort for an amendment of the Federal system. Nothing has prevented a dissolution of it, but the appointment of this Convention; and he could not express his alarms for the consequence of such an event. He read his motion to form the States into classes, with an apportionment of Senators among them.

General PINCKNEY[2] was willing the motion might be considered. He did not entirely approve it. . . . Some compromise seemed to be necessary, the States being exactly divided on the question for an equality of votes in the second branch. He proposed that a Committee consisting of a member from each State should be appointed to devise and report some compromise.

Mr. L. MARTIN had no objection to a commitment, but no modifications whatever could reconcile the smaller States to the least diminution of their equal sovereignty.

Mr. SHERMAN.[3] We are now at a full stop; and nobody, he supposed, meant that we should break up without doing something. A committee he thought most likely to hit on some expedient.

Mr. GOUVERNEUR MORRIS[4] thought a Committee advisable, as the Convention had been equally divided. He had a stronger reason also. The mode of appointing the second branch tended, he was sure, to defeat the object of it. What is this object? To check the precipitation, changeableness,

---

[1] Charles Pinckney of South Carolina

[2] Charles Cotesworth Pinckney of South Carolina, an elder second cousin of Charles Pinckney

[3] Roger Sherman of Connecticut

[4] Gouverneur Morris of Pennsylvania

and excesses, of the first branch. . . . Every man of observation had seen in the democratic branches of the State Legislatures, precipitation — in Congress, changeableness — in every department, excesses against personal liberty, private property, and personal safety. What qualities are necessary to constitute a check in this case? *Abilities* and *virtue* are equally necessary in both branches. Something more, then, is now wanted. In the first place, the checking branch must have a personal interest in checking the other branch. One interest must be opposed to another interest. Vices, as they exist, must be turned against each other. . . .

Doctor WILLIAMSON.[5] If we do not concede on both sides, our business must soon be at an end. He approved of the commitment, supposing that, as the Committee would be a smaller body, a compromise would be pursued with more coolness.

Mr. WILSON[6] objected to the Committee, because it would decide according to that very rule of voting[7] which was opposed on one side. Experience in Congress had also proved the inutility of Committees consisting of members from each State.

Mr. LANSING[8] would not oppose the commitment, though expecting little advantage from it.

Mr. MADISON opposed the commitment. He had rarely seen any other effect than delay from *such* committees in Congress. Any scheme of compromise that could be proposed in the Committee might as easily be proposed in the House; and the report of the Committee, where it contained merely the *opinion* of the Committee, would neither shorten the discussion, nor influence the decision of the House.

Mr. GERRY[9] was for the commitment. Something must be done, or we shall disappoint not only America, but the whole world. He suggested a consideration of the state we should be thrown into by the failure of the Union. We should be without an umpire to decide controversies, and must be at the mercy of events. What, too, is to become of our treaties — what of our foreign debts — what of our domestic? We must make concessions on both sides. Without these, the Constitutions of the several States would never have been formed.

---

5 Hugh Williamson of North Carolina

6 James Wilson of Pennsylvania

7 by states

8 John Lansing, Jr. of New York

9 Elbridge Gerry of Massachusetts

On the question for committing, generally, — Massachusetts, Connecticut, New York, Pennsylvania, Maryland, Virginia, North Carolina, South Carolina, Georgia, aye — 9; New Jersey, Delaware, no — 2.

On the question for committing it "to a member from each state," — Massachusetts, Connecticut, New York, New Jersey, Delaware, Maryland, Virginia, North Carolina, South Carolina, Georgia, aye — 10; Pennsylvania, no — 1.

The Committee, elected by ballot, were, Mr. GERRY, Mr. ELLSWORTH, Mr. YATES, Mr. PATTERSON, Dr. FRANKLIN, Mr. BEDFORD, Mr. MARTIN, Mr. MASON, Mr. DAVIE, Mr. RUTLEDGE, Mr. BALDWIN.

That time might be given to the Committee, and to such as choose to attend to the celebrations on the anniversary of Independence, the Convention adjourned till Thursday.

July 5

In Convention, — Mr. GERRY delivered in, from the Committee appointed on Monday last, the following Report:

"The Committee to whom was referred the eighth Resolution of the Report from the Committee of the Whole House, and so much of the seventh as has not been decided on, submit the following Report:

"That the subsequent propositions be recommended to the Convention on condition that both shall be generally adopted.

"1. That in the first branch of the Legislature each of the States now in the Union shall be allowed one member for every forty thousand inhabitants, of the description reported in the seventh Resolution of the Committee of the Whole House: that each State not containing that number shall be allowed one member: that all bills for raising or appropriating money, and for fixing the salaries of the officers of the Government of the United States, shall originate in the first branch of the Legislature, and shall not be altered or amended by the second branch; and that no money shall be drawn from the public Treasury but in pursuance of appropriations to be originated in the first branch.

"2. That in the second branch, each State shall have an equal vote."

Mr. GORHAM[10] observed, that, as the report consisted of propositions mutually conditional, he wished to hear some explanations touching the grounds on which the conditions were estimated.

---

[10] Nathaniel Gorham of Massachusetts

Mr. GERRY[11]. The Committee were of different opinions, as well as the Deputations from which the Committee were taken; and agreed to the Report merely in order that some ground of accommodation might be proposed. Those opposed to the equality of votes have only assented conditionally; and if the other side do not generally agree, will not be under any obligation to support the Report.

Mr. WILSON thought the Committee had exceeded their powers.

Mr. MARTIN was for taking the question on the whole Report.

Mr. WILSON was for a division of the question; otherwise it would be a leap in the dark.

Mr. MADISON could not regard the privilege of originating money bills as any concession on the side of the small States. Experience proved that it had no effect. If seven States in the upper branch wished a bill to be originated, they might surely find some member from some of the same States in the lower branch, who would originate it. The restriction as to amendments was of as little consequence. Amendments could be handed privately by the Senate to members in the other House. Bills could be negatived, that they might be sent up in the desired shape. If the Senate should yield to the obstinacy of the first branch, the use of that body, as a check, would be lost. If the first branch should yield to that of the Senate, the privilege would be nugatory. Experience had also shown, both in Great Britain, and the States having a similar regulation, that it was a source of frequent and obstinate altercations. These considerations had produced a rejection of a like motion on a former occasion, when judged by its own merits. It could not, therefore, be deemed any concession on the present, and left in force all the objections which had prevailed against allowing each State an equal voice. He conceived that the Convention was reduced to the alternative of either departing from justice in order to conciliate the smaller States, and the minority of the people of the United States, or of displeasing these, by justly gratifying the larger States and the majority of the people. He could not himself hesitate as to the option he ought to make. The Convention, with justice and a majority of the people on their side, had nothing to fear. With injustice and the minority on their side, they had every thing to fear. It was in vain to purchase concord in the Convention on terms which would perpetuate discord among their constituents. . . . Harmony in the Convention was, no doubt, much to be desired. Satisfaction to all the States, in the first instance, still more so. But if the principal States comprehending a majority of the people of the United

[11] Elbridge Gerry of Massachusetts

States, should concur in a just and judicious plan, he had the firmest hopes that all the other States would by degrees accede to it.

Mr. BUTLER[12] said he could not let down his idea of the people of America so far as to believe they would, from mere respect to the Convention, adopt a plan evidently unjust. He did not consider the privilege concerning money bills as of any consequence. He urged, that the second branch ought to represent the States according to their property.

Mr. GOUVERNEUR MORRIS thought the form as well as the matter of the Report objectionable. It seemed, in the first place, to render amendment impracticable. In the next place, it seemed to involve a pledge to agree to the second part, if the first should be agreed to. He conceived the whole aspect of it to be wrong. He came here as a Representative of America; he flattered himself he came here in some degree as a Representative of the whole human race; for the whole human race will be affected by the proceedings of this Convention. He wished gentlemen to extend their views beyond the present moment of time; beyond the narrow limits of place from which they derive their political origin. If he were to believe some things which he had heard, he should suppose that we were assembled to truck and bargain for our particular States. He cannot descend to think that any gentlemen are really actuated by these views. We must look forward to the effects of what we do. These alone ought to guide us. Much has been said of the sentiments of the people. They were unknown. They could not be known. All that we can infer is, that, if the plan we recommend be reasonable and right, all who have reasonable minds and sound intentions will embrace it, notwithstanding what had been said by some gentlemen. . . .

But returning to the Report, he could not think it in any respect calculated for the public good. As the second branch is now constituted, there will be constant disputes and appeals to the States, which will undermine the General Government, and control and annihilate the first branch. . . . He wished our ideas to be enlarged to the true interest of man, instead of being circumscribed within the narrow compass of a particular spot. And, after all, how little can be the motive yielded by selfishness for such a policy? Who can say, whether he himself, much less whether his children, will the next year be an inhabitant of this or that State?

Mr. BEDFORD. . . . The condition of the United States requires that something should be immediately done. It will be better that a defective plan should be adopted, than that none should be recommended. He saw no reason

---

[12] Pierce Butler of South Carolina

why defects might not be supplied by meetings ten, fifteen or twenty years hence.

Mr. ELLSWORTH said, he had not attended the proceedings of the Committee,[13] but was ready to accede to the compromise they had reported. Some compromise was necessary; and he saw none more convenient or reasonable.

Mr. WILLIAMSON hoped that the expressions of individuals would not be taken for the sense of their colleagues, much less of their States, which was not and could not be known. He hoped, also, that the meaning of those expressions would not be misconstrued or exaggerated. He did not conceive that (Mr. GOUVERNEUR MORRIS) meant that the sword ought to be drawn against the smaller States. He only pointed out the probable consequences of anarchy in the United States. A similar exposition ought to be given of the expressions of (Mr. GORHAM). He was ready to hear the Report discussed; but thought the propositions contained in it the most objectionable of any he had yet heard.

Mr. PATTERSON said that he had, when the report was agreed to in the Committee, reserved to himself the right of freely discussing it. He acknowledged that the warmth complained of was improper; but he thought the sword and the gallows little calculated to produce conviction. He complained of the manner in which Mr. MADISON and Mr. G. MORRIS had treated the small States.

Mr. GERRY. Though he had assented to the Report in the Committee, he had very material objections to it. We were, however, in a peculiar situation. We were neither the same nation, nor different nations. We ought not, therefore, to pursue the one or the other of these ideas too closely. If no compromise should take place, what will be the consequence? A secession he foresaw would take place; for some gentlemen seemed decided on it. Two different plans will be proposed, and the result no man could foresee. If we do not come to some agreement among ourselves, some foreign sword will probably do the work for us.

Mr. MASON. The Report was meant not as specific propositions to be adopted, but merely as a general ground of accommodation. There must be some accommodation on this point, or we shall make little further progress in

---

[13] According to a footnote Madison made to his notes on the debates of July 5, Roger Sherman attended the Gerry committee meetings in the place of Ellsworth, who "was kept away by indisposition," that is, a slight illness.

the work. Accommodation was the object of the House in the appointment of the Committee, and of the Committee in the Report they had made. . . .

The first proposition in the Report for fixing the representation in the first branch, "one member for every forty thousand inhabitants," being taken up, —

Mr. GOUVERNEUR MORRIS objected to that scale of apportionment. He thought property ought to be taken into the estimate as well as the number of inhabitants. Life and liberty were generally said to be of more value than property. An accurate view of the matter would, nevertheless, prove that property was the main object of society. . . .

Mr. RUTLEDGE. The gentleman last up had spoken some of his sentiments precisely. Property was certainly the principal object of society. If numbers should be made the rule of representation, the Atlantic States would be subjected to the Western.[14] He moved that the first proposition in the Report be postponed, in order to take up the following, viz.[15]: "That the suffrages of the several States be regulated and proportioned according to the sums to be paid towards the general revenue by the inhabitants of each State respectively: that an apportionment of suffrages, according to the ratio aforesaid shall be made and regulated at the end of — years from the first meeting of the Legislature of the United States, and at the end of every — years; but that for the present, and until the period above mentioned, the suffrages shall be for New Hampshire —, for Massachusetts —, &c."

Col. MASON said, the case of new States was not unnoticed in the Committee: but it was thought, and he was himself decidedly of opinion, that if they made a part of the Union, they ought to be subject to no unfavorable discriminations. Obvious considerations required it.

Mr. RANDOLPH concurred with Mr. MASON.

On the question on Mr. RUTLEDGE'S motion, — South Carolina, aye — 1; Massachusetts, Connecticut, New York, New Jersey, Pennsylvania, Delaware, Maryland, Virginia, North Carolina, no — 9; Georgia, not on the floor.

---

[14] The Western States that Rutledge is probably referring to are the states to be carved out of the Northwest Territories ceded earlier primarily by Virginia. The Northwest Ordinance had been debated in the existing Confederation Congress during the 1780s and the debate was about to come to an end. The existing Congress passed the Northwest Ordinance a few days after July 5, 1787. Rutledge did not explain why he thought states arising in the then sparsely occupied western territory would subject the existing states to their will.

[15] Abbreviation of the Latin *videlicet:* that is, namely

Document 11

The Three-Fifths Clause Revisited

July 11 - 14 and 16, 1787

More than one argument over principle was at stake in the debates leading to the Connecticut Compromise. Document 10 in this collection illuminated the opposing concerns of two parties: those who saw proportional representation in the legislative branch as required by justice, and those whose concern to protect state sovereignty caused them to insist on equal representation for each state. But during the final days of the discussion over representation, the difference between small and large states receded in comparison to the difference between states holding large populations of slaves and those in which the overwhelming majority of laborers were free. This issue had already arisen (see Document 6).

The North and South Carolina delegates reiterated their concern that wealth be represented, since the purpose of government, they held, was to protect property. Slaves were the specific property they had in mind, and the South Carolina delegates now contended that counting merely three-fifths of the slave population when determining a number of representatives proportional to population would not adequately protect that species of property. Other delegates remarked on the inconsistency in counting three fifths of the slave population for purposes of taxation and the entire population for purposes of apportioning representation. Some wondered why slave property was to be counted, but not other kinds of property. And still other delegates recoiled at the suggestion of counting slaves as "property" at all.

The delegates did seem to move toward consensus on one point: if population were to determine representation, a periodic census would need to be taken. Consideration of this point brought the delegates once again to disputing whether representation should be proportional to population or accorded equally to each state. While Madison insisted on the justice of proportional representation, Roger Sherman of Connecticut argued that equal representation of each state was important not as a principle of justice, but rather to insure the survival of independent state governments.

Despite the differing positions, and the occasionally heated language, the long journey over representation that started in earnest on June 11 would come to an end on July 16. On that date, despite the "no" votes of Virginia, Pennsylvania, South

Carolina, and Georgia, delegates approved what (because of the roles played by Roger Sherman and Oliver Ellsworth of Connecticut in bringing it about) came to be called the Connecticut Compromise. Five states voted to affirm it; and due to the division of the Massachusetts delegation and the absence of the New York delegation, the compromise passed, allowing the Convention to begin discussing the powers to be granted Congress.

Source: Gordon Lloyd, ed., Debates in the Federal Convention of 1787 by James Madison, a Member *(Ashland, Ohio: Ashbrook Center, 2014), 208-23 and 234-235.*

July 11

Mr. WILLIAMSON[1]. . . . moved. . ."that in order to ascertain the alterations that may happen in the population and wealth of the several States, a census shall be taken of the free white inhabitants, and three-fifths of those of other descriptions on the first year after this government shall have been adopted, and every — year thereafter; and that the representation be regulated accordingly."

. . . Mr. BUTLER[2] and General PINCKNEY[3] insisted that blacks be included in the rule of representation *equally* with the whites; and for that purpose moved that the words "three-fifths" be struck out.

Mr. GERRY[4] thought that three-fifths of them was, to say the least, the full proportion that could be admitted.

Mr. GORHAM.[5] This ratio was fixed by Congress as a rule of taxation. Then it was urged, by the Delegates representing the States having slaves, that the blacks were still more inferior to freemen. At present, when the ratio of representation is to be established, we are assured that they are equal to freemen. The arguments on the former occasion had convinced him that three-fifths was pretty near the just proportion, and he should vote according to the same opinion now.

Mr. BUTLER insisted that the labor of a slave in South Carolina was as productive and valuable as that of a freeman in Massachusetts; that as wealth

---

[1] Hugh Williamson of North Carolina

[2] Pierce Butler of South Carolina

[3] Charles Cotesworth Pinckney of South Carolina

[4] Elbridge Gerry of Massachusetts

[5] Nathaniel Gorham of Massachusetts

was the great means of defense and utility to the nation, they were equally valuable to it with freemen; and that consequently an equal representation ought to be allowed for them in a government which was instituted principally, for the protection of property, and was itself to be supported by property. . . .

. . . Mr. WILLIAMSON reminded Mr. GORHAM that if the Southern States contended for the inferiority of blacks to whites when taxation was in view, the Eastern States, on the same occasion, contended for their equality. He did not, however, either then or now, concur in either extreme, but approved of the ratio of three-fifths.

On Mr. BUTLER'S motion, for considering blacks as equal to whites in the apportionment of representation, — Delaware, South Carolina, Georgia, aye — 3; Massachusetts, Connecticut, New Jersey, Pennsylvania, Maryland, Virginia, North Carolina, no — 7; New York, not on the floor.

Mr. RUTLEDGE[6] contended for the admission of wealth in the estimate by which representation should be regulated. . . . He moved that, "at the end of — years after the first meeting of the Legislature, and of every — years thereafter, the Legislature shall proportion the representation according to the principles of wealth and population."

. . . Mr. GORHAM. If the Convention, who are comparatively so little biased by local views, are so much perplexed, how can it be expected that the Legislature hereafter, under the full bias of those views will be able to settle a standard? He was convinced, by the arguments of others and his own reflections, that the Convention ought to fix some standard or other.

Mr. GOUVERNEUR MORRIS. The arguments of others and his own reflections had led him to a very different conclusion. If we cannot agree on a rule that will be just at this time, how can we expect to find one that will be just in all times to come? Surely those who come after us will judge better of things present than we can of things future. . . .

Mr. MADISON . . . would admit that in no situation numbers of inhabitants were an accurate measure of wealth. He contended, however, that in the United States it was sufficiently so for the object in contemplation. Although their climate varied considerably, yet as the governments, the laws, and the manners of all, were nearly the same, and the intercourse between different parts perfectly free, population, industry, arts, and the value of labor, would constantly tend to equalize themselves. The value of labor might be considered as the principal criterion of wealth and ability to support taxes; and this would find its level in different places, where the intercourse should be

---

[6] John Rutledge of South Carolina

easy and free, with as much certainty as the value of money or any other thing. Wherever labor would yield most, people would resort; till the competition should destroy the inequality. Hence it is that the people are constantly swarming from the more to the less, populous places — from Europe to America — from the Northern and middle parts of the United States to the Southern and Western. They go where land is cheaper, because there labor is dearer. . . .

. . . On the question for postponing Mr. WILLIAMSON'S motion, in order to consider that of Mr. RUTLEDGE, it passed in the negative, — Massachusetts, Pennsylvania, Delaware, South Carolina, Georgia, aye — 5; Connecticut, New Jersey, Maryland, Virginia, North Carolina, no — 5.[7]

On the question on the first clause of Mr. WILLIAMSON'S motion, as to taking a census of the free inhabitants, it passed in the affirmative, — Massachusetts, Connecticut, New Jersey, Pennsylvania, Virginia, North Carolina, aye — 6; Delaware, Maryland, South Carolina, Georgia, no — 4.

The next clause as to three-fifths of the negroes being considered, —

Mr. KING,[8] being much opposed to fixing numbers as the rule of representation, was particularly so on account of the blacks. He thought the admission of them along with whites at all, would excite great discontents among the States having no slaves. He had never said, as to any particular point, that he would in no event acquiesce in and support it; but he would say that if in any case such a declaration was to be made by him, it would be in this. He remarked that in the temporary allotment of representatives made by the Committee, the Southern States had received more than the number of their white and three-fifths of their black inhabitants entitled them to.

. . . Mr. GORHAM . . . . recollected that when the proposition of Congress for changing the eighth Article of the Confederation was before the Legislature of Massachusetts, the only difficulty then was, to satisfy them that the negroes ought not to have been counted equally with the whites, instead of being counted in the ratio of three-fifths only.

Mr. WILSON[9] did not well see, on what principle the admission of blacks in the proportion of three-fifths, could be explained. Are they admitted as citizens — then why are they not admitted on an equality with white citizens? Are they admitted as property — then why is not other property admitted into

---

[7] A tie vote on a proposition was not counted as an affirmative vote. Thus, the motion "passed in the negative," or failed.

[8] Rufus King of Massachusetts

[9] James Wilson of Pennsylvania

the computation? These were difficulties, however, which he thought must be overruled by the necessity of compromise. He had some apprehensions also, from the tendency of the blending of the blacks with the whites, to give disgust to the people of Pennsylvania. . . .

Mr. GOUVERNEUR MORRIS was compelled to declare himself reduced to the dilemma of doing injustice to the Southern States, or to human nature; and he must therefore do it to the former. For he could never agree to give such encouragement to the slave trade, as would be given by allowing them a representation for their negroes; and he did not believe those States would ever confederate on terms that would deprive them of that trade.

On the question for agreeing to include three-fifths of the blacks, — Connecticut, Virginia, North Carolina, Georgia, aye — 4; Massachusetts, New Jersey, Pennsylvania, Delaware, Maryland, South Carolina, no — 6. . . .

July 12

Mr. GOUVERNEUR MORRIS moved to add to the clause empowering the Legislature to vary the representation according to the principles of wealth and numbers of inhabitants, a proviso, "that taxation shall be in proportion to representation."

Mr. BUTLER contended again, that representation should be according to the full number of inhabitants including all the blacks.

Mr. MASON[10] also admitted the justice of the principle, but was afraid embarrassments might be occasioned to the Legislature by it. . . .

Mr. GOUVERNEUR MORRIS admitted that some objections lay against his motion, but supposed they would be removed by restraining the rule to *direct* taxation. . . .

General PINCKNEY liked the idea. . . . He was alarmed at what was said yesterday, concerning the negroes. . . .

. . . Mr. DAVIE[11] said it was high time now to speak out. He saw that it was meant by some gentlemen to deprive the Southern States of any share of representation for their blacks. He was sure that North Carolina would never confederate on any terms that did not rate them at least as three-fifths. If the Eastern States meant, therefore, to exclude them altogether, the business was at an end.

---

[10] George Mason of Virginia

[11] William Davie of North Carolina

Doctor JOHNSON[12] thought that wealth and population were the true, equitable rules of representation; but he conceived that these two principles resolved themselves into one, population being the best measure of wealth. . . .

Mr. GOUVERNEUR MORRIS. It had been said that it is high time to speak out. As one member, he would candidly do so. He came here to form a compact for the good of America. He was ready to do so with all the States. He hoped and believed that all would enter into such a compact. If they would not, he was ready to join with any States that would. But as the compact was to be voluntary, it is in vain for the Eastern States to insist on what the Southern States will never agree to. It is equally vain for the latter to require what the other States can never admit; and he verily believed the people of Pennsylvania will never agree to a representation of negroes. What can be desired by these States more than has been already proposed — that the Legislature shall from time to time regulate representation according to population and wealth?

General PINCKNEY desired that the rule of wealth should be ascertained, and not left to the pleasure of the Legislature; and that property in slaves should not be exposed to danger, under a government instituted for the protection of property.

. . . Mr. ELLSWORTH[13] . . . moved to add to the last clause adopted by the House the words following, "and that the rule of contribution by direct taxation, for the support of the Government of the United States, shall be the number of white inhabitants and three-fifths of every other description in the several States, until some other rule that shall more accurately ascertain the wealth of the several States can be devised and adopted by the Legislature."

Mr. BUTLER seconded the motion, in order that it might be committed.

Mr. RANDOLPH[14] was not satisfied with the motion. . . . He proposed, in lieu of Mr. ELLSWORTH's motion, "that in order to ascertain the alterations in representation that may be required, from time to time, by changes in the relative circumstances of the States, a census shall be taken within two years from the first meeting of the General Legislature of the United States, and once within the term of every — years afterwards, of all the inhabitants, in the manner and according to the ratio recommended by Congress in their Resolution of the eighteenth day of April, 1783, (rating the blacks at three-fifths of their number); and that the Legislature of the United States shall arrange the representation accordingly." He urged strenuously that express

---

[12] William Samuel Johnson of Connecticut

[13] Oliver Ellsworth of Connecticut

[14] Edmund Randolph of Virginia

security ought to be provided for including slaves in the ratio of representation. He lamented that such a species of property existed. But as it did exist, the holders of it would require this security. It was perceived that the design was entertained by some of excluding slaves altogether; the Legislature therefore ought not to be left at liberty.

Mr. ELLSWORTH withdraws his motion, and seconds that of Mr. RANDOLPH.

Mr. WILSON observed that less umbrage would perhaps be taken against an admission of the slaves into the rule of representation, if it should be so expressed as to make them indirectly only an ingredient in the rule, by saying that they should enter into the rule of taxation; and as representation was to be according to taxation, the end would be equally attained. He accordingly moved, and was seconded, so to alter the last clause adopted by the House, that, together with the amendment proposed, the whole should read as follows: "provided always that the representation ought to be proportioned according to direct taxation; and in order to ascertain the alterations in the direct taxation which may be required from time to time by the changes in the relative circumstances of the States, *Resolved*, that a census be taken within two years from the first meeting of the legislature of the United States, and once within the term of every — years afterwards, of all the inhabitants of the United States, in the manner and according to the ratio recommended by Congress in their Resolution of the eighteenth day of April, 1783; and that the Legislature of the United States shall proportion the direct taxation accordingly."[15]

Mr. KING. Although this amendment varies the aspect somewhat, he had still two powerful objections against tying down the Legislature to the rule of numbers, — first, they were at this time an uncertain index of the relative

---

[15] See Document 6 where, on June 11, Mr. Wilson, seconded by Mr. Pinckney, noted that the 3/5[ths] clause had its roots in the Confederation Congress for apportioning support of the general government. Three-fifths was the "rule in the act of Congress, agreed to by eleven States, for apportioning quotas of revenue on the States. . . . " Under the Articles, representation was not the issue: each State had one vote. The issue was to find a formula to raise revenue. That is the origin the three-fifths clause. At the Constitutional Convention, there was overwhelming support to bestow the power of taxation on Congress in order to raise the revenue necessary for running the government. The issue was how to settle the issue of representation. Wilson introduced a solution with which the delegates were familiar, if they had the sense to apply it to representation.

wealth of the States; secondly, if they were a just index at this time, it cannot be supposed always to continue so. He was far from wishing to retain any unjust advantage whatever in one part of the Republic. If justice was not the basis of the connection, it could not be of long duration. He must be short-sighted indeed who does not foresee, that, whenever the Southern States shall be more numerous than the Northern, they can and will hold a language that will awe them into justice. If they threaten to separate now in case injury shall be done them, will their threats be less urgent or effectual when force shall back their demands? Even in the intervening period there will be no point of time at which they will not be able to say, do us justice or we will separate. He urged the necessity of placing confidence, to a certain degree in every government, and did not conceive that the proposed confidence, as to a periodical re-adjustment of the representation, exceeded[16] that degree.

Mr. PINCKNEY[17] moved to amend Mr. RANDOLPH'S motion, so as to make "blacks equal to the whites in the ratio of representation." This he urged, was nothing more than justice. The blacks are the laborers, the peasants, of the Southern States. They are as productive of pecuniary resources as those of the Northern States. They add equally to the wealth, and, considering money as the sinew of war, to the strength, of the nation. It will also be politic with regard to the Northern States, as taxation is to keep pace with representation.

. . . On Mr. PINCKNEY'S motion, for rating blacks as equal to whites, instead of as three-fifths, — South Carolina, Georgia, aye — 2; Massachusetts, Connecticut, (Doctor JOHNSON, aye), New Jersey, Pennsylvania, (three against two), Delaware, Maryland, Virginia, North Carolina, no — 8. . . .

On the question on the whole proposition, as proportioning representation to direct taxation, and both to the white and three-fifths of the black inhabitants, and requiring a census within six years, and within every ten years afterwards, — Connecticut, Pennsylvania, Maryland, Virginia, North Carolina, Georgia, aye — 6; New Jersey, Delaware, no — 2; Massachusetts, South Carolina, divided.

July 13

On the motion of Mr. RANDOLPH, the vote of Monday last, authorizing the Legislature to adjust, from time to time, the representation upon the principles of *wealth* and numbers of inhabitants, was reconsidered by common

---

[16] Mr. King seems to mean that the proposed census would not *increase* Southerners' confidence in the government.

[17] Charles Pinckney of South Carolina

consent, in order to strike out *wealth* and adjust the resolution to that requiring periodical revisions according to the number of whites and three-fifths of the blacks.

The motion was in the words following: — "But as the present situation of the States may probably alter in the number of their inhabitants, that the Legislature of the United States be authorized, from time to time, to apportion the number of Representatives; and in case any of the States shall hereafter be divided, or any two or more States united, or new States created within the limits of the United States, the Legislature of the United States shall possess authority to regulate the number of Representatives in any of the foregoing cases, upon the principle of their number of inhabitants, according to the provisions hereafter mentioned."

Mr. GOUVERNEUR MORRIS opposed the alteration, as leaving still an incoherence. If negroes were to be viewed as inhabitants, and the revision was to proceed on the principle of numbers of inhabitants, they ought to be added in their entire number, and not in the proportion of three-fifths. If as property, the word *wealth* was right; and striking it out would produce the very inconsistency which it was meant to get rid of. The train of business, and the late turn which it had taken, had led him, he said, into deep meditation on it, and he would candidly state the result. A distinction had been set up, and urged, between the Northern and Southern States. He had hitherto considered this doctrine as heretical. He still thought the distinction groundless. He sees, however, that it is persisted in; and the Southern gentlemen will not be satisfied unless they see the way open to their gaining a majority in the public councils. The consequence of such a transfer of power from the maritime to the interior and landed interest, will, he foresees, be such an oppression to commerce, that he shall be obliged to vote for the vicious principle of equality in the second branch, in order to provide some defense for the Northern States against it. But, to come more to the point, either this distinction is fictitious or real; if fictitious, let it be dismissed, and let us proceed with due confidence. If it be real, instead of attempting to blend incompatible things, let us at once take a friendly leave of each other. . . .

Mr. BUTLER. The security the Southern States want is, that their negroes may not be taken from them, which some gentlemen within or without doors have a very good mind to do. . . .

Mr. WILSON. If a general declaration would satisfy any gentleman, he had no indisposition to declare his sentiments. Conceiving that all men, wherever placed, have equal rights, and are equally entitled to confidence, he viewed without apprehension the period when a few States should contain the superior number of people. The majority of people, wherever found, ought in all questions to govern the minority. If the interior country should acquire this majority, it will not only have the right, but will avail itself of it, whether we will or no. . . .

On the question to strike out *wealth*, and to make the change as moved by Mr. RANDOLPH, it passed in the affirmative, — Massachusetts, Connecticut, New Jersey, Pennsylvania, Maryland, Virginia, North Carolina, South Carolina, Georgia, aye — 9; Delaware, divided.

Mr. READ[18] moved to insert, after the word "divided," "or enlarged by addition of territory;" which was agreed to, nem. con.[19]

July 14

Mr. L. MARTIN urged the question on the whole. He did not like many parts of it. He did not like having two branches, nor the inequality of votes in the first branch. He was willing, however, to make trial of the plan, rather than do nothing.

Mr. WILSON traced the progress of the report through its several stages; remarking, that when, on the question concerning an equality of votes the House was divided, our constituents, had they voted as their Representatives did, would have stood as two thirds against the equality, and one third only in favor of it. This fact would ere long be known, and it would appear that this fundamental point has been carried by one third against two thirds. What hopes will our constituents entertain, when they find that the essential principles of justice have been violated in the outset of the Government? . . . The equality of votes was a point of such critical importance, that every opportunity ought to be allowed for discussing and collecting the mind of the Convention upon it.

Mr. L. MARTIN denies that there were two-thirds against the equality of votes. The States that please to call themselves large are the weakest in the Union. Look at Massachusetts — look at Virginia — are they efficient States? He was for letting a separation take place, if they desired it. He had rather there should be two confederacies, than one founded on any other principle than an equality of votes in the second branch at least.

Mr. WILSON was not surprised that those who say that a minority does more than a majority, should say the minority is stronger than the majority. He supposed the next assertion will be, that they are richer also; though he hardly

---

[18] George Read of Delaware

[19] an abbreviation of *nemine contradicente*, Latin for "no one dissenting"

expected it would be persisted in, when the States shall be called on for taxes and troops.

Mr. GERRY . . . . The Report was not altogether to his mind; but he would agree to it as it stood, rather than throw it out altogether.

The reconsideration being tacitly agreed to, —

Mr. PINCKNEY moved, that, instead of an equality of votes, the States should be represented in the second branch as follows: New Hampshire by two members; Massachusetts, four; Rhode Island, one; Connecticut, three; New York, three; New Jersey, two; Pennsylvania, four; Delaware, one; Maryland, three; Virginia, five; North Carolina, three; South Carolina, three; Georgia, two; making in the whole, thirty-six.

Mr. WILSON seconds the motion.

Mr. DAYTON.[20] The smaller States can never give up their equality. For himself, he would in no event yield that security for their rights.

Mr. SHERMAN[21] urged the equality of votes, not so much as a security for the small States, as for the State Governments, which could not be preserved unless they were represented, and had a negative in the General Government. He had no objection to the members in the second branch voting *per capita*,[22] as had been suggested by (Mr. GERRY).

Mr. MADISON concurred in this motion of Mr. PINCKNEY, as a reasonable compromise.

Mr. GERRY said, he should like the motion, but could see no hope of success. An accommodation must take place, and it was apparent from what had been seen, that it could not do so on the ground of the motion. He was utterly against a partial confederacy, leaving other States to accede or not accede, as had been intimated.

Mr. KING said, it was always with regret that he differed from his colleagues, but it was his duty to differ from (Mr. GERRY) on this occasion. He considered the proposed Government as substantially and formally a General and National Government over the people of America. There never will be a case in which it will act as a Federal Government, on the States and not on the individual citizens. And is it not a clear principle, that in a free government, those who are to be the objects of a government, ought to influence the operations of it? What reason can be assigned, why the same rule of representation should not prevail in the second, as in the first, branch? He

---

[20] Jonathan Dayton of New Jersey

[21] Roger Sherman of Connecticut

[22] as individuals

could conceive none. On the contrary, every view of the subject that presented itself seemed to require it. . . .

It was his firm belief that Massachusetts would never be prevailed on to yield to an equality of votes. In New York, (he was sorry to be obliged to say any thing relative to that State in the absence of its representatives, but the occasion required it), in New York he had seen that the most powerful argument used by the considerate opponents to the grant of the Impost to Congress was pointed against the vicious constitution of Congress with regard to representation and suffrage. He was sure that no government would last that was not founded on just principles. He preferred the doing of nothing, to an allowance of an equal vote to all the States. It would be better, he thought, to submit to a little more confusion and convulsion, than to submit to such an evil. It was difficult to say what the views of different gentlemen might be. Perhaps there might be some who thought no Government co-extensive with the United States could be established with a hope of its answering the purpose. Perhaps there might be other fixed opinions incompatible with the object we are pursuing. If there were, he thought it but candid, that gentlemen should speak out, that we might understand one another.

Mr. STRONG.[23] The Convention had been much divided in opinion. In order to avoid the consequences of it, an accommodation had been proposed. A committee had been appointed; and though some of the members of it were averse to an equality of votes, a report had been made in favor of it. It is agreed, on all hands, that Congress are nearly at an end. If no accommodation takes place, the Union itself must soon be dissolved. It has been suggested that if we cannot come to any general agreement, the principal States may form and recommend a scheme of government. But will the small States, in that case, ever accede to it? Is it probable that the large States themselves will, under such circumstances, embrace and ratify it? He thought the Small states had made a considerable concession, in the article of money bills,[24] and that they might naturally expect some concessions on the other side. From this view of the matter, he was compelled to give his vote for the Report taken altogether.

Mr. MADISON expressed his apprehensions that if the proper foundation of government was destroyed, by substituting an equality in place of a proportional representation, no proper superstructure would be raised. . . .

But it had been said that the Government would, in its operation, be partly federal, partly national; that although in the latter respect the representatives of

---

[23] Caleb Strong of Massachusetts

[24] Strong refers to the decision that these bills originate in the first branch.

the people ought to be in proportion to the people, yet in the former, it ought to be according to the number of States. If there was any solidity in this distinction, he was ready to abide by it; if there was none, it ought to be abandoned. . . .

. . . On the question for agreeing to Mr. PINCKNEY'S motion, for allowing New Hampshire two; Massachusetts, four, &c. it passed in the negative, — Pennsylvania, Maryland, Virginia, South Carolina, aye — 4; Massachusetts, (Mr. KING, aye, Mr. GORHAM absent), Connecticut, New Jersey, Delaware, North Carolina, Georgia, no — 6.

July 16

In Convention, — On the question for agreeing to the whole Report, as amended, and including the equality of votes in the second branch, it passed in the affirmative, — Connecticut, New Jersey, Delaware, Maryland, North Carolina (Mr. SPAIGHT no) aye — 5; Pennsylvania, Virginia, South Carolina, Georgia, no — 4; Massachusetts, divided (Mr. GERRY, Mr. STRONG, aye; Mr. KING, Mr. GORHAM, no). . . .

Document 12

The Committee of Detail Report

July 23 - 24 and August 6, 1787

The first two months of the Convention were devoted mainly to discussing and settling the issue of representation of people, states, and wealth in the new government. By the end of this discussion, the doctrine of bicameralism had been firmly established, with each branch of the legislature having its own source of election and scheme of representation. But there were other issues that were deliberated but not completely settled during June and July. For example, should the powers of Congress be listed or unlisted, and if listed, should they be interpreted as expressly listed — that is, as precluding any implied powers? It was also time to make progress on the creation of the Presidency and the Judiciary, as well as on how the document should be adopted and altered. Each of these issues were addressed by the five-member Committee on Detail. Also of considerable interest is the warning issued on July 23 by General Charles Cotesworth Pinckney of South Carolina just as the Convention was ready to pursue a course of reconciliation. By this point, the difference of interests between north and south, rather than between large and small states, was emerging as the critical obstacle the Convention had to overcome.

On July 24, the Convention chose a five-member Committee of Detail that issued its Report on August 6. Nathaniel Gorham of Massachusetts, James Wilson of Pennsylvania, Oliver Ellsworth of Connecticut, Edmund Randolph of Virginia, and John Rutledge of South Carolina were selected to the Committee.

Source: Gordon Lloyd, ed., Debates in the Federal Convention of 1787 by James Madison, a Member *(Ashland, Ohio: Ashbrook Center, 2014) 284, 290, 308-319.*

July 23

General PINCKNEY reminded the Convention, that if the Committee should fail to insert some security to the Southern States against an emancipation of slaves, and taxes on exports, he should be bound by duty to his State to vote against their report.

The appointment of a Committee, as moved by Mr. GERRY, was agreed to, *nem. con.*[1]

On the question, Shall the Committee consist of ten members, one from each State present? — all the States were *no*, except Delaware, *aye*.

Shall it consist of seven members? — New Hampshire, Massachusetts, Connecticut, Maryland, South Carolina, aye — 5; Pennsylvania, Delaware, Virginia, North Carolina, Georgia, no — 5.

The question being lost by an equal division of votes, it was agreed, *nem. con.*, that the Committee should consist of five members, to be appointed to-morrow.

July 24

On a ballot for a committee to report a Constitution conformable to the Resolutions passed by the Convention, the members chosen were: —

Mr. RUTLEDGE, Mr. RANDOLPH, Mr. GORHAM, Mr. ELLSWORTH, Mr. WILSON.[2]

On motion to discharge the Committee of the Whole from the propositions submitted to the Convention by Mr. C. PINCKNEY[3] as the basis of a Constitution, and to refer them to the Committee of Detail just appointed, it was agreed to, *nem. con.*

A like motion was then made and agreed to, *nem. con.*, with respect to the propositions of Mr. PATTERSON.[4]

Adjourned.

August 6

Mr. RUTLEDGE delivered in the Report of the Committee of Detail, as follows — a printed copy being at the same time furnished to each member:

---

[1] an abbreviation of *nemine contradicente*, Latin for "no one dissenting"

[2] Very rarely did the delegates choose a committee that included fewer than one member from each State present. The Committee on Detail is an important exception. One delegate came from each of the three most populous States: Massachusetts, Pennsylvania, and Virginia. One delegate was selected from Connecticut, probably to keep the Connecticut Compromise secure, and one delegate, Rutledge, from South Carolina was chosen to resist the apparently growing effort to involve the new government in the slavery question. Thus, special attention needs to be paid to the slavery provisions of the Committee on Detail Report and how the whole convention responds to the slave trade resolutions.

[3] Charles Pinckney of South Carolina

[4] William Patterson of New Jersey

We the people of the States of New Hampshire, Massachusetts, Rhode Island and Providence Plantations, Connecticut, New York, New Jersey, Pennsylvania, Delaware, Maryland, Virginia, North Carolina, South Carolina, and Georgia, do ordain, declare, and establish, the following Constitution for the government of ourselves and our posterity.

ARTICLE I.

The style of the Government shall be, "The United States of America."

ARTICLE II.

The Government shall consist of supreme Legislative, Executive, and Judicial powers.

ARTICLE III.

The legislative power shall be vested in a Congress, to consist of two separate and distinct bodies of men, a House of Representatives and a Senate; each of which shall in all cases have a negative on the other. The Legislature shall meet on the first Monday in December in every year.

ARTICLE IV.

Sect. 1. The members of the House of Representatives shall be chosen every second year, by the people of the several States comprehended within this Union. The qualifications of the electors shall be the same from time to time, as those of the electors in the several States, of the most numerous branch of their own Legislatures.

Sect. 2. Every member of the House of Representatives shall be of the age of twenty-five years at least; shall have been a citizen in the United States for at least three years before his election; and shall be, at the time of his election, a resident of the State in which he shall be chosen.

Sect. 3. The House of Representatives shall, at its first formation, and until the number of citizens and inhabitants shall be taken in the manner hereinafter described, consist of sixty-five members, of whom three shall be chosen in New Hampshire, eight in Massachusetts, one in Rhode Island and Providence Plantations, five in Connecticut, six in New York, four in New Jersey, eight in Pennsylvania, one in Delaware, six in Maryland, ten in Virginia, five in North Carolina, five in South Carolina, and three in Georgia.

Sect. 4. As the proportions of numbers in different States will alter from time to time; as some of the States may hereafter be divided: as others may be enlarged by addition of territory; as two or more States may be united; as new States will be erected within the limits of the United States, the legislature shall, in each of these cases, regulate the number of Representatives by the number of inhabitants, according to the provisions hereinafter made, at the rate of one for every forty thousand.

Sect. 5. All bills for raising or appropriating money, and for fixing the salaries of the officers of government, shall originate in the House of Representatives, and shall not be altered or amended by the Senate. No money shall be drawn from the public treasury, but in pursuance of appropriations that shall originate in the House of Representatives.

Sect. 6. The House of Representatives shall have the sole power of impeachment. It shall choose its speaker and other officers.

Sect. 7. Vacancies in the House of Representatives shall be supplied by writs of election from the Executive authority of the state in the representation from which they shall happen.

ARTICLE V.

Sect. 1. The Senate of the United States shall be chosen by the Legislatures of the several States. Each Legislature shall choose two members. Vacancies may be supplied by the Executive until the next meeting of the Legislature. Each member shall have one vote.

Sect. 2. The Senators shall be chosen for six years; but immediately after the first election, they shall be divided, by lot, into three classes, as nearly as may be, numbered one, two, and three. The seats of the members of the first class shall be vacated at the expiration of the second year; of the second class at the expiration of the fourth year; of the third class at the expiration of the sixth year; so that a third part of the members may be chosen every second year.

Sect. 3. Every member of the Senate shall be of the age of thirty years at least; shall have been a citizen in the United States for at least four years before his election; and shall be, at the time of his election, a resident of the State for which he shall be chosen.

Sect. 4. The Senate shall choose its own President and other officers.

ARTICLE VI.

Sect. 1. The times, and places, and manner of holding the elections of the members of each House, shall be prescribed by the Legislature of each State; but their provisions concerning them may at any time, be altered by the Legislature of the United States.

Sect. 2. The Legislature of the United States shall have authority to establish such uniform qualifications of the members of each House, with regard to property, as to the said Legislature shall seem expedient.

Sect. 3. In each House a majority of the members shall constitute a quorum to do business; but a smaller number may adjourn from day to day.

Sect. 4. Each House shall be the judge of the elections, returns, and qualifications, of its own members.

Sect. 5. Freedom of speech and debate in the Legislature shall not be impeached or questioned in any court or place out of the Legislature; and the members of each House shall, in all cases, except treason, felony, and breach of the peace, be privileged from arrest during their attendance at Congress, and in going to and returning from it.

Sect. 6. Each House may determine the rules of its proceedings; may punish its members for disorderly behavior; and may expel a member.

Sect. 7. The House of Representatives, and the Senate when it shall be acting in a legislative capacity, shall keep a journal of their proceedings; and shall, from time to time, publish them; and the yeas and nays of the members of each House, on any question, shall, at the desire of one fifth part of the members present, be entered on the Journal.

Sect. 8. Neither House, without the consent of the other, shall adjourn for more than three days, nor to any other place than that at which the two Houses are sitting. But this regulation shall not extend to the Senate when it shall exercise the powers mentioned in the — Article.

Sect. 9. The members of each House shall be ineligible to, and incapable of holding, any office under the authority of the United States, during the time for which they shall respectively be elected: and the members of the Senate shall be ineligible to, and incapable of holding, any such office for one year afterwards.

Sect. 10. The members of each House shall receive a compensation for their services to be ascertained and paid by the State in which they shall be chosen.

Sec. 11. The enacting style of the laws of the United States shall be, "Be it enacted, and it is hereby enacted, by the House of Representatives, and by the Senate of the United States, in Congress assembled."

Sect. 12. Each House shall possess the right of originating bills, except in the cases before mentioned.

Sect. 13. Every bill, which shall have passed the House of Representatives and the Senate, shall, before it becomes a law, be presented to the President of the United States for his revision. If, upon such revision, he approve of it, he shall signify his approbation by signing it. But if, upon such revision, it shall appear to him improper for being passed into a law, he shall return it, together with his objections against it, to that House in which it shall have originated;

who shall enter the objections at large on their Journal, and proceed to reconsider the bill. But if, after such reconsideration, two-thirds of that House shall, notwithstanding the objections of the President, agree to pass it, it shall, together with his objections, be sent to the other House, by which it shall likewise be re-considered, and if approved by two-thirds of the other House also, it shall become a law. But in all such cases the votes of both Houses shall be determined by Yeas and Nays; and the names of the persons voting for or against the bill, shall be entered on the Journal of each House respectively. If any bill shall not be returned by the President within seven days after it shall have been presented to him, it shall be a law, unless the Legislature, by their adjournment, prevent its return; in which case it shall not be a law.

ARTICLE VII.

Sect. 1. The Legislature of the United States shall have the power to lay and collect taxes, duties, imposts and excises;

To regulate commerce with foreign nations, and among the several States;

To establish an uniform rule of naturalization throughout the United States;

To coin money;

To regulate the value of foreign coin;

To fix the standard of weights and measures;

To establish post-offices;

To borrow money, and emit bills on the credit of the United States;

To appoint a Treasurer by ballot;

To constitute tribunals inferior to the Supreme Court;

To make rules concerning captures on land and water;

To declare the law and punishment of piracies and felonies committed on the high seas, and the punishment of counterfeiting the coin of the United States, and of offences against the law of nations;

To subdue a rebellion in any State, on the application of its Legislature;

To make war;

To raise armies;

To build and equip fleets;

To call forth the aid of the militia, in order to execute the laws of the Union, enforce treaties, suppress insurrections, and repel invasions;

And to make all laws that shall be necessary and proper for carrying into execution the foregoing powers, and all other powers vested by this Constitution in the Government of the United States, or in any department or office thereof.

Sect. 2. Treason against the United States shall consist only in levying war against the United States, or any of them; and in adhering to the enemies of the United States, or any of them. The Legislature of the United States shall have power to declare the punishment of treason. No person shall be convicted of treason, unless on the testimony of two witnesses. No attainder of treason shall work corruption of blood, nor forfeiture, except during the life of the person attained.[5]

Sect. 3. The proportions of direct taxation shall be regulated by the whole number of white and other free citizens and inhabitants of every age, sex and condition, including those bound to servitude for a term of years, and three-fifths of all other persons not comprehended in the foregoing description, (except Indians not paying taxes); which number shall, within six years after the first meeting of the Legislature, and within the term of every ten years afterwards, be taken in such a manner as the said Legislature shall direct.

Sect. 4. No tax or duty shall be laid by the Legislature on articles exported from any State; nor on the migration or importation of such persons as the several States shall think proper to admit; nor shall such migration or importation be prohibited.

Sect. 5. No capitation tax[6] shall be laid, unless in proportion to the census hereinbefore directed to be taken.

Sect. 6. No navigation act shall be passed without the assent of two-thirds of the members present in each House.

Sect. 7. The United States shall not grant any title of nobility.

ARTICLE VIII.

The acts of the Legislature of the United States made in pursuance of this Constitution, and all treaties made under the authority of the United States, shall be the supreme law of the several States, and of their citizens and inhabitants; and the Judges in the several States shall be bound thereby in their decisions, any thing in the constitutions or laws of the several States to the contrary notwithstanding.

ARTICLE IX.

Sect. 1. The Senate of the United States shall have power to make treaties, and to appoint ambassadors, and Judges of the Supreme Court.

---

[5] This clause means that the children of a person convicted of treason do not inherit his guilt.

[6] A capitation tax, sometimes called a "poll tax," is levied on each inhabitant.

Sect. 2. In all disputes and controversies now subsisting, or that may hereafter subsist, between two or more States, respecting jurisdiction or territory, the Senate shall possess the following powers: — Whenever the Legislature or the Executive authority, or lawful agent of any State, in controversy with another, shall, by memorial to the Senate, state the matter in question, and apply for a hearing, notice of such memorial and application shall be given, by order of the Senate, to the Legislature, or the Executive authority, of the other State in controversy. The Senate shall also assign a day for the appearance of the parties, by their agents, before that House. The agents shall be directed to appoint, by joint consent, commissioners or judges to constitute a court for hearing and determining the matter in question. But if the agents cannot agree, the Senate shall name three persons out of each of the several States; and from the list of such persons, each party shall alternately strike out one, until the number shall be reduced to thirteen; and from that number, not less than seven, nor more than nine, names, as the Senate shall direct, shall, in their presence, be drawn out by lot; and the persons whose names shall be so drawn, or any five of them, shall be commissioners or judges to hear and finally determine the controversy; provided a majority of the judges who shall hear the cause agree in the determination. If either party shall neglect to attend at the day assigned, without showing sufficient reasons for not attending, or being present shall refuse to strike, the Senate shall proceed to nominate three persons out of each State, and the Clerk of the Senate shall strike in behalf of the party absent or refusing. If any of the parties shall refuse to submit to the authority of such court, or shall not appear to prosecute or defend their claim or cause, the court shall nevertheless proceed to pronounce judgment. The judgment shall be final and conclusive. The proceedings shall be transmitted to the President of the Senate, and shall be lodged among the public records for the security of the parties concerned. Every commissioner shall, before he sit in judgment, take an oath to be administered by one of the Judges of the Supreme or Superior Court of the State where the cause shall be tried, "well and truly to hear and determine the matter in question, according to the best of his judgment, without favor, affection, or hope of reward."

Sect. 3. All controversies concerning lands claimed under different grants of two or more States, whose jurisdictions, as they respect such lands, shall have been decided or adjusted subsequently to such grants, or any of them, shall, on application to the Senate, be finally determined, as near as may be, in the same manner as is before prescribed for deciding controversies between different States.

ARTICLE X.

Sect. 1. The Executive power of the United States shall be vested in a single person. His style shall be, "The President of the United States of America," and his title shall be, "His Excellency." He shall be elected by ballot by the Legislature. He shall hold his office during the term of seven years; but shall not be elected a second time.

Sect. 2. He shall, from time to time, give information to the Legislature, of the state of the Union. He may recommend to their consideration such measures as he shall judge necessary, and expedient. He may convene them on extraordinary occasions. In case of disagreement between the two Houses, with regard to the time of adjournment, he may adjourn them to such time as he thinks proper. He shall take care that the laws of the United States be duly and faithfully executed. He shall commission all the officers of the United States; and shall appoint officers in all cases not otherwise provided for by this Constitution. He shall receive Ambassadors, and may correspond with the supreme executives of the several States. He shall have power to grant reprieves and pardons, but his pardon shall not be pleadable in bar of an impeachment. He shall be Commander-in-chief of the army and navy of the United States, and of the militia of the several States. He shall, at stated times, receive for his services a compensation, which shall neither be increased nor diminished during his continuance in office. Before he shall enter on the duties of his department, he shall take the following oath or affirmation, "I — solemnly swear, (or affirm) that I will faithfully execute the office of President of the United States of America." He shall be removed from his office on impeachment by the House of Representatives, and conviction, in the Supreme Court, of treason, bribery or corruption. In case of his removal, as aforesaid, death, resignation, or disability to discharge the powers and duties of his office, the President of the Senate shall exercise those powers and duties until another President of the United States be chosen, or until the disability of the President be removed.

ARTICLE XI.

Sect. 1. The Judicial power of the United States shall be vested in one Supreme Court, and in such inferior courts, as shall, when necessary, from time to time, be constituted by the Legislature of the United States.

Sect. 2. The Judges of the Supreme Court, and of the inferior courts, shall hold their offices during good behavior. They shall, at stated times, receive for their services a compensation, which shall not be diminished during their continuance in office.

Sect. 3. The jurisdiction of the Supreme Court shall extend to all cases arising under laws passed by the Legislature of the United States; to all cases affecting ambassadors, other public ministers and consuls; to the trial of impeachments of officers of the United States; to all cases of admiralty and maritime jurisdiction; to controversies between two or more States, (except such as shall regard territory or jurisdiction); between a state and citizens of another State; between citizens of different States; and between a state, or the citizens thereof, and foreign states, citizens or subjects. In cases of impeachment, cases affecting ambassadors, other public ministers and consuls, and those in which a State shall be party, this jurisdiction shall be original. In all the other cases before mentioned, it shall be appellate, with such exceptions, and under such regulations, as the Legislature shall make. The Legislature may assign any part of the jurisdiction above mentioned (except the trial of the President of the United States) in the manner and under the limitations which it shall think proper, to such inferior courts as it shall constitute from time to time.

Sect. 4. The trial of all criminal offences (except in cases of impeachment) shall be in the State where they shall be committed; and shall be by jury.

Sect. 5. Judgment, in cases of impeachment, shall not extend further than to removal from office, and disqualification to hold and enjoy any office of honor, trust or profit, under the United States. But the party convicted shall nevertheless be liable and subject to indictment, trial, judgment and punishment according to law.

ARTICLE XII.

No State shall coin money; nor grant letters of marque and reprisal;[7] nor enter into any treaty, alliance or confederation; nor grant any title of nobility.

ARTICLE XIII.

No State, without the consent of the Legislature of the United States, shall emit bills of credit, or make any thing but specie a tender in payment of debts; nor lay imposts or duties on imports; nor keep troops or ships of war in time of peace; nor enter into any agreement or compact with another state, or with any foreign power; nor engage in any war, unless it shall be actually invaded by

---

[7] These are warrants authorizing private citizens to capture the merchant ships of another nation—actions that would normally be deemed piracy but, because of the warrant granted, implicitly become acts of war.

enemies, or the danger of invasion be so imminent as not to admit of a delay until the Legislature of the United States can be consulted.

ARTICLE XIV.

The citizens of each State shall be entitled to all privileges and immunities of citizens in the several States.

ARTICLE XV.

Any person charged with treason, felony or high misdemeanor in any State, who shall flee from justice, and shall be found in any other State, shall, on demand of the Executive power of the State from which he fled, be delivered up and removed to the State having jurisdiction of the offence.

ARTICLE XVI.

Full faith shall be given in each State to the acts of the Legislatures, and to the records and judicial proceedings of the courts and magistrates, of every other State.

Article XVII.

New States lawfully constituted or established within the limits of the United States may be admitted, by the Legislature, into this government; but to such admission the consent of two-thirds of the members present in each House shall be necessary. If a new State shall arise within the limits of any of the present States, the consent of the Legislatures of such States shall be also necessary to its admission. If the admission be consented to, the new States shall be admitted on the same terms with the original States. But the Legislature may make conditions with the new States concerning the public debt which shall be then subsisting.

Article XVIII.

The United States shall guarantee to each State a republican form of government; and shall protect each State against foreign invasions, and, on the application of its Legislature, against domestic violence.

Article XIX.

On the application of the Legislatures of two-thirds of the States in the Union, for an amendment of this Constitution, the Legislature of the United States shall call a convention for that purpose.

Article XX.

The members of the Legislatures, and the Executive and Judicial officers of the United States, and of the several States, shall be bound by oath to support this Constitution.

ARTICLE XXI.

The ratification of the conventions of — States shall be sufficient for organizing this Constitution.

ARTICLE XXII.

This Constitution shall be laid before the United States in Congress assembled, for their approbation; and it is the opinion of this Convention, that it should be afterwards submitted to a Convention chosen in each State, under the recommendation of its Legislature, in order to receive the ratification of such Convention.

ARTICLE XXIII.

To introduce this government, it is the opinion of this Convention, that each assenting convention should notify its assent and ratification to the United States in Congress assembled; that Congress, after receiving the assent and ratification of the Conventions of — States, should appoint and publish a day, as early as may be, and appoint a place, for commencing proceedings under this Constitution; that after such publication, the Legislatures of the several States should elect members of the Senate and direct the election of members of the House of Representatives; and that the members of the Legislature should meet at the time and place assigned by Congress, and should, as soon as may be after their meeting, choose the President of the United States, and proceed to execute this Constitution. . . .

Document 13

The Slave Trade Clause

August 21, 22, 24 and 25, 1787

The Committee of Detail Report presented on August 6 listed, for the first time, 18 powers of Congress. Among those powers was the power to regulate international trade. And a vital part of international trade was the slave trade. Without a specific restriction, it would be constitutionally possible for Congress, under the Committee of Detail draft, to regulate the international slave trade. But the five member Committee — chaired by John Rutledge of South Carolina — were well aware of the warning issued by General Charles Cotesworth Pinckney of South Carolina on July 23 that South Carolina would not sign the Constitution if there were a move toward "the emancipation of slaves." Both sides in the debate over slavery accepted the premise that slave trade policy would have a major impact on the future of slavery in the new nation.

Sections 4, 5 and 6 of Article VII of the Committee of Detail Report shaped the discussion in August over what Congress could and could not do with respect to the slave trade. There were three identifiable groups at the Convention with respect to the Slave Trade clause in the COD Report.

1. John Langdon of New Hampshire "was strenuous for giving the power to the general government" to control the slave trade. John Dickinson of Delaware, Luther Martin of Maryland, and Madison wanted an end to the slave trade on the grounds of principle. So did James Wilson and Gouverner Morris of Pennsylvania.

2. Charles Pinckney, from South Carolina, and Hugh Williamson, from North Carolina, reminded the delegates of political reality: be careful not to drive the Deep South into bolting the union. Abraham Baldwin of Georgia was not interested in "an attempt to abridge (Georgia) one of her favorite prerogatives."

3. Roger Sherman of Connecticut asserted: "it was better to let the Southern States import slaves than to part with [those states], if they made that a sine qua non." Massachusetts seemed accommodating. Rufus King of Massachusetts said the whole "subject should be considered in a political light only."

To deal with these differences, in late August, the delegates established a Committee of 11 to alter the recommendation of the Committee of Detail so the entire convention could agree and move forward to other matters.

What did the Committee of 11 come up with concerning the ability of Congress to eventually regulate the slave trade?

Source: Gordon Lloyd, ed., Debates in the Federal Convention of 1787 by James Madison, a Member *(Ashland, Ohio: Ashbrook Center, 2014), 404-419, 428, 435-437.*

August 21

Mr. L. MARTIN proposed to vary Article 7, Section 4, so as to allow a prohibition or tax on the importation of slaves. In the first place, as five slaves are to be counted as three freemen, in the apportionment of Representatives, such a clause would leave an encouragement to this traffic. In the second place, slaves weakened one part of the Union, which the other parts were bound to protect; the privilege of importing them was therefore unreasonable. And in the third place, it was inconsistent with the principles of the Revolution, and dishonorable to the American character, to have such a feature in the Constitution.

Mr. RUTLEDGE[1] did not see how the importation of slaves could be encouraged by this section. He was not apprehensive of insurrections, and would readily exempt the other States from the obligation to protect the Southern against them. Religion and humanity had nothing to do with this question. Interest alone is the governing principle with nations. The true question at present is, whether the Southern States shall or shall not be parties to the Union. If the Northern States consult their interest, they will not oppose the increase of slaves, which will increase the commodities of which they will become the carriers.

Mr. ELLSWORTH[2] was for leaving the clause as it stands. Let every State import what it pleases. The morality or wisdom of slavery are considerations belonging to the States themselves. What enriches a part enriches the whole, and the States are the best judges of their particular interest. The old Confederation had not meddled with this point; and he did not see any greater necessity for bringing it within the policy of the new one.

Mr. PINCKNEY. South Carolina can never receive the plan if it prohibits the slave-trade. In every proposed extension of the powers of Congress, that State has expressly and watchfully excepted that of meddling with the importation of negroes. If the States be all left at liberty on this subject, South

---

[1] John Rutledge of South Carolina

[2] Oliver Ellsworth of Connecticut

Carolina may perhaps, by degrees do of herself what is wished, as Virginia and Maryland already have done.[3]

Adjourned.

August 22

In Convention. — Article 7, Section 4, was resumed.

Mr. SHERMAN was for leaving the clause as it stands. He disapproved of the slave-trade; yet as the States were now possessed of the right to import slaves, as the public good did not require it to be taken from them, and as it was expedient to have as few objections as possible to the proposed scheme of government, he thought it best to leave the matter as we find it. He observed that the abolition of slavery seemed to be going on in the United States, and that the good sense of the several States would probably by degrees complete it. He urged on the Convention the necessity of dispatching its business.

Colonel MASON.[4] This infernal traffic originated in the avarice of British merchants. The British Government constantly checked the attempts of Virginia to put a stop to it. The present question concerns not the importing States alone, but the whole Union. The evil of having slaves was experienced during the late war. Had slaves been treated as they might have been by the enemy, they would have proved dangerous instruments in their hands. But their folly dealt by the slaves as it did by the tories.[5] He mentioned the dangerous insurrections of the slaves in Greece and Sicily; and the instructions given by Cromwell to the commissioners sent to Virginia, to arm the servants and slaves, in case other means of obtaining its submission should fail. Maryland and Virginia, he said, had already prohibited the importation of slaves expressly. North Carolina had done the same in substance. All this would be in vain, if South Carolina and Georgia be at liberty to import. The Western people are already calling out for slaves for their new lands; and will fill that country with slaves, if they can be got through South Carolina and Georgia. Slavery discourages arts and manufactures. The poor despise labor when performed by slaves. They prevent the emigration of whites, who really enrich and strengthen a country. They produce the most pernicious effect on manners. Every master of slaves is born a petty tyrant. They bring the

---

[3] See George Mason's comments on the decision of Maryland and Virginia (August 22, below).

[4] George Mason of Virginia

[5] The British failed to make effective use of slaves to foment insurrections in the American states, as they also failed to do with Tories in the states.

judgment of Heaven on a country. As nations cannot be rewarded or punished in the next world, they must be in this. By an inevitable chain of causes and effects, Providence punishes national sins by national calamities. He lamented that some of our Eastern brethren had, from a lust of gain, embarked in this nefarious traffic. As to the States being in possession of the right to import, this was the case with many other rights, now to be properly given up. He held it essential in every point of view, that the General Government should have power to prevent the increase of slavery.

Mr. ELLSWORTH, as he had never owned a slave, could not judge of the effects of slavery on character. He said, however, that if it was to be considered in a moral light, we ought to go further and free those already in the country. As slaves also multiply so fast in Virginia and Maryland that it is cheaper to raise than import them, whilst in the sickly rice swamps foreign supplies are necessary, if we go no further than is urged, we shall be unjust towards South Carolina and Georgia. Let us not intermeddle. As population increases, poor laborers will be so plenty as to render slaves useless. Slavery in time, will not be a speck in our country. Provision is already made in Connecticut for abolishing it. And the abolition has already taken place in Massachusetts. As to the danger of insurrections from foreign influence, that will become a motive to kind treatment of the slaves.

Mr. PINCKNEY. If slavery be wrong, it is justified by the example of all the world. He cited the case of Greece, Rome, and other ancient states; the sanction given by France, England, Holland, and other modern states. In all ages one half of mankind have been slaves. If the Southern States were let alone, they will probably of themselves stop importations. He would himself, as a citizen of South Carolina, vote for it. An attempt to take away the right, as proposed, will produce serious objections to the Constitution, which he wished to see adopted.

General PINCKNEY[6] declared it to be his firm opinion, that if himself and all his colleagues were to sign the Constitution, and use their personal influence, it would be of no avail towards obtaining the assent of their constituents. South Carolina and Georgia cannot do without slaves. As to Virginia, she will gain by stopping the importations. Her slaves will rise in value, and she has more than she wants. It would be unequal, to require South Carolina and Georgia to confederate on such unequal terms. He said the Royal assent, before the Revolution, had never been refused to South Carolina, as to

---

[6] Charles Cotesworth Pinckney, the elder second cousin of Charles Pinckney; both were from South Carolina

Virginia. He contended, that the importation of slaves would be for the interest of the whole Union. The more slaves, the more produce to employ the carrying trade; the more consumption also; and the more of this, the more revenue for the common treasury. He admitted it to be reasonable that slaves should be dutied like other imports; but should consider a rejection of the clause as an exclusion of South Carolina from the Union.

Mr. BALDWIN had conceived national objects alone to be before the Convention; not such as, like the present, were of a local nature. Georgia was decided on this point. That State has always hitherto supposed a General Government to be the pursuit of the central States, who wished to have a vortex[7] for every thing; that her distance would preclude her from equal advantage; and that she could not prudently purchase it by yielding national powers. From this it might be understood, in what light she would view an attempt to abridge one of her favorite prerogatives. If left to herself, she may probably put a stop to the evil. As one ground for this conjecture, he took notice of the sect of —; which he said was a respectable class of people, who carried their ethics beyond the mere *equality of men*, extending their humanity to the claims of the whole animal creation.

Mr. WILSON observed, that if South Carolina and Georgia were themselves disposed to get rid of the importation of slaves in a short time, as had been suggested, they would never refuse to unite because the importation might be prohibited. As the section now stands, all articles imported are to be taxed. Slaves alone are exempt. This is in fact a bounty on that article.

Mr. GERRY[8] thought we had nothing to do with the conduct of the States as to slaves, but ought to be careful not to give any sanction to it.

Mr. DICKINSON considered it as inadmissible, on every principle of honor and safety, that the importation of slaves should be authorized to the States by the Constitution. The true question was, whether the national happiness would be promoted or impeded by the importation; and this question ought to be left to the National Government, not to the States particularly interested. If England and France permit slavery, slaves are, at the same time, excluded from both those kingdoms. Greece and Rome were made unhappy by their slaves. He could not believe that the Southern States would refuse to confederate on the account apprehended; especially as the power was not likely to be immediately exercised by the General Government.

---

[7] Baldwin seems to say that Georgia believes that the central states seek a way of drawing the entire country into an arrangement that would best suit the central states.

[8] Elbridge Gerry of Massachusetts

Mr. WILLIAMSON stated the law of North Carolina on the subject, to wit, that it did not directly prohibit the importation of slaves. It imposed a duty of £5 on each slave imported from Africa; £10 on each from elsewhere; and £50 on each from a State licensing manumission.[9] He thought the Southern States could not be members of the Union, if the clause should be rejected; and that it was wrong to force any thing down not absolutely necessary, and which any State must disagree to.

Mr. KING thought the subject should be considered in a political light only. If two States will not agree to the Constitution, as stated on one side, he could affirm with equal belief on the other, that great and equal opposition would be experienced from the other States. He remarked on the exemption of slaves from duty, whilst every other import was subjected to it, as an inequality that could not fail to strike the commercial sagacity of the Northern and Middle States.

Mr. LANGDON was strenuous for giving the power to the General Government. He could not, with a good conscience, leave it with the States, who could then go on with the traffic, without being restrained by the opinions here given, that they will themselves cease to import slaves.

General PINCKNEY thought himself bound to declare candidly, that he did not think South Carolina would stop her importations of slaves in any short time; but only stop them occasionally, as she now does. He moved to commit the clause, that slaves might be made liable to an equal tax with other imports; which he thought right, and which would remove one difficulty that had been started.

Mr. RUTLEDGE. If the Convention thinks that North Carolina, South Carolina, and Georgia, will ever agree to the plan, unless their right to import slaves be untouched, the expectation is vain. The people of those States will never be such fools as to give up so important an interest. He was strenuous against striking out the section, and seconded the motion of General PINCKNEY for a commitment.

Mr. GOUVERNEUR MORRIS wished the whole subject to be committed,[10] including the clauses relating to taxes on exports and to a navigation act. These things may form a bargain among the Northern and Southern States.

---

[9] allowing the freeing of slaves

[10] That is, Morris wished that all these issues be referred to a committee, who would study them and make recommendations.

Mr. BUTLER[11] declared, that he never would agree to the power of taxing exports.

Mr. SHERMAN said it was better to let the Southern States import slaves than to part with them, if they made that a *sine qua non*. He was opposed to a tax on slaves imported, as making the matter worse, because it implied they were *property*. He acknowledged that if the power of prohibiting the importation should be given to the General Government, it would be exercised. He thought it would be its duty to exercise the power.

Mr. READ[12] was for the commitment, provided the clause concerning taxes on exports should also be committed.

Mr. SHERMAN observed, that that clause had been agreed to, and therefore could not be committed.

Mr. RANDOLPH[13] was for committing, in order that some middle ground might, if possible, be found. He could never agree to the clause as it stands. He would sooner risk the Constitution. He dwelt on the dilemma to which the Convention was exposed. By agreeing to the clause, it would revolt the Quakers, the Methodists, and many others in the States having no slaves. On the other hand, two States might be lost to the Union. Let us then, he said, try the chance of a commitment.

On the question for committing the remaining part of Sections 4 and 5 of Article 7, — Connecticut, New Jersey, Maryland, Virginia, North Carolina, South Carolina, Georgia, aye, — 7; New Hampshire, Pennsylvania, Delaware, no, — 3; Massachusetts, absent.

Mr. PINCKNEY and Mr. LANGDON moved to commit Section 6, as to a navigation act by two thirds of each House.

Mr. GORHAM[14] did not see the propriety of it. Is it meant to require a greater proportion of votes? He desired it to be remembered, that the Eastern States had no motive to union but a commercial one. They were able to protect themselves. They were not afraid of external danger, and did not need the aid of the Southern States.

Mr. WILSON wished for a commitment, in order to reduce the proportion of votes required.

Mr. ELLSWORTH was for taking the plan as it is. This widening of opinions had a threatening aspect. If we do not agree on this middle and

---

[11] Pierce Butler of South Carolina

[12] George Read of Delaware

[13] Edmund Randolph of Virginia

[14] Nathaniel Gorham of Massachusetts

moderate ground, he was afraid we should lose two States, with such others as may be disposed to stand aloof; should fly into a variety of shapes and directions, and most probably into several confederations, — and not without bloodshed.

On the question for committing Section 6, as to a navigation act, to a member from each State, — New Hampshire, Massachusetts, Pennsylvania, Delaware, Maryland, Virginia, North Carolina, South Carolina, Georgia, aye, — 9; Connecticut, New Jersey no, — 2.

The Committee appointed were, Messrs. LANGDON, KING, JOHNSON,[15] LIVINGSTON,[16] CLYMER,[17] DICKINSON, L. MARTIN, MADISON, WILLIAMSON, C. C. PINCKNEY, and BALDWIN.

To this committee were referred also the two clauses, above mentioned of the fourth and fifth Sections of Article 7.

August 24

In Convention, — Governor LIVINGSTON, from the Committee of eleven, to whom were referred the two remaining clauses of the fourth Section, and the fifth and sixth Sections of the seventh Article, delivered the following Report:

"Strike out so much of the fourth Section as was referred to the Committee, and insert, 'The migration or importation of such persons as the several States, now existing, shall think proper to admit, shall not be prohibited by the Legislature prior to the year 1800; but a tax or duty may be imposed on such migration or importation, at a rate not exceeding the average of the duties laid on imports.'

"The fifth section to remain as in the Report."

"The sixth Section to be stricken out. . . ."

August 25

The Report of the Committee of eleven being taken up, —

General PINCKNEY moved to strike out the words, "the year eighteen hundred," as the year limiting the importation of slaves; and to insert the words "the year eighteen hundred and eight."

Mr. GORHAM seconded the motion.

---

[15] William Samuel Johnson of Connecticut

[16] William Livingston of New Jersey, then Governor of the state

[17] George Clymer of Pennsylvania

Mr. MADISON. Twenty years will produce all the mischief that can be apprehended from the liberty to import slaves. So long a term will be more dishonorable to the American character than to say nothing about it in the Constitution.

On the motion, which passed in the affirmative, — New Hampshire, Massachusetts, Connecticut, Maryland, North Carolina, South Carolina, Georgia, aye, — 7; New Jersey, Pennsylvania, Delaware, Virginia, no, — 4.

Mr. GOUVERNEUR MORRIS was for making the clause read at once, "the importation of slaves into North Carolina, South Carolina, and Georgia, shall not be prohibited, &c." This he said would be most fair, and would avoid the ambiguity by which, under the power with regard to naturalization, the liberty reserved to the States might be defeated. He wished it to be known, also, that this part of the Constitution was a compliance with those States. If the change of language, however, should be objected to, by the members from those states, he should not urge it.

Colonel MASON was not against using the term "slaves," but against naming North Carolina, South Carolina, and Georgia, lest it should give offence to the people of those States.

Mr. SHERMAN liked a description better than the terms proposed, which had been declined by the old Congress, and were not pleasing to some people.

Mr. CLYMER concurred with Mr. SHERMAN.

Mr. WILLIAMSON said, that both in opinion and practice he was against slavery; but thought it more in favor of humanity, from a view of all circumstances, to let in South Carolina and Georgia on those terms, than to exclude them from the Union.

Mr. GOUVERNEUR MORRIS withdrew his motion.

Mr. DICKINSON wished the clause to be confined to the States which had not themselves prohibited the importation of slaves; and for that purpose moved to amend the clause, so as to read: "The importation of slaves into such of the states as shall permit the same, shall not be prohibited by the legislature of the United States until the year 1808; which was disagreed to, *nem. con.*[18]

The first part of the Report was then agreed to, amended as follows: "The migration or importation of such persons as the several states now existing shall think proper to admit, shall not be prohibited by the legislature prior to the year 1808," —

---

[18] an abbreviation of *nemine contradicente,* Latin for "no one dissenting"

New Hampshire, Massachusetts, Connecticut, Maryland, North Carolina. South Carolina, Georgia, aye, — 7; New Jersey, Pennsylvania, Delaware, Virginia, no, — 4.

Mr. BALDWIN, in order to restrain and more explicitly define, "the average duty," moved to strike out of the second part the words, "average of the duties laid on imports," and insert "common impost on articles not enumerated"; which was agreed to, *nem. con.*

Mr. SHERMAN was against this second part, as acknowledging men to be property, by taxing them as such under the character of slaves.

Mr. KING and Mr. LANGDON considered this as the price of the first part.

General PINCKNEY admitted that it was so.

Colonel MASON. Not to tax, will be equivalent to a bounty on, the importation of slaves.

Mr. GORHAM thought that Mr. SHERMAN should consider the duty, not as implying that slaves are property, but as a discouragement to the importation of them.

Mr. GOUVERNEUR MORRIS remarked, that, as the clause now stands, it implies that the Legislature may tax freemen imported.

Mr. SHERMAN, in answer to Mr. GORHAM, observed, that the smallness of the duty showed revenue to be the object, not the discouragement of the importation.

Mr. MADISON thought it wrong to admit in the Constitution the idea that there could be property in men. The reason of duties did not hold, as slaves are not, like merchandise, consumed, &c.

Colonel MASON, in answer to Mr. GOUVERNEUR MORRIS. The provision, as it stands, was necessary for the case of convicts, in order to prevent the introduction of them.

It was finally agreed, *nem. con.*, to make the clause read: "but a tax or duty may be imposed on such importation, not exceeding ten dollars for each person"; and then the second part, as amended, was agreed to.

Article 7, Sect. 5, was agreed to, *nem. con.*, as reported.

Article 7, Sect. 6, in the Report was postponed. . . .

Document 14

The Fugitive Slave Clause

July 14; August 6, 28 and 29; and September 12, 15 and 17, 1787

The Fugitive Slave Clause of the Constitution was the outcome of discussions and negotiations between Northern and Southern delegates, occurring from mid-July until mid-September. There are seven important dates to bear in mind when considering its adoption. On each date, a decision was made and recorded in the documents excerpted below. We list these in chronological order, under their dates.

Here is a brief history: (1) In the conversations and documents of the American Founding, the Fugitive Slave Clause first appeared in the last article in the Northwest Ordinance. That ordinance was passed on July 14, 1787. The news of the Northwest Ordinance reached the Constitutional Convention at the time the delegates were passing the Connecticut Compromise on federal representation and Congressional powers. (2) On August 6, the Committee of Detail issued its Report. There was no mention of the fugitive slave clause, but Article XV addressed what became popularly known as the Extradition Clause. (3) During the discussion of this clause on August 28, the South Carolina delegation attempted, unsuccessfully, to include "fugitive slaves" in the "fugitive" provision of the extradition clause. So (4) on August 29 that delegation came up with a separate fugitive clause that was accepted and (5) placed right under the original extradition clause in the Committee of Style Report. (On September 8, the delegates appointed a Committee of Style "to revise the style of, and arrange, the articles which have been agreed to by the House.") (6) On September 15, the delegates agreed to a change in the language of the Fugitive Slave Clause. (7) The Constitution was signed by 39 of the 55 delegates attending the Convention on September 17, 1787.

The language and contiguous location of the Extradition Clause and the Fugitive Slave Clause in the Constitution invite the reader to compare and contrast them.

Source: Gordon Lloyd ed., Debates in the Federal Convention of 1787 by James Madison, a Member *(Ashland, Ohio: Ashbrook Center, 2014), 317, 448-449, 454, 521, 542, 561.*

(1) North West Ordinance, July 14

ARTICLE VI

There shall be neither slavery nor involuntary servitude in the said territory, otherwise than in the punishment of crimes, whereof the party shall have been duly convicted: Provided, always, That any person escaping into the same, from whom labor or service is lawfully claimed in any one of the original States, such fugitive may be lawfully reclaimed, and conveyed to the person claiming his or her labor or service as aforesaid.

(2) Committee of Detail Report, August 6

ARTICLE XV

Any person charged with treason, felony or high misdemeanor in any State, who shall flee from justice, and shall be found in any other State, shall, on demand of the Executive power of the State from which he fled, be delivered up and removed to the State having jurisdiction of the offence.

(3) Madison's Account of Debates in the Constitutional Convention, August 28

Article XV being then taken up, the words, "high misdemeanor," were struck out, and the words, "other crime," inserted, in order to comprehend all proper cases; it being doubtful whether "high misdemeanor" had not a technical meaning too limited.

Mr. BUTLER[1] and Mr. PINCKNEY[2] moved to require "fugitive slaves and servants to be delivered up like criminals."

Mr. WILSON.[3] This would oblige the Executive of the State to do it at the public expense.

Mr. SHERMAN[4] saw no more propriety in the public seizing and surrendering a slave or servant than a horse.

Mr. BUTLER withdrew his proposition, in order that some particular provision might be made, apart from this article.

Article 15, as amended, was then agreed to, *nem. con.*[5]

Adjourned.

---

[1] Pierce Butler of South Carolina

[2] Charles Pinckney of South Carolina

[3] James Wilson of Pennsylvania

[4] Roger Sherman of Connecticut

[5] an abbreviation of *nemine contradicente,* Latin for "no one dissenting"

(4) Madison's Account of Debates in the Constitutional Convention, August 29

Mr. BUTLER moved to insert after Article 15, "If any person bound to service or labor in any of the United States, shall escape into another State, he or she shall not be discharged from such service or labor, in consequence of any regulations subsisting in the State to which they escape, but shall be delivered up to the person justly claiming their service or labor," — which was agreed to, *nem. con.*

(5) Committee of Style Report, September 12

Article IV. Sect. 2.

A person charged in any State with treason, felony, or other crime, who shall flee from justice, and be found in another State, shall, on demand of the executive authority of the State from which he fled, be delivered up, and removed to the State having jurisdiction of the crime.

No person legally held to service or labor in one State, escaping into another, shall, in consequence of regulations subsisting therein, be discharged from such service or labor; but shall be delivered up, on claim of the party to whom such service or labor may be due.

(6) Madison's Account of Debates in the Constitutional Convention, September 15

Article 4, Sect. 2, (the third paragraph,) the term "legally" was struck out; and the words "under the laws thereof," inserted after the word "State," in compliance with the wish of some who thought the term *legal* equivocal, and favoring the idea that slavery was legal in a moral view.

(7) The Constitution, September 17

Article IV, Sect 2

Extradition Clause

A Person charged in any State with Treason, Felony, or other Crime, who shall flee from Justice, and be found in another State, shall on Demand of the executive Authority of the State from which he fled, be delivered up, to be removed to the State having Jurisdiction of the Crime.

Fugitive Slave Clause

No Person held to Service or Labor in one State, under the Laws thereof, escaping into another, shall, in Consequence of any Law or Regulation therein, be discharged from such Service or Labor, but shall be delivered up on Claim of the Party to whom such Service or Labor may be due.

Document 15

Gerry, Mason, and Randolph Decline to Sign the Constitution

September 10, 12, 15 and 17, 1787

Edmund Randolph and George Mason of Virginia, and Elbridge Gerry of Massachusetts, played leading roles in the Convention, arriving at the beginning and staying to the very end. During their 88 days at the Convention, their opinions changed dramatically. All three of these influential delegates supported the initial Virginia plan, but declined to support the Constitution. Is it possible to locate the moment or issue when they started to have reservations about the direction of the conversation? Randolph was the first to state his objections. He did so on September 10, when Gerry raised a question about the provisions for ratifying the new Constitution. Gerry disliked the removal of a phrase from the current draft of that document that would have required that it be approved by Congress before being submitted to the state conventions. Randolph went further, declaring that the Constitution should give the state ratifying conventions the power to propose amendments. Later in that day's discussion, Randolph revealed a lengthy series of complaints against what he considered inadequate provisions for limiting the power of the executive and the legislature.

Mason and Gerry seemed to suggest on September 12 that Randolph's concerns could be resolved if the Convention added a Bill of Rights to the Constitution. Their motion was immediately rejected by all the state delegations present. On September 15, Randolph elaborated his concerns. He was joined on that day by Mason and then by Gerry. Mason also wrote his objections (repeating some of those Randolph and Gerry had raised but adding others) on his copy of the Committee of Style Report. The decision of Randolph, Mason and Gerry to withhold their signatures became important in the debate over the ratification of the Constitution.

Source: Gordon Lloyd ed., Debates in the Federal Convention of 1787 by James Madison, a Member *(Ashland, Ohio: Ashbrook Center, 2014), 508-511, 544-546; "George Mason's Objsctions to the Constitution," George Mason Manuscript Collection, Gunston Hall Library and Archives, available online from http://www.gunstonhall.org/library/archives/manuscripts/objections.html.*

September 10

Mr. GERRY moved to reconsider Articles 21 and 22; from the latter of which "for the approbation of Congress," had been struck out.[1] He objected to proceeding to change the Government without the approbation of Congress, as being improper, and giving just umbrage to that body. He repeated his objections, also, to an annulment of the Confederation with so little scruple or formality.

Mr. HAMILTON[2] concurred with Mr. GERRY as to the indecorum of not requiring the approbation of Congress. He considered this as a necessary ingredient in the transaction. He thought it wrong, also, to allow nine States, as provided by Article 21, to institute a new Government on the ruins of the existing one. He would propose, as a better modification of the two Articles (21 and 22,) that the plan should be sent to Congress, in order that the same, if approved by them, may be communicated to the State Legislatures, to the end that they may refer it to State conventions; each Legislature declaring, that, if the convention of the State should think the plan ought to take effect among nine ratifying States, the same should take effect accordingly.

Mr. GORHAM.[3] Some States will say that nine States shall be sufficient to establish the plan; others will require unanimity for the purpose, and the different and conditional ratifications will defeat the plan altogether.

Mr. HAMILTON. No convention convinced of the necessity of the plan will refuse to give it effect, on the adoption by nine States. He thought this mode less exceptionable than the one proposed in the article: while it would attain the same end.

Mr. FITZSIMONS[4] remarked, that the words, "for their approbation," had been struck out in order to save Congress from the necessity of an act inconsistent with the Articles of Confederation under which they held their authority.

Mr. RANDOLPH declared if no change should be made in this part of the plan, he should be obliged to dissent from the whole of it. He had from the beginning, he said, been convinced that radical changes in the system of the Union were necessary. Under this conviction he had brought forward a set of republican propositions, as the basis and outline of a reform. These republican

---

[1] For these articles, see the Committee of Detail Report, Document 12.

[2] Alexander Hamilton of New York

[3] Nathaniel Gorham of Massachusetts

[4] Thomas Fitzsimons of Pennsylvania

propositions had, however, much to his regret, been widely, and, in his opinion, irreconcilably departed from. In this state of things, it was his idea, and he accordingly meant to propose, that the State conventions should be at liberty to offer amendments to the plan; and that these should be submitted to a second General Convention, with full power to settle the Constitution finally. He did not expect to succeed in this proposition, but the discharge of his duty in making the attempt would give quiet to his own mind.

Mr. WILSON[5] was against a reconsideration for any of the purposes which had been mentioned.

Mr. KING[6] thought it would be more respectful to Congress, to submit the plan generally to them than in such a form as expressly and necessarily to require their approbation or disapprobation. The assent of nine States he considered as sufficient; and that it was more proper to make this a part of the Constitution itself, than to provide for it by a supplemental or distinct recommendation.

Mr. GERRY urged the indecency and pernicious tendency of dissolving, in so slight a manner, the solemn obligations of the Articles of Confederation. If nine out of thirteen can dissolve the compact, six out of nine will be just as able to dissolve the new one hereafter.

Mr. SHERMAN[7] was in favor of Mr. KING'S idea of submitting the plan generally to Congress. He thought nine States ought to be made sufficient; but that it would be better to make it a separate act, and in some such form as that intimated by Col. HAMILTON, than to make it a particular article of the Constitution.

On the question for reconsidering the two articles, 21 and 22, —

Connecticut, New Jersey, Delaware, Maryland, Virginia, North Carolina, Georgia, aye, — 7; Massachusetts, Pennsylvania, South Carolina, no, — 3; New Hampshire, divided.

. . . Mr. RANDOLPH took this opportunity to state his objections to the system. They turned on the Senate's being made the court of impeachment for trying the Executive, — on the necessity of three fourths instead of two thirds of each House to overrule the negative of the President, — on the smallness of the number of the Representative branch, — on the want of limitation to a standing army, — on the general clause concerning necessary and proper laws, — on the want of some particular restraint on navigation acts, — on the power

---

[5] James Wilson of Pennsylvania

[6] Rufus King of Massachusetts

[7] Roger Sherman of Connecticut

to lay duties on exports, — on the authority of the General Legislature to interpose on the application of the *Executives* of the States, — on the want of a more definite boundary between the General and State Legislatures, — and between the General and State Judiciaries, — on the unqualified power of the President to pardon treasons, — on the want of some limit to the power of the Legislature in regulating their own compensations. With these difficulties in his mind, what course, he asked, was he to pursue? Was he to promote the establishment of a plan which he verily believed would end in tyranny? He was unwilling, he said, to impede the wishes and judgment of the Convention, but he must keep himself free, in case he should be honored with a seat in the Convention of his State, to act according to the dictates of his judgment. The only mode in which his embarrassment could be removed was that of submitting the plan to Congress, to go from them to the State Legislatures, and from these to State Conventions, having power to adopt, reject, or amend; the process to close with another General Convention, with full power to adopt or reject the alterations proposed by the State Conventions, and to establish finally the Government. He accordingly proposed a resolution to this effect.

Doctor FRANKLIN[8] seconded the motion.

Colonel MASON urged and obtained that the motion should lie on the table for a day or two, to see what steps might be taken with regard to the parts of the system objected to by Mr. RANDOLPH.

Mr. PINCKNEY moved, "that it be an instruction to the Committee for revising the style and arrangement of the articles agreed on, to prepare an address to the people, to accompany the present Constitution, and to be laid, with the same, before the United States in Congress."

The motion itself was referred to the Committee, *nem. con.*

Mr. RANDOLPH moved to refer to the Committee, also, a motion relating to pardons in cases of treason; which was agreed to, *nem. con.*

Adjourned.

September 12

Colonel MASON . . . wished the plan had been prefaced with a Bill of Rights, & would second a Motion if made for the purpose. It would give great quiet to the people; and with the aid of the State declarations, a bill might be prepared in a few hours.

Mr. GERRY concurred in the idea & moved for a Committee to prepare a Bill of Rights.

---

[8] Benjamin Franklin of Pennsylvania

Colonel MASON 2ded. the motion.

Mr. SHERMAN, was for securing the rights of the people where requisite. The State Declarations of Rights are not repealed by this Constitution; and being in force are sufficient. There are many cases where juries are proper which can not be discriminated. The Legislature may be safely trusted.

Colonel MASON. The Laws of the U. S. are to be paramount to State Bills of Rights.

On the question for a Committee to prepare a Bill of Rights, —

N.H. no. Mas. absent. Ct. no. N. J. no. Pa. no. Del no. Md. no. Va. no. N. C. no. S. C. no. Geo. no

September 15

Mr. RANDOLPH animadverting[9] on the indefinite and dangerous power given by the Constitution to Congress, expressing the pain he felt at differing from the body of the Convention on the close of the great and awful subject of their labors, and anxiously wishing for some accommodating expedient which would relieve him from his embarrassments, made a motion importing, "that amendments to the plan might be offered by the State conventions, which should be submitted to, and finally decided on by, another general Convention." Should this proposition be disregarded, it would, he said, be impossible for him to put his name to the instrument. Whether he should oppose it afterwards, he would not then decide; but he would not deprive himself of the freedom to do so in his own State, if that course should be prescribed by his final judgment.

Colonel MASON seconded and followed Mr. RANDOLPH in animadversions on the dangerous power and structure of the Government, concluding that it would end either in monarchy, or a tyrannical aristocracy; which, he was in doubt, but one or other, he was sure. This Constitution had been formed without the knowledge or idea of the people. A second Convention will know more of the sense of the people, and be able to provide a system more consonant to it. It was improper to say to the people, take this or nothing. As the Constitution now stands, he could neither give it his support or vote in Virginia; and he could not sign here what he could not support there. With the expedient of another Convention, as proposed, he could sign.

Mr. PINCKNEY.[10] These declarations from members so respectable, at the close of this important scene, give a peculiar solemnity to the present

---

[9] pointing critically to

[10] Charles Pinckney of South Carolina

moment. He descanted[11] on the consequences of calling forth the deliberations and amendments of the different States, on the subject of government at large. Nothing but confusion and contrariety will spring from the experiment. The States will never agree in their plans, and the deputies to a second convention, coming together under the discordant impressions of their constituents, will never agree. Conventions are serious things, and ought not to be repeated. He was not without objections, as well as others, to the plan. He objected to the contemptible weakness and dependence of the Executive. He objected to the power of a majority, only, of Congress, over commerce. But apprehending the danger of a general confusion, and an ultimate decision by the sword, he should give the plan his support.

Mr. GERRY stated the objections which determined him to withhold his name from the Constitution:

1. the duration and re-eligibility of the Senate; 2. the power of the House of Representatives to conceal their Journals; 3. the power of Congress over the places of election; 4. the unlimited power of Congress over their own compensation; 5. that Massachusetts has not a due share of representatives allotted to her; 6. that three fifths of the blacks are to be represented, as if they were freemen; 7. that under the power over commerce, monopolies may be established; 8. the Vice President being made head of the Senate.

He could, however, he said, get over all these, if the rights of the citizens were not rendered insecure, — first, by the general power of the Legislature to make what laws they may please to call "necessary and proper"; secondly, to raise armies and money without limit; thirdly, to establish a tribunal without juries, which will be a Star Chamber[12] as to civil cases. Under such a view of the Constitution, the best that could be done, he conceived, was to provide for a second general Convention.

On the question, on the proposition of Mr. RANDOLPH, all the States answered, no.

On the question to agree to the Constitution, as amended, all the States, aye. The Constitution was then ordered to be engrossed, and the House Adjourned.

---

[11] spoke at length

[12] The Star Chamber existed as an English court of law between the late 15th and mid 17th centuries. Designed as a supplement to common-law courts that would ensure speedier trial and stricter judgments against prominent people, it dispensed with indictments and substituted appointive judges for a jury of commoners. It came to be seen as a tool by which the monarch could enforce his arbitrary will.

Mason's Objections to the Constitution
September 17

[1] There is no declaration of rights: and the laws of the general government being paramount to the laws and constitutions of the several states, the declarations of rights, in the separate states, are no security. Nor are the people secured even in the enjoyment of the benefit of the common law, which stands here upon no other foundation than its having been adopted by the respective acts forming the constitutions of the several states.

[2] In the House of Representatives there is not the substance, but the shadow only of representation; which can never produce proper information in the legislature, or inspire confidence in the people. — The laws will, therefore, be generally made by men little concerned in, and unacquainted with, their effects and consequences.

[3] The Senate have the power of altering all money-bills, and of originating appropriations of money, and the salaries of the officers of their own appointment, in conjunction with the President of the United States — Although they are not the representatives of the people, or amenable to them. These, with their other great powers (viz.[13] their powers in the appointment of ambassadors, and all public officers, in making treaties, and in trying all impeachments), their influence upon, and connection with, the supreme executive from these causes, their duration of office, and their being a constant existing body, almost continually sitting, joined with their being one complete branch of the legislature, will destroy any balance in the government, and enable them to accomplish what usurpations they please upon the rights and liberties of the people.

[4] The judiciary of the United States is so constructed and extended, as to absorb and destroy the judiciaries of the several states; thereby rendering laws as tedious, intricate, and expensive, and justice as unattainable by a great part of the community, as in England; and enabling the rich to oppress and ruin the poor.

[5] The President of the United States has no constitutional council (a thing unknown in any safe and regular government.) He will therefore be unsupported by proper information and advice; and will generally be directed by minions and favorites — or he will become a tool to the Senate — or a council of state will grow out of the principal officers of the great departments — the worst and most dangerous of all ingredients for such a council, in a free country; for they may be induced to join in any dangerous or oppressive

[13] Abbreviation of the Latin *videlicet*: that is, namely

measures, to shelter themselves, and prevent an inquiry into their own misconduct in office. Whereas, had a constitutional council been formed (as was proposed) of six members, viz., two from the eastern, two from the middle, and two from the southern states, to be appointed by vote of the states in the House of Representatives, with the same duration and rotation of office as the Senate, the executive would always have had safe and proper information and advice; the president of such a council might have acted as Vice-President of the United States, *pro tempore,*[14] upon any vacancy or disability of the chief magistrate, and long continued sessions of the Senate, would in a great measure have been prevented. From this fatal defect of a constitutional council, has arisen the improper power of the Senate, in the appointment of the public officers, and the alarming dependence and connection between that branch of the legislature and the supreme executive. Hence, also, sprung that unnecessary officer, the Vice-President, who, for want of other employment, is made President of the Senate, thereby dangerously blending the executive and legislative powers; besides always giving to some one of the states an unnecessary and unjust pre-eminence over the others.

[6] The President of the United States has the unrestrained power of granting pardon for treason; which may be sometimes exercised to screen from punishment those whom he had secretly instigated to commit the crime, and thereby prevent a discovery of his own guilt. By declaring all treaties supreme laws of the land, the executive and the Senate have, in many cases, an exclusive power of legislation, which might have been avoided, by proper distinctions with respect to treaties, and requiring the assent of the House of Representatives, where it could be done with safety.

[7] By requiring only a majority to make all commercial and navigation laws, the five southern states (whose produce and circumstances are totally different from those of the eight northern and eastern States) will be ruined: for such rigid and premature regulations may be made, as will enable the merchants of the northern and eastern states not only to demand an exorbitant freight, but to monopolize the purchase of the commodities, at their own price, for many years, to the great injury of the landed interest, and the impoverishment of the people: and the danger is the greater, as the gain on one side will be in proportion to the loss on the other. Whereas, requiring two-thirds of the members present in both houses, would have produced mutual moderation, promoted the general interest, and removed an insuperable objection to the adoption of the government.

---

[14] temporarily

[8] Under their own construction of the general clause at the end of the enumerated powers, the Congress may grant monopolies in trade and commerce, constitute new crimes, inflict unusual and severe punishments, and extend their power as far as they shall think proper; so that the state legislatures have no security for the powers now presumed to remain to them, or the people for their rights. There is no declaration of any kind for preserving the liberty of the press, the trial by jury in civil cases, nor against the danger of standing armies in time of peace.

[9] The state legislatures are restrained from laying export duties on their own produce — the general legislature is restrained from prohibiting the further importation of slaves for twenty odd years, though such importations render the United States weaker, more vulnerable, and less capable of defense. Both the general legislature, and the state legislatures are expressly prohibited making *ex post facto* laws, though there never was, nor can be, a legislature but must and will make such laws, when necessity and the public safety require them, which will hereafter be a breach of all the constitutions in the union, and afford precedents for other innovations.

[10] This government will commence in a moderate aristocracy; it is at present impossible to foresee whether it will, in its operation, produce a monarchy, or a corrupt oppressive aristocracy; it will most probably vibrate some years between the two, and then terminate in the one or the other.

Document 16

Centinel I

October 5, 1787

There is a difference of opinion with respect to what to call the opponents of the Constitution. The Federalist Papers *referred to them as the antifederalists, degrading them to a position of irrelevance and incoherence. Some modern scholars, by contrast, capitalize their name but then hyphenate it, making them Anti-federalists—relevant, but incoherent. We have chosen the nomenclature "Antifederalist" in order to encourage the reader to see their remarks as both relevant and coherent.*

This essay of "Centinel" offered one of the earliest public Antifederalist critiques of the Constitutional framers' work as the ratification process began. He opens his remarks, addressed to the Freemen of Pennsylvania, with a reminder and a question: the essential liberties of the people are secured in the Pennsylvania Bill of Rights; are they secure under the proposed Constitution? He suggests that "all the blessings of liberty and the dearest privileges of freemen are now at stake and dependent on your present conduct."

Beware, he adds, the work of "artful and designing men." Unfortunately, Centinel contends, the Convention was inspired by John Adams's political thought on "good government," which presumed a balancing of the three functions of government—legislative, executive, and judicial—in three branches. According to Centinel, this means that the Constitution does not rely on the virtue of the people; it simply balances the powers of those governing them. "A republican, or free government, can only exist where the body of the people are virtuous, and where property is pretty equally divided," Centinel maintains. Furthermore, the plan encourages the exercise of extensive powers by the general government—see the general welfare clause and the supremacy clause—over an extensive territory, which is a recipe not "for a regular balanced government" but for "a permanent ARISTOCRACY."

Centinel concludes that 1) the new Constitution does not include a bill of rights to ward off future crises and 2) no such crisis exists compelling adoption of the Constitution right away. That we are in crisis "is the argument of tyrants." We need to follow the wisdom of the French political theorist Montesquieu (whose Spirit of the Laws *was widely read among the Framers) concerning the size and homogeneity of republics; if they were to remain free, they need to be small, and their citizens had to have common interests.*

The "Centinel" series comprised 24 separate essays, published in the Philadelphia Independent Gazetteer *and the Philadelphia* Freeman's Journal, *the last appearing November 4, 1788. This first Centinel essay was republished in several other newspapers.*

Source: Herbert J. Storing, ed., The Complete Anti-Federalist, *vol. 2, 136-143.*

To the Freemen of Pennsylvania

Friends, Countrymen and Fellow Citizens, Permit one of yourselves to put you in mind of certain *liberties* and *privileges* secured to you by the constitution of this commonwealth, and to beg your serious attention to his uninterested opinion upon the plan of federal government submitted to your consideration, before you surrender these great and valuable privileges up forever. Your present frame of government, secures to you a right to hold yourselves, houses, papers and possessions free from search and seizure, and therefore warrants granted without oaths or affirmations first made, affording sufficient foundation for them, whereby any officer or messenger may be commanded or required to search your houses or seize your persons or property, not particularly described in such warrant, shall not be granted. Your constitution further provides "that in controversies respecting property, and in suits between man and man, the parties have a right *to trial by jury, which ought to be held sacred.*" It also provides and declares "*that the people have a right of* FREEDOM OF SPEECH, *and of* WRITING *and* PUBLISHING *their sentiments, therefore* THE FREEDOM OF THE PRESS OUGHT NOT TO BE RESTRAINED." The constitution of Pennsylvania is *yet* in existence, *as yet* you have the right to *freedom of speech,* and of *publishing your sentiments.* How long those rights will appertain to you, you yourselves are called upon to say, whether your *houses* shall continue to be your *castles;* whether your *papers,* your *persons* and your *property,* are to be held sacred and free from *general warrants,* you are now to determine. Whether the *trial by jury* is to continue as your birth-right, the freemen of Pennsylvania, nay, of all America, are now called upon to declare.

Without presuming upon my own judgment, I cannot think it an unwarrantable presumption to offer my private opinion, and call upon others for theirs; and if I use my pen with the boldness of a freeman, it is because I know that *the liberty of the press yet remains unviolated,* and *juries yet are judges.*

The late Convention have submitted to your consideration a plan of a new federal government — The subject is highly interesting to your future welfare — Whether it be calculated to promote the great ends of civil society, *viz.*[1] the happiness and prosperity of the community; it behoves you well to consider, uninfluenced by the authority of names. Instead of that frenzy of enthusiasm, that has actuated the citizens of Philadelphia, in their approbation of the proposed plan, before it was possible that it could be the result of a rational investigation into its principles; it ought to be dispassionately and deliberately examined, and its own intrinsic merit the only criterion of your patronage. If ever free and unbiased discussion was proper or necessary, it is on such an occasion. — All the blessings of liberty and the dearest privileges of freemen, are now at stake and dependent on your present conduct. Those who are competent to the task of developing the principles of government, ought to be encouraged to come forward, and thereby the better enable the people to make a proper judgment; for the science of government is so abstruse, that few are able to judge for themselves; without such assistance the people are too apt to yield an implicit assent to the opinions of those characters, whose abilities are held in the highest esteem, and to those in whose integrity and patriotism they can confide; not considering that the love of domination is generally in proportion to talents, abilities, and superior acquirements; and that the men of the greatest purity of intention may be made instruments of despotism in the hands of the *artful and designing*. If it were not for the stability and attachment which time and habit gives to forms of government it would be in the power of the enlightened and aspiring few, if they should combine, at any time to destroy the best establishments, and even make the people the instruments of their own subjugation. . . .

I am fearful that the principles of government inculcated in Mr. [John] Adams's treatise,[2] and enforced in the numerous essays and paragraphs in the newspapers, have misled some well designing members of the late Convention. But it will appear in the sequel, that the construction of the proposed plan of government is infinitely more extravagant.

I have been anxiously expecting that some enlightened patriot would, ere this, have taken up the pen to expose the futility, and counteract the baneful tendency of such principles. Mr. Adams's *sine qua non*[3] of a good government is three balancing powers, whose repelling qualities are to produce an

---

[1] Abbreviation of the Latin *videlicet*: that is, namely

[2] The essay "Thoughts on Government" was written by John Adams in April of 1776.

[3] essential requirement (in Latin, literally "without which not")

equilibrium of interests, and thereby promote the happiness of the whole community. He asserts that the administrators of every government, will ever be actuated by views of private interest and ambition, to the prejudice of the public good; that therefore the only effectual method to secure the rights of the people and promote their welfare, is to create an opposition of interests between the members of two distinct bodies, in the exercise of the powers of government, and balanced by those of a third. This hypothesis supposes human wisdom competent to the task of instituting three co-equal orders in government, and a corresponding weight in the community to enable them respectively to exercise their several parts, and whose views and interests should be so distinct as to prevent a coalition of any two of them for the destruction of the third. Mr. Adams, although he has traced the constitution of every form of government that ever existed, as far as history affords materials, has not been able to adduce a single instance of such a government; he indeed says that the British constitution is such in theory, but this is rather a confirmation that his principles are chimerical[4] and not to be reduced to practice. If such an organization of power were practicable, how long would it continue? not a day — for there is so great a disparity in the talents, wisdom and industry of mankind, that the scale would presently preponderate to one or the other body, and with every accession of power the means of further increase would be greatly extended. The state of society in England is much more favorable to such a scheme of government than that of America. There they have a powerful hereditary nobility, and real distinctions of rank and interests; but even there, for want of that perfect equality of power and distinction of interests, in the three orders of government, they exist but in name; the only operative and efficient check, upon the conduct of administration, is the sense of the people at large.

Suppose a government could be formed and supported on such principles, would it answer the great purposes of civil society; If the administrators of every government are actuated by views of private interest and ambition, how is the welfare and happiness of the community to be the result of such jarring adverse interests?

Therefore, as different orders in government will not produce the good of the whole, we must recur to other principles. I believe it will be found that the form of government, which holds those entrusted with power, in the greatest responsibility to their constituents, the best calculated for freemen. A republican, or free government, can only exist where the body of the people are

---

[4] imaginary and unrealistic

virtuous, and where property is pretty equally divided; in such a government the people are the sovereign and their sense or opinion is the criterion of every public measure; for when this ceases to be the case, the nature of the government is changed, and an aristocracy, monarchy or despotism will rise on its ruin. The highest responsibility is to be attained, in a simple structure of government, for the great body of the people never steadily attend to the operations of government, and for want of due information are liable to be imposed on — If you complicate the plan by various orders, the people will be perplexed and divided in their sentiments about the source of abuses or misconduct, some will impute it to the senate, others to the house of representatives, and so on, that the interposition of the people may be rendered imperfect or perhaps wholly abortive. But if, imitating the constitution of Pennsylvania, you vest all the legislative power in one body of men (separating the executive and judicial) elected for a short period, and necessarily excluded by rotation from permanency, and guarded from precipitancy and surprise by delays imposed on its proceedings, you will create the most perfect responsibility, for then, whenever the people feel a grievance they cannot mistake the authors, and will apply the remedy with certainty and effect, discarding them at the next election. This tie of responsibility will obviate all the dangers apprehended from a single legislature, and will the best secure the rights of the people.

Having premised this much, I shall now proceed to the examination of the proposed plan of government, and I trust, shall make it appear to the meanest capacity, that it has none of the essential requisites of a free government; that it is neither founded on those balancing restraining powers, recommended by Mr. Adams and attempted in the British constitution, or possessed of that responsibility to its constituents, which, in my opinion, is the only effectual security for the liberties and happiness of the people; but on the contrary, that it is the most daring attempt to establish a despotic aristocracy among freemen, that the world has ever witnessed.

I shall previously consider the extent of the powers intended to be vested in Congress, before I examine the construction of the general government.

It will not be controverted[5] that the legislative is the highest delegated power in government, and that all others are subordinate to it. The celebrated *Montesquieu*[6] establishes it as a maxim, that legislation necessarily follows the power of taxation. By sect. 8, of the first article of the proposed plan of

---

[5] denied

[6] French political philosopher who lived from 1689 to 1755

government, "the Congress are to have power to lay and collect taxes, duties, imposts and excises, to pay the debts and provide for the common defense and *general welfare* of the United States, but all duties, imposts and excises, shall be uniform throughout the United States." Now what can be more comprehensive than these words; not content by other sections of this plan, to grant all the great executive powers of a confederation, and a STANDING ARMY IN TIME OF PEACE, that grand engine of oppression, and moreover the absolute control over the commerce of the United States and all external objects of revenue, such as unlimited imposts upon imports, etc. — they are to be vested with every species of *internal* taxation — whatever taxes, duties and excises that they may deem requisite for the *general welfare,* may be imposed on the citizens of these states, levied by the officers of Congress, distributed through every district in America; and the collection would be enforced by the standing army, however grievous or improper they may be. The Congress may construe every purpose for which the state legislatures now lay taxes, to be for the *general welfare,* and thereby seize upon every object of revenue.

The judicial power by 1st sect. of article 3 "shall extend to all cases, in law and equity, arising under this constitution, the laws of the United States, and treaties made or which shall be made under their authority; to all cases affecting ambassadors, other public ministers and consuls; to all cases of admiralty and maritime jurisdiction, to controversies to which the United States shall be a party, to controversies between two or more states, between a state and citizens of another state, between citizens of different states, between citizens of the same state claiming lands under grants of different states, and between a state, or the citizens thereof, and foreign states, citizens or subjects."

The judicial power to be vested in one Supreme Court, and in such Inferior Courts as the Congress may from time to time ordain and establish.

The objects of jurisdiction recited above, are so numerous, and the shades of distinction between civil causes are oftentimes so slight, that it is more than probable that the state judicatories would be wholly superseded; for in contests about jurisdiction, the federal court, as the most powerful, would ever prevail. Every person acquainted with the history of the courts in England, knows by what ingenious sophisms they have, at different periods, extended the sphere of their jurisdiction over objects out of the line of their institution, and contrary to their very nature; courts of a criminal jurisdiction obtaining cognizance in civil causes.

To put the omnipotency of Congress over the state government and judicatories out of all doubt, the 6th article ordains that "this constitution and the laws of the United States which shall be made in pursuance thereof, and all treaties made, or which shall be made under the authority of the United States, shall be the *supreme law of the land*, and the judges in every state shall be bound thereby, any thing in the constitution or laws of any state to the contrary notwithstanding."

By these sections the all-prevailing power of taxation, and such extensive legislative and judicial powers are vested in the general government, as must in their operation, necessarily absorb the state legislatures and judicatories; and that such was in the contemplation of the framers of it, will appear from the provision made for such event, in another part of it; (but that, fearful of alarming the people by so great an innovation, they have suffered the forms of the separate governments to remain, as a blind.) By sect. 4th of the 1st article, "the times, places and manner of holding elections for senators and representatives, shall be prescribed in each state by the legislature thereof; but *the Congress may at any time, by law, make or alter such regulations, except as to the place of choosing senators.*" The plain construction of which is, that when the state legislatures drop out of sight, from the necessary operation [of] this government, then Congress are to provide for the election and appointment of representatives and senators.

If the foregoing be a just comment — if the united states are to be melted down into one empire, it becomes you to consider, whether such a government, however constructed, would be eligible in so extended a territory; and whether it would be practicable, consistent with freedom? It is the opinion of the greatest writers, that a very extensive country cannot be governed on democratical principles, on any other plan, than a confederation of a number of small republics, possessing all the powers of internal government, but united in the management of their foreign and general concerns.

It would not be difficult to prove, that any thing short of despotism, could not bind so great a country under one government; and that whatever plan you might, at the first setting out, establish, it would issue in a despotism.

If one general government could be instituted and maintained on principles of freedom, it would not be so competent to attend to the various local concerns and wants, of every particular district, as well as the peculiar governments, who are nearer the scene, and possessed of superior means of information, besides, if the business of the *whole* union is to be managed by one government, there would not be time. Do we not already see, that the inhabitants in a number of larger states, who are remote from the seat of government, are loudly complaining of the inconveniencies and disadvantages they are subjected to on this account, and that, to enjoy the comforts of local government, they are separating into smaller divisions.

Having taken a review of the powers, I shall now examine the construction of the proposed general government.

Art. 1. Sect. 1. "All legislative powers herein granted shall be vested in a Congress of the United States, which shall consist of a senate and house of representatives." By another section, the president (the principal executive officer) has a conditional control over their proceedings.

Sect. 2. "The house of representatives shall be composed of members chosen every second year, by the people of the several states. The number of representatives shall not exceed one for every 30,000 inhabitants."

The senate, the other constituent branch of the legislature, is formed by the legislature of each state appointing two senators, for the term of six years.

The executive power by Art. 2, Sect. 1. is to be vested in a president of the United States of America, elected for four years: Sect. 2. gives him "power, by and with the consent of the senate to make treaties, provided two thirds of the senators present concur; and he shall nominate, and by and with the advice and consent of the senate, shall appoint ambassadors, other public ministers and consuls, judges of the Supreme Court, and all other officers of the United States, whose appointments are not herein otherwise provided for, and which shall be established by law," etc. And by another section he has the absolute power of granting reprieves and pardons for treason and all other high crimes and misdemeanors, except in case of impeachment.

The foregoing are the outlines of the plan.

Thus we see, the house of representatives, are on the part of the people to balance the senate, who I suppose will be composed of the *better sort*, the *well born*, etc. The number of the representatives (being only one for every 30,000 inhabitants) appears to be too few, either to communicate the requisite information, of the wants, local circumstances and sentiments of so extensive an empire, or to prevent corruption and undue influence, in the exercise of such great powers; the term for which they are to be chosen, too long to preserve a due dependence and accountability to their constituents; and the mode and places of their election not sufficiently ascertained, for as Congress have the control over both, they may govern the choice, by ordering the *representatives* of a *whole* state, to be *elected* in *one* place, and that too may be the most *inconvenient*.

The senate, the great efficient body in this plan of government, is constituted on the most unequal principles. The smallest state in the union has equal weight with the great states of Virginia, Massachusetts, or Pennsylvania—The Senate, besides its legislative functions, has a very considerable share in the Executive; none of the principal appointments to office can be made without its advice and consent. The term and mode of its appointment, will lead to permanency; the members are chosen for six years, the mode is under the control of Congress, and as there is no exclusion by rotation, they may be continued for life, which, from their extensive means of influence, would follow of course. The President, who would be a mere pageant of state, unless he coincides with the views of the Senate, would either become the head of the aristocratic junto in that body, or its minion, besides, their influence being the most predominant, could the best secure his re-election to office. And from his power of granting pardons, he might screen from punishment the most treasonable attempts on liberties of the people, when instigated by the Senate.

From this investigation into the organization of this government, it appears that it is devoid of all responsibility or accountability to the great body of the people, and that so far from being a regular balanced government, it would be in practice a *permanent* ARISTOCRACY.

The framers of it, actuated by the true spirit of such a government, which ever abominates and suppresses all free enquiry and discussion, have made no provision for the *liberty of the press,* that grand *palladium of freedom,* and *scourge of tyrants,* but observed a total silence on that head. It is the opinion of some great writers, that if the liberty of the press, by an institution of religion, or otherwise, could be rendered *sacred,* even in *Turkey,* that despotism would fly before it.

And it is worthy of remark, that there is no declaration of personal rights, premised in most free constitutions; and that trial by *jury* in *civil* cases is taken away; for what other construction can be put on the following, *viz.* Article 3. Sect. 2d. "In all cases affecting ambassadors, other public ministers and consuls, and those in which a State shall be party, the Supreme Court shall have original jurisdiction. In all the other cases above mentioned, the Supreme Court shall have *appellate* jurisdiction, both as to *law and fact*"? It would be a novelty in jurisprudence, as well as evidently improper to allow an appeal from the verdict of a jury, on the matter of fact; therefore, it implies and allows of a dismissal of the jury in civil cases, and especially when it is considered, that jury trial in criminal cases is expressly stipulated for, but not in civil cases.

But our situation is represented to be so *critically* dreadful that, however reprehensible and exceptionable the proposed plan of government may be, there is no alternative, between the adoption of it and absolute ruin.

My fellow citizens, things are not at that crisis, it is the argument of tyrants; the present distracted state of Europe secures us from injury on that quarter, and as to domestic dissensions, we have not so much to fear from them, as to precipitate us into this form of government, without it is[7] a safe and a proper one. For remember, of all *possible* evils that of *despotism is* the *worst* and the most to be *dreaded.*

Besides, it cannot be supposed, that the first essay on so difficult a subject, is so well digested, as it ought to be, — if the proposed plan, after a mature deliberation, should meet the approbation of the respective States, the matter will end, but if it should be found to be fraught with dangers and inconveniencies, a future general Convention being in possession of the objections, will be the better enabled to plan a suitable government.

> Who's here so base, that would a bondsman be?
>
> If any, speak; for him have I offended.
>
> Who's here so vile, that will not love his country?
>
> If any, speak; for him have I offended.
>
> —*Julius Caesar,* Act 3, Scene 2

Centinel.

[7] unless it is

Document 17

Brutus I

October 18, 1787

"Brutus," a New York Antifederalist, or opponent of the proposed Constitution (generally assumed to have been Robert Yates, a New York delegate to the Constitutional Convention), anticipated by two weeks the opening paragraph of Federalist *1, also addressed to the people of New York. As would "Publius" — author of* The Federalist, *a collection of newspaper essays published in New York City defending the Constitution — he introduced his own first essay with the observation that "the most important question that was ever proposed to your decision, or to the decision of any people under heaven, is before you." Nothing less than "the dignity of human nature" and the blessings of liberty are at stake. Brutus then argues that "although the government reported by the convention does not go to a perfect and entire consolidation, yet it approaches so near to it, that it must, if executed, certainly and infallibly terminate in it." The necessary and proper clause, the supremacy clause, and the judicial power have the potentiality to transform America from a system of confederated states into a "complete consolidated government." Anticipating the distinction between a democracy and a republic in* Federalist 10 *and 63, and agreeing that a representative government is to be preferred to a pure democracy, Brutus then argued that, contrary to the wisdom of the French political theorist Montesquieu (whose* Spirit of the Laws *was widely read among the Framers) and contrary to the experience of history, the Framers have given us "an extensive republic" rather than a confederation of small republics. A "free republic" over "such vast extent" of territory is impracticable because, in time, the people will become "acquainted with very few of their rulers" and lose "confidence" in, and control over, the government.*

Brutus voiced a concern shared by many Americans: Could a widely dispersed and diverse people be united under one government without sacrificing the blessings of liberty and self-government? Brutus' powerful arguments prompted Federalists to articulate a more thorough explanation of what the Constitution meant and why it should be ratified.

Source: Herbert J. Storing, ed., The Complete Anti-Federalist *(Chicago: The University of Chicago Press, 1981), 2:363-372.*

To the Citizens of the State of New-York.

When the public is called to investigate and decide upon a question in which not only the present members of the community are deeply interested, but upon which the happiness and misery of generations yet unborn is in great measure suspended, the benevolent mind cannot help feeling itself peculiarly interested in the result.

In this situation, I trust the feeble efforts of an individual, to lead the minds of the people to a wise and prudent determination, cannot fail of being acceptable to the candid and dispassionate part of the community. Encouraged by this consideration, I have been induced to offer my thoughts upon the present important crisis of our public affairs.

Perhaps this country never saw so critical a period in their political concerns. We have felt the feebleness of the ties by which these United States are held together, and the want of sufficient energy in our present confederation, to manage, in some instances, our general concerns. Various expedients have been proposed to remedy these evils, but none have succeeded. At length a Convention of the states has been assembled, they have formed a constitution which will now, probably, be submitted to the people to ratify or reject, who are the fountain of all power, to whom alone it of right belongs to make or unmake constitutions, or forms of government, at their pleasure. The most important question that was ever proposed to your decision, or to the decision of any people under heaven, is before you, and you are to decide upon it by men of your own election, chosen specially for this purpose. If the constitution, offered to [your acceptance], be a wise one, calculated to preserve the invaluable blessings of liberty, to secure the inestimable rights of mankind, and promote human happiness, then, if you accept it, you will lay a lasting foundation of happiness for millions yet unborn; generations to come will rise up and call you blessed. You may rejoice in the prospects of this vast extended continent becoming filled with freemen, who will assert the dignity of human nature. You may solace yourselves with the idea, that society, in this favored land, will fast advance to the highest point of perfection; the human mind will expand in knowledge and virtue, and the golden age be, in some measure, realized. But if, on the other hand, this form of government contains principles that will lead to the subversion of liberty — if it tends to establish a despotism, or, what is worse, a tyrannic aristocracy; then, if you adopt it, this only remaining asylum for liberty will be [shut] up, and posterity will execrate your memory....

With these few introductory remarks I shall proceed to a consideration of this constitution:

The first question that presents itself on the subject is, whether a confederated government be the best for the United States or not? Or in other words, whether the thirteen United States should be reduced to one great republic, governed by one legislature, and under the direction of one executive and judicial; or whether they should continue thirteen confederated republics, under the direction and control of a supreme federal head for certain defined national purposes only?

This inquiry is important, because, although the government reported by the convention does not go to a perfect and entire consolidation, yet it approaches so near to it, that it must, if executed, certainly and infallibly terminate in it.

This government is to possess absolute and uncontrollable power, legislative, executive and judicial, with respect to every object to which it extends, for by the last clause of section 8th, article 1st, it is declared "that the Congress shall have power to make all laws which shall be necessary and proper for carrying into execution the foregoing powers, and all other powers vested by this constitution, in the government of the United States; or in any department or office thereof." And by the 6th article, it is declared "that this constitution, and the laws of the United States, which shall be made in pursuance thereof, and the treaties made, or which shall be made, under the authority of the United States, shall be the supreme law of the land; and the judges in every state shall be bound thereby, any thing in the constitution, or law of any state to the contrary notwithstanding." It appears from these articles that there is no need of any intervention of the state governments, between the Congress and the people, to execute any one power vested in the general government, and that the constitution and laws of every state are nullified and declared void, so far as they are or shall be inconsistent with this constitution, or the laws made in pursuance of it, or with treaties made under the authority of the United States. — The government then, so far as it extends, is a complete one, and not a confederation. It is as much one complete government as that of New-York or Massachusetts, has as absolute and perfect powers to make and execute all laws, to appoint officers, institute courts, declare offences, and annex penalties, with respect to every object to which it extends, as any other in the world. So far therefore as its powers reach, all ideas of confederation are given up and lost. It is true this government is limited to certain objects, or to speak more properly, some small degree of power is still left to the states, but a little attention to the powers vested in the general government, will convince every candid man, that if it is capable of being executed, all that is reserved for the individual states must very soon be annihilated, except so far as they are barely necessary to the organization of the general government. The powers of the general legislature extend to every case that is of the least importance — there is nothing valuable to human nature, nothing dear to freemen, but what is within its power. It has authority to make laws which will affect the lives, the liberty, and property of every man in the United States; nor can the constitution or laws of any state, in any way prevent or impede the full and complete execution of every power given. The legislative power is competent to lay taxes, duties, imposts, and excises; — there is no limitation to this power, unless it be said that the clause which directs the use to which those taxes, and duties shall be applied, may be said to be a limitation; but this is no restriction of the power at all, for by this clause they are to be applied to pay the debts and provide for the common defense and general welfare of the United States; but the legislature have authority to contract debts at their discretion; they are the sole judges of what is necessary to provide for the common defense, and they only are to determine what is for the general welfare: this power therefore is neither more nor less, than a power to lay and collect taxes, imposts, and excises, at their pleasure; not only the power to lay taxes unlimited, as to the amount they may require, but it is perfect and absolute to raise them in any mode they please. No state legislature, or any power in the state governments, have any more to do in carrying this into effect, than the authority of one state has to do with that of another. In the business therefore of laying and collecting taxes, the idea of confederation is totally lost, and that of one entire republic is embraced. It is proper here to remark, that the authority to lay and collect taxes is the most important of any power that can be granted; it connects with it almost all other powers, or at least will in process of time draw all other after it; it is the great mean of protection, security, and defense, in a good government, and the great engine of oppression and tyranny in a bad one. This cannot fail of being the case, if we consider the contracted limits which are set by this constitution, to the late governments, on this article of raising money. No state can emit paper money — lay any duties, or imposts, on imports, or exports, but by consent of the Congress; and then the net produce shall be for the benefit of the United States. The only mean therefore left, for any state to support its government and discharge its debts, is by direct taxation; and the United States have also power to lay and collect taxes, in any way they please. Every one who has thought on the subject, must be convinced that but small sums of money can be collected in any country, by direct taxes[; hence,] when the federal government begins to exercise the right of taxation in all its parts, the legislatures of the several states will find it impossible to raise monies to support their governments. Without money they cannot be supported, and they must dwindle away, and, as before observed, their powers [will be] absorbed in that of the general government.

It might be here shown, that the power in the federal legislative, to raise and support armies at pleasure, as well in peace as in war, and their control over the militia, tend, not only to a consolidation of the government, but the destruction of liberty. — I shall not, however, dwell upon these, as a few observations upon the judicial power of this government, in addition to the preceding, will fully evince the truth of the position.

The judicial power of the United States is to be vested in a supreme court, and in such inferior courts as Congress may from time to time ordain and establish. The powers of these courts are very extensive; their jurisdiction comprehends all civil causes, except such as arise between citizens of the same state; and it extends to all cases in law and equity arising under the constitution. One inferior court must be established, I presume, in each state at least, with the necessary executive officers appendant thereto. It is easy to see, that in the common course of things, these courts will eclipse the dignity, and take away from the respectability, of the state courts. These courts will be, in themselves, totally independent of the states, deriving their authority from the United States, and receiving from them fixed salaries; and in the course of human events it is to be expected, that they will swallow up all the powers of the courts in the respective states.

How far the clause in the 8th section of the 1st article may operate to do away all idea of confederated states, and to effect an entire consolidation of the whole into one general government, it is impossible to say. The powers given by this article are very general and comprehensive, and it may receive a construction to justify the passing almost any law. A power to make all laws, which shall be necessary and proper, for carrying into execution, all powers vested by the constitution in the government of the United States, or any department or officer thereof, is a power very comprehensive and definite, and may, for ought I know, be exercised in a such manner as entirely to abolish the state legislatures. Suppose the legislature of a state should pass a law to raise money to support their government and pay the state debt, may the Congress repeal this law, because it may prevent the collection of a tax which they may think proper and necessary to lay, to provide for the general welfare of the United States? For all laws made, in pursuance of this constitution, are the supreme law of the land, and the judges in every state shall be bound thereby, any thing in the constitution or laws of the different states to the contrary notwithstanding. — By such a law, the government of a particular state might be overturned at one stroke, and thereby be deprived of every means of its support.

It is not meant, by stating this case, to insinuate that the constitution would warrant a law of this kind; or unnecessarily to alarm the fears of the people, by suggesting, that the federal legislature would be more likely to pass the limits assigned them by the constitution, than that of an individual state, further than they are less responsible to the people. But what is meant is, that the legislature of the United States are vested with the great and uncontrollable powers, of laying and collecting taxes, duties, imposts, and excises; of regulating trade, raising and supporting armies, organizing, arming, and disciplining the militia, instituting courts, and other general powers. And are by this clause invested with the power of making all laws, proper and necessary, for carrying all these into execution; and they may so exercise this power as entirely to annihilate all the state governments, and reduce this country to one single government. And if they may do it, it is pretty certain they will; for it will be found that the power retained by individual states, small as it is, will be a clog upon the wheels of the government of the United States; the latter therefore will be naturally inclined to remove it out of the way. Besides, it is a truth confirmed by the unerring experience of ages, that every man, and every body of men, invested with power, are ever disposed to increase it, and to acquire a superiority over every thing that stands in their way. This disposition, which is implanted in human nature, will operate in the federal legislature to lessen and ultimately to subvert the state authority, and having such advantages, will most certainly succeed, if the federal government succeeds at all. It must be very evident then, that what this constitution wants of being a complete consolidation of the several parts of the union into one complete government, possessed of perfect legislative, judicial, and executive powers, to all intents and purposes, it will necessarily acquire in its exercise and operation.

Let us now proceed to inquire, as I at first proposed, whether it be best the thirteen United States should be reduced to one great republic, or not? It is here taken for granted, that all agree in this, that whatever government we adopt, it ought to be a free one; that it should be so framed as to secure the liberty of the citizens of America, and such an one as to admit of a full, fair, and equal representation of the people. The question then will be, whether a government thus constituted, and founded on such principles, is practicable, and can be exercised over the whole United States, reduced into one state?

If respect is to be paid to the opinion of the greatest and wisest men who have ever thought or wrote on the science of government, we shall be constrained to conclude, that a free republic cannot succeed over a country of such immense extent, containing such a number of inhabitants, and these increasing in such rapid progression as that of the whole United States. Among the many illustrious authorities which might be produced to this point, I shall content myself with quoting only two.

The one is the Baron de Montesquieu, *Spirit of the Laws,*[1] Chap. xvi. Vol. I [Book VIII]. "It is natural to a republic to have only a small territory, otherwise it cannot long subsist. In a large republic there are men of large fortunes, and consequently of less moderation; there are trusts too great to be placed in any single subject; he has interest of his own; he soon begins to think that he may be happy, great and glorious, by oppressing his fellow citizens; and that he may raise himself to grandeur on the ruins of his country. In a large republic, the public good is sacrificed to a thousand views; it is subordinate to exceptions, and depends on accidents. In a small one, the interest of the public is easier perceived, better understood, and more within the reach of every citizen; abuses are of less extent, and of course are less protected." Of the same opinion is the Marquis Beccarari.[2]

History furnishes no example of a free republic, anything like the extent of the United States. The Grecian republics were of small extent; so also was that of the Romans. Both of these, it is true, in process of time, extended their conquests over large territories of country; and the consequence was, that their governments were changed from that of free governments to those of the most tyrannical that ever existed in the world.

Not only the opinion of the greatest men, and the experience of mankind, are against the idea of an extensive republic, but a variety of reasons may be drawn from the reason and nature of things, against it. In every government, the will of the sovereign is the law. In despotic governments, the supreme authority being lodged in one, his will is law, and can be as easily expressed to a large extensive territory as to a small one. In a pure democracy the people are the sovereign, and their will is declared by themselves; for this purpose they must all come together to deliberate, and decide.

This kind of government cannot be exercised, therefore, over a country of any considerable extent; it must be confined to a single city, or at least limited to such bounds as that the people can conveniently assemble, be able to debate, understand the subject submitted to them, and declare their opinion concerning it.

---

[1] This major work by the French political theorist was first published in 1748.

[2] Cesare Beccaria, 18th century political and economic theorist, lived from 1738 to 1794.

In a free republic, although all laws are derived from the consent of the people, yet the people do not declare their consent by themselves in person, but by representatives, chosen by them, who are supposed to know the minds of their constituents, and to be possessed of integrity to declare this mind.

In every free government, the people must give their assent to the laws by which they are governed. This is the true criterion between a free government and an arbitrary one. The former are ruled by the will of the whole, expressed in any manner they may agree upon; the latter by the will of one, or a few. If the people are to give their assent to the laws, by persons chosen and appointed by them, the manner of the choice and the number chosen, must be such, as to possess, be disposed, and consequently qualified to declare the sentiments of the people; for if they do not know, or are not disposed to speak the sentiments of the people, the people do not govern, but the sovereignty is in a few. Now, in a large extended country, it is impossible to have a representation, possessing the sentiments, and of integrity, to declare the minds of the people, without having it so numerous and unwieldy, as to be subject in great measure to the inconveniency of a democratic government.

The territory of the United States is of vast extent; it now contains near three millions of souls, and is capable of containing much more than ten times that number. Is it practicable for a country, so large and so numerous as they will soon become, to elect a representation, that will speak their sentiments, without their becoming so numerous as to be incapable of transacting public business? It certainly is not.

In a republic, the manners, sentiments, and interests of the people should be similar. If this be not the case, there will be a constant clashing of opinions; and the representatives of one part will be continually striving against those of the other. This will retard the operations of government, and prevent such conclusions as will promote the public good. If we apply this remark to the condition of the United States, we shall be convinced that it forbids that we should be one government. The United States includes a variety of climates. The productions of the different parts of the union are very variant, and their interests, of consequence, diverse. Their manners and habits differ as much as their climates and productions; and their sentiments are by no means coincident. The laws and customs of the several states are, in many respects, very diverse, and in some opposite; each would be in favor of its own interests and customs, and, of consequence, a legislature, formed of representatives from the respective parts, would not only be too numerous to act with any care or decision, but would be composed of such heterogeneous and discordant principles, as would constantly be contending with each other.

The laws cannot be executed in a republic, of an extent equal to that of the United States, with promptitude.

The magistrates in every government must be supported in the execution of the laws, either by an armed force, maintained at the public expense for that purpose; or by the people turning out to aid the magistrate upon his command, in case of resistance.

In despotic governments, as well as in all the monarchies of Europe, standing armies are kept up to execute the commands of the prince or the magistrate, and are employed for this purpose when occasion requires: But they have always proved the destruction of liberty, and [are] abhorrent to the spirit of a free republic. In England, where they depend upon the parliament for their annual support, they have always been complained of as oppressive and unconstitutional, and are seldom employed in executing of the laws; never except on extraordinary occasions, and then under the direction of a civil magistrate.

A free republic will never keep a standing army to execute its laws. It must depend upon the support of its citizens. But when a government is to receive its support from the aid of the citizens, it must be so constructed as to have the confidence, respect, and affection of the people. Men who, upon the call of the magistrate, offer themselves to execute the laws, are influenced to do it either by affection to the government, or from fear; where a standing army is at hand to punish offenders, every man is actuated by the latter principle, and therefore, when the magistrate calls, will obey: but, where this is not the case, the government must rest for its support upon the confidence and respect which the people have for their government and laws. The body of the people being attached, the government will always be sufficient to support and execute its laws, and to operate upon the fears of any faction which may be opposed to it, not only to prevent an opposition to the execution of the laws themselves, but also to compel the most of them to aid the magistrate; but the people will not be likely to have such confidence in their rulers, in a republic so extensive as the United States, as necessary for these purposes. The confidence which the people have in their rulers, in a free republic, arises from their knowing them, from their being responsible to them for their conduct, and from the power they have of displacing them when they misbehave: but in a republic of the extent of this continent, the people in general would be acquainted with very few of their rulers: the people at large would know little of their proceedings, and it would be extremely difficult to change them. The people in Georgia and New-Hampshire would not know one another's mind, and therefore could not act in concert to enable them to effect a general change of representatives. The different parts of so extensive a country could not possibly be made acquainted with the conduct of their representatives, nor be informed of the reasons upon which measures were founded. The consequence will be, they will have no confidence in their legislature, suspect them of ambitious views, be jealous of every measure they adopt, and will not support the laws they pass. Hence the government will be nerveless and inefficient, and no way will be left to render it otherwise, but by establishing an armed force to execute the laws at the point of the bayonet — a government of all others the most to be dreaded.

In a republic of such vast extent as the United-States, the legislature cannot attend to the various concerns and wants of its different parts. It cannot be sufficiently numerous to be acquainted with the local condition and wants of the different districts, and if it could, it is impossible it should have sufficient time to attend to and provide for all the variety of cases of this nature, that would be continually arising.

In so extensive a republic, the great officers of government would soon become above the control of the people, and abuse their power to the purpose of aggrandizing themselves, and oppressing them. The trust committed to the executive offices, in a country of the extent of the United-States, must be various and of magnitude. The command of all the troops and navy of the republic, the appointment of officers, the power of pardoning offences, the collecting of all the public revenues, and the power of expending them, with a number of other powers, must be lodged and exercised in every state, in the hands of a few. When these are attended with great honor and emolument, as they always will be in large states, so as greatly to interest men to pursue them, and to be proper objects for ambitious and designing men, such men will be ever restless in their pursuit after them. They will use the power, when they have acquired it, to the purposes of gratifying their own interest and ambition, and it is scarcely possible, in a very large republic, to call them to account for their misconduct, or to prevent their abuse of power.

These are some of the reasons by which it appears, that a free republic cannot long subsist over a country of the great extent of these states. If then this new constitution is calculated to consolidate the thirteen states into one, as it evidently is, it ought not to be adopted.

Though I am of opinion, that it is a sufficient objection to this government, to reject it, that it creates the whole union into one government, under the form of a republic, yet if this objection was obviated, there are exceptions to it, which are so material and fundamental, that they ought to determine every man, who is a friend to the liberty and happiness of mankind, not to adopt it. I beg the candid and dispassionate attention of my countrymen while I state these objections — they are such as have obtruded themselves upon my mind upon a careful attention to the matter, and such as I sincerely believe are well founded. There are many objections, of small moment, of which I shall take no notice — perfection is not to be expected in any thing that is the production of man — and if I did not in my conscience believe that this scheme was defective in the fundamental principles — in the foundation upon which a free and equal government must rest — I would hold my peace.

Brutus.

Document 18

Federalist 1

Publius (Alexander Hamilton)
October 27, 1787

The Federalist Papers *were originally newspaper essays written by Alexander Hamilton, James Madison, and John Jay under the pseudonym Publius, whose immediate goal was to persuade the people of New York to ratify the Constitution. Hamilton opened* Federalist *1 by raising the momentousness of the choice that lay before New Yorkers and the American people as a whole. If Americans failed to deliberate and choose well, they would prove forever that humans are incapable of founding just and successful governments based on "reflection and choice" — that in fact, governments necessarily come into existence by "accident and force". Publius also provides an outline of the topics to be covered in this series of newspaper articles as well as a not too subtle warning to be aware that the Antifederalists are really in favor of disunion.*

Source: George W. Carey and James McClellan, eds., The Federalist: The Gideon Edition, *(Indianapolis: Liberty Fund, 2001), 1-4.*

After full experience of the insufficiency of the subsisting federal government, you are invited to deliberate on a New Constitution for the United States of America. The subject speaks its own importance; comprehending in its consequences, nothing less than the existence of the UNION, the safety and welfare of the parts of which it is composed, the fate of an empire, in many respects, the most interesting in the world. It has been frequently remarked, that it seems to have been reserved to the people of this country to decide, by their conduct and example, the important question, whether societies of men are really capable or not, of establishing good government from reflection and choice, or whether they are forever destined to depend, for their political constitutions, on accident and force. If there be any truth in the remark, the crisis at which we are arrived may, with propriety, be regarded as the period when that decision is to be made; and a wrong election of the part we shall act may, in this view, deserve to be considered as the general misfortune of mankind.

This idea, by adding the inducements of philanthropy to those of patriotism, will heighten the solicitude which all considerate and good men must feel for the event. Happy will it be if our choice should be directed by a judicious estimate of our true interests, uninfluenced by considerations foreign to the public good. But this is more ardently to be wished for, than seriously to be expected. The plan offered to our deliberations, affects too many particular interests, innovates upon too many local institutions, not to involve in its discussion a variety of objects extraneous to its merits, and of views, passions and prejudices little favorable to the discovery of truth.

Among the most formidable of the obstacles which the new constitution will have to encounter may readily be distinguished the obvious interest of a certain class of men in every state to resist all changes which may hazard a diminution of the power, emolument and consequence of the offices they hold under the state establishments . . . and the perverted ambition of another class of men, who will either hope to aggrandize themselves by the confusions of their country, or will flatter themselves with fairer prospects of elevation from the subdivision of the empire into several partial confederacies, than from its union under one government.

It is not, however, my design to dwell upon observations of this nature. I am aware that it would be disingenuous to resolve indiscriminately the opposition of any set of men into interested or ambitious views, merely because their situations might subject them to suspicion. Candor will oblige us to admit, that even such men may be actuated by upright intentions; and it cannot be doubted, that much of the opposition, which has already shown itself, or that may hereafter make its appearance, will spring from sources blameless at least, if not respectable — the honest errors of minds led astray by preconceived jealousies and fears. So numerous indeed and so powerful are the causes which serve to give a false bias to the judgment, that we, upon many occasions, see wise and good men on the wrong as well as on the right side of questions, of the first magnitude to society. This circumstance, if duly attended to, would always furnish a lesson of moderation to those, who are engaged in any controversy, however well persuaded of being in the right. And a further reason for caution, in this respect, might be drawn from the reflection, that we are not always sure, that those who advocate the truth are activated by purer principles than their antagonists. Ambition, avarice, personal animosity, party opposition, and many other motives, not more laudable than these, are apt to operate as well upon those who support, as those who oppose, the right side of a question. Were there not even these inducements to moderation, nothing could be more ill judged than that intolerant spirit, which has, at all times, characterized political parties. For, in politics as in religion, it is equally absurd to aim at making proselytes by fire and sword. Heresies in either can rarely be cured by persecution.

And yet, just as these sentiments must appear to candid men, we have already sufficient indications, that it will happen in this as, in all former cases of great national discussion. A torrent of angry and malignant passions will be let loose. To judge from the conduct of the opposite parties, we shall be led to conclude, that they will mutually hope to evince the justness of their opinions, and to increase the number of their converts, by the loudness of their declamations, and by the bitterness of their invectives. An enlightened zeal for the energy and efficiency of government, will be stigmatized as the offspring of a temper fond of power and hostile to the principles of liberty. An over scrupulous jealousy of danger to the rights of the people, which is more commonly the fault of the head than of the heart, will be represented as mere pretense and artifice, the stale bait for popularity at the expense of public good. It will be forgotten, on the one hand, that jealousy is the usual concomitant of violent love, and that the noble enthusiasm of liberty is too apt to be infected with a spirit of narrow and illiberal distrust. On the other hand, it will be equally forgotten, that the vigor of government is essential to the security of liberty; that, in the contemplation of a sound and well informed judgment, their interests can never be separated; and that a dangerous ambition more often lurks behind the specious mask of zeal for the rights of the people, than under the forbidding appearances of zeal for the firmness and efficiency of government. History will teach us, that the former has been found a much more certain road to the introduction of despotism, than the latter, and that of those men who have overturned the liberties of republics, the greatest number have begun their career, by paying an obsequious court to the people; commencing demagogues, and ending tyrants.

In the course of the preceding observations, it has been my aim, my fellow-citizens, to put you upon your guard against all attempts, from whatever quarter, to influence your decision in a matter of the utmost moment to your welfare, by any impressions, other than those which may result from the evidence of truth. You will, no doubt, at the same time, have collected from the general scope of them, that they proceed from a source not unfriendly to the new constitution. Yes, my countrymen, I own to you, that, after having given it an attentive consideration, I am clearly of opinion it is your interest to adopt it. I am convinced, that this is the safest course for your liberty, your dignity, and your happiness. I affect not reserves,[1] which I do not feel. I will not amuse you with an appearance of deliberation, when I have decided. I frankly acknowledge to you my convictions, and I will freely lay before you the reasons on which they are founded. The consciousness of good intentions disdains ambiguity. I shall not however multiply professions on this head. My motives must remain in the depository of my own breast: my arguments will be open to all and may be judged of by all. They shall at least be offered in a spirit, which will not disgrace the cause of truth.

I propose, in a series of papers, to discuss the following interesting particulars . . . *The utility of the UNION to your political prosperity . . . The insufficiency of the present confederation to preserve that Union . . . The necessity of a government at least equally energetic with the one proposed, to the attainment of this object . . . The conformity of the proposed constitution to the true principles of republican government . . . Its analogy to your own state constitution . . . and lastly, The additional security, which its adoption will afford to the preservation of that species of government, to liberty and to property.*

In the progress of this discussion, I shall endeavor to give a satisfactory answer to all the objections which shall have made their appearance, that may seem to have any claim to attention.

It may perhaps be thought superfluous to offer arguments to prove the utility of the UNION, a point, no doubt, deeply engraved on the hearts of the great body of the people in every state, and one which, it may be imagined, has no adversaries. But the fact is, that we already hear it whispered in the private circles of those who oppose the new constitution, that the Thirteen States are of too great extent for any general system, and that we must of necessity resort to separate confederacies of distinct portions of the whole. This doctrine will, in all probability, be gradually propagated, till it has votaries enough to countenance its open avowal. For nothing can be more evident, to those who are able to take an enlarged view of the subject, than the alternative of an adoption of the constitution, or a dismemberment of the Union. It may, therefore, be essential to examine particularly the advantages of that Union, the certain evils, and so the probable dangers, to which every state will be exposed from its dissolution. This shall accordingly be done.

PUBLIUS

---

[1] reservations, that is, unexpressed doubts

Document 19

Federalist 9

Publius (Alexander Hamilton)

November 21, 1787

In this essay, Publius notes five developments in "the science of politics" that were "either not known at all, or imperfectly understood by the ancients." They form the "broad and solid" foundation for the claim that America will succeed where previous republics have failed. The improvements are 1) legislative checks and balances, 2) the separation of powers, 3) an independent judiciary, 4) a scheme of representation, and 5) a more recent innovation which Hamilton, the author of Federalist 9, *calls "the enlargement of the orbit within which [republican]systems are to revolve."*

Elaborating on the last, Publius suggests that it is not clear that the French political theorist Montesquieu, regarded by many as the 18th century "oracle" on political theory, has a definitive and relevant teaching on it. Publius acknowledges that, as the Antifederalist Brutus had already noted, Montesquieu maintained that republican systems flourish best when they govern small territories, since in those cases citizens are more likely to share common interests and are better able to closely observe their elected leaders, guarding against abuses of authority. Yet Hamilton demonstrates that Montesquieu's observation is irrelevant to the American case, since the size of territory Montesquieu had in mind — based on the history of ancient city-states — was "of dimensions far short of the limits of almost every one of these States." America had already outgrown the classical example of republican government.

However, Publius points out, Montesquieu had discussed the utility of a "confederate republic" as a way of extending the reach of a democratic system, giving it sufficient resources to withstand attacks by foreign powers. The French theorist had even maintained that in such a federation, no single person aspiring to tyrannical control of the whole would be likely to seize power, since the political base of each strongman would be in his own local district. Hence a federation of republics might best protect the independence of its constituent small states and at the same time the liberty of the citizens in these states.

Source: George W. Carey and James McClellan, eds., The Federalist: The Gideon Edition, *(Indianapolis: Liberty Fund, 2001), 37-41.*

A FIRM Union will be of the utmost moment to the peace and liberty of the States as a barrier against domestic faction and insurrection. It is impossible to read the history of the petty republics of Greece and Italy without feeling sensations of horror and disgust at the distractions with which they were continually agitated, and at the rapid succession of revolutions by which they were kept in a state of perpetual vibration between the extremes of tyranny and anarchy. If they exhibit occasional calms, these only serve as short-lived contrasts to the furious storms that are to succeed. If now and then intervals of felicity open themselves to view, we behold them with a mixture of regret, arising from the reflection that the pleasing scenes before us are soon to be overwhelmed by the tempestuous waves of sedition and party rage. If momentary rays of glory break forth from the gloom, while they dazzle us with a transient and fleeting brilliancy, they at the same time admonish us to lament that the vices of government should pervert the direction and tarnish the luster of those bright talents and exalted endowments for which the favored soils that produced them have been so justly celebrated.

From the disorders that disfigure the annals of those republics the advocates of despotism have drawn arguments, not only against the forms of republican government, but against the very principles of civil liberty. They have decried all free government as inconsistent with the order of society, and have indulged themselves in malicious exultation over its friends and partisans. Happily for mankind, stupendous fabrics reared on the basis of liberty, which have flourished for ages, have, in a few glorious instances, refuted their gloomy sophisms. And, I trust, America will be the broad and solid foundation of other edifices, not less magnificent, which will be equally permanent monuments of their errors.

But it is not to be denied that the portraits they have sketched of republican government were too just copies of the originals from which they were taken. If it had been found impracticable to have devised models of a more perfect structure, the enlightened friends to liberty would have been obliged to abandon the cause of that species of government as indefensible. The science of politics, however, like most other sciences, has received great improvement. The efficacy of various principles is now well understood, which were either not known at all, or imperfectly known to the ancients. The regular distribution of power into distinct departments; the introduction of legislative balances and checks; the institution of courts composed of judges holding their offices during good behavior; the representation of the people in the legislature by deputies of their own election: these are either wholly new discoveries, or have made their principal progress towards perfection in modern times. They are means, and powerful means, by which the excellencies of republican government may be retained and its imperfections lessened or avoided.

To this catalogue of circumstances that tend to the amelioration of popular systems of civil government, I shall venture, however novel it may appear to some, to add one more, on a principle which has been made the foundation of an objection to the new Constitution, I mean the ENLARGEMENT of the ORBIT within which such systems are to revolve, either in respect to the dimensions of a single State, or to the consolidation of several smaller States into one great Confederacy. The latter is that which immediately concerns the object under consideration. It will, however, be of use to examine the principle in its application to a single State, which shall be attended to in another place.

The utility of a Confederacy, as well to suppress faction and to guard the internal tranquility of States as to increase their external force and security, is in reality not a new idea. It has been practiced upon in different countries and ages, and has received the sanction of the most applauded writers on the subjects of politics. The opponents of the PLAN proposed have, with great assiduity, cited and circulated the observations of Montesquieu on the necessity of a contracted territory for a republican government. But they seem not to have been apprised of the sentiments of that great man expressed in another part of his work, nor to have adverted to the consequences of the principle to which they subscribe with such ready acquiescence.

When Montesquieu recommends a small extent for republics, the standards he had in view were of dimensions far short of the limits of almost every one of these States. Neither Virginia, Massachusetts, Pennsylvania, New York, North Carolina, nor Georgia can by any means be compared with the models from which he reasoned and to which the terms of his description apply. If we therefore take his ideas on this point as the criterion of truth, we shall be driven to the alternative either of taking refuge at once in the arms of monarchy, or of splitting ourselves into an infinity of little, jealous, clashing, tumultuous commonwealths, the wretched nurseries of unceasing discord and the miserable objects of universal pity or contempt. Some of the writers who have come forward on the other side of the question seem to have been aware of the dilemma; and have even been bold enough to hint at the division of the larger States, as a desirable thing. Such an infatuated policy, such a desperate expedient, might, by the multiplication of petty offices, answer the views of men who possess not qualifications to extend their influence beyond the narrow circles of personal intrigue, but it could never promote the greatness or happiness of the people of America.

Referring the examination of the principle itself to another place, as has been already mentioned, it will be sufficient to remark here that, in the sense of the author who has been most emphatically quoted upon the occasion, it would only dictate a reduction of the SIZE of the more considerable MEMBERS of the Union, but would not militate against their being all comprehended in one confederate government. And this is the true question, in the discussion of which we are at present interested.

So far are the suggestions of Montesquieu from standing in opposition to a general Union of the States that he explicitly treats of a CONFEDERATE REPUBLIC as the expedient for extending the sphere of popular government and reconciling the advantages of monarchy with those of republicanism.

"It is very probable (says he) that mankind would have been obliged at length to live constantly under the government of a SINGLE PERSON, had they not contrived a kind of constitution that has all the internal advantages of a republican, together with the external force of a monarchial, government. I mean a CONFEDERATE REPUBLIC.

"This form of government is a convention, by which several smaller *states* agree to become members of a larger *one,* which they intend to form. It is a kind of assemblage of societies that constitute a new one, capable of increasing, by means of new associations, till they arrive to such a degree of power as to be able to provide for the security of the united body.

"A republic of this kind, able to withstand an external force, may support itself without any internal corruption. The form of this society prevents all manner of inconveniences.

"If a single member should attempt to usurp the supreme authority, he could not be supposed to have an equal authority and credit in all the confederate states. Were he to have too great influence over one, this would alarm the rest. Were he to subdue a part, that which would still remain free might oppose him with forces independent of those which he had usurped, and overpower him before he could be settled in his usurpation.

"Should a popular insurrection happen in one of the confederate States, the others are able to quell it. Should abuses creep into one part, they are reformed by those that remain sound. The state may be destroyed on one side, and not on the other; the confederacy may be dissolved, and the confederates preserve their sovereignty.

"As this government is composed of small republics, it enjoys the internal happiness of each; and with respect to its external situation, it is possessed, by means of the association, of all the advantages of large monarchies."[1]

I have thought it proper to quote at length these interesting passages, because they contain a luminous abridgement of the principal arguments in favor of the Union, and must effectually remove the false impressions which a misapplication of other parts of the work was calculated to produce. They have, at the same time, an intimate connection with the more immediate design of this paper, which is to illustrate the tendency of the Union to repress domestic faction and insurrection.

A distinction, more subtle than accurate, has been raised between a *confederacy* and a *consolidation* of the States. The essential characteristic of the first is said to be the restriction of its authority to the members in their collective capacities, without reaching to the individuals of whom they are composed. It is contended that the national council ought to have no concern with any object of internal administration. An exact equality of suffrage between the members has also been insisted upon as a leading feature of a confederate government. These positions are, in the main, arbitrary; they are supported neither by principle nor precedent. It has indeed happened that governments of this kind have generally operated in the manner which the distinction, taken notice of, supposes to be inherent in their nature; but there have been in most of them extensive exceptions to the practice, which serve to prove, as far as example will go, that there is no absolute rule on the subject. And it will be clearly shown, in the course of this investigation, that as far as the principle contended for has prevailed, it has been the cause of incurable disorder and imbecility in the government.

The definition of a *confederate republic* seems simply to be an "assemblage of societies" or an association of two or more states into one state. The extent, modifications, and objects of the Federal authority are mere matters of discretion. So long as the separate organization of the members be not abolished; so long as it exists, by a constitutional necessity, for local purposes; though it should be in perfect subordination to the general authority of the union, it would still be, in fact and in theory, an association of states, or a confederacy. The proposed Constitution, so far from implying an abolition of the State governments, makes them constituent parts of the national sovereignty, by allowing them a direct representation in the Senate, and leaves

---

[1] These passages are quoted from Montesquieu's *The Spirit of the Laws* (Vol. I, Book IX, Ch. 1).

in their possession certain exclusive and very important portions of sovereign power. This fully corresponds, in every rational import of the terms, with the idea of a federal government.

In the Lycian confederacy,[2] which consisted of twenty-three CITIES, or republics, the largest were entitled to *three* votes in the COMMON COUNCIL, those of the middle class to *two,* and the smallest to *one.* The COMMON COUNCIL had the appointment of all the judges and magistrates of the respective CITIES. This was certainly the most delicate species of interference in their internal administration; for if there be any thing that seems exclusively appropriated to the local jurisdictions, it is the appointment of their own officers. Yet Montesquieu, speaking of this association, says: "Were I to give a model of an excellent Confederate Republic, it would be that of Lycia."[3] Thus we perceive that the distinctions insisted upon were not within the contemplation of this enlightened civilian; and we shall be led to conclude that they are the novel refinements of an erroneous theory.

PUBLIUS

---

[2] The Lycian confederacy was an ancient league of city-state republics on the peninsula of Lycia on the southern coast of Turkey.

[3] Here, Publius quotes *Spirit of the Laws,* Vol. I, Book IX, Ch. 3.

Document 20

Federalist 10

Publius (James Madison)
November 22, 1787

Federalist *10 (authored by Madison) claims that the "violence of faction" is the "mortal disease" of popular governments. Even today, he says, pointing to the experience of the states, the divisions between rival parties too often lead not to reasonable compromises but to decisions made "not according to the rules of justice, and the rights of the minor party, but by the superior force of an interested and overbearing majority." Unless it remedies this problem on the national level, the new Constitution will not cement "a well constructed union" of the states.*

We can cure the disease of faction either by "removing its causes" or by "controlling its effects." There are but two ways to remove the causes of faction: to destroy "the liberty essential to its existence," or to give "to every citizen the same opinions, the same passions, and the same interests." Since, in other words, the causes of faction are "sown in the nature of man," we must design popular government to control its effects.

Fortunately, Publius points out, among the various options for popular government — a pure democracy, a small republic, or a large republic — the Constitution is designed not only for the actual American situation but also for that most likely to mitigate the problem of faction. It is designed for a large republic extending over a geographically large and diverse territory and comprehending within its limits a diverse and constantly shifting and reconfiguring array of interest groups. This very diversity will prevent any single faction from acquiring the power to tyrannize over the others.

Source: George W. Carey and James McClellan, eds., The Federalist: The Gideon Edition, *(Indianapolis: Liberty Fund, 2001), 42-49.*

Among the numerous advantages promised by a well constructed union, none deserves to be more accurately developed, than its tendency to break and control the violence of faction. The friend of popular governments, never finds himself so much alarmed for their character and fate, as when he contemplates their propensity to this dangerous vice. He will not fail, therefore, to set a due value on any plan which, without violating the principles to which he is attached, provides a proper cure for it. The instability, injustice, and confusion, introduced into the public councils, have, in truth, been the mortal diseases under which popular governments have every where perished; as they continue to be the favorite and fruitful topics from which the adversaries to liberty derive their most specious declamations. The valuable improvements made by the American constitutions on the popular models, both ancient and modern, cannot certainly be too much admired; but it would be an unwarrantable partiality, to contend that they have as effectually obviated the danger on this side, as was wished and expected. Complaints are every where heard from our most considerate and virtuous citizens, equally the friends of public and private faith, and of public and personal liberty, that our governments are too unstable; that the public good is disregarded in the conflicts of rival parties; and that measures are too often decided, not according to the rules of justice, and the rights of the minor party, but by the superior force of an interested and overbearing majority. However anxiously we may wish that these complaints had no foundation, the evidence of known facts will not permit us to deny that they are in some degree true. It will be found, indeed, on a candid review of our situation, that some of the distresses under which we labor, have been erroneously charged on the operation of our governments; but it will be found, at the same time, that other causes will not alone account for many of our heaviest misfortunes; and, particularly, for that prevailing and increasing distrust of public engagements, and alarm for private rights, which are echoed from one end of the continent to the other. These must be chiefly, if not wholly, effects of the unsteadiness and injustice, with which a factious spirit has tainted our public administrations.

By a faction, I understand a number of citizens, whether amounting to a majority or minority of the whole, who are united and actuated by some common impulse of passion, or of interest, adverse to the rights of other citizens, or to the permanent and aggregate interests of the community.

There are two methods of curing the mischiefs of faction: The one, by removing its causes; the other, by controlling its effects.

There are again two methods of removing the causes of faction: The one, by destroying the liberty which is essential to its existence; the other, by giving to every citizen the same opinions, the same passions, and the same interests.

It could never be more truly said, than of the first remedy, that it is worse than the disease. Liberty is to faction, what air is to fire, an aliment, without which it instantly expires. But it could not be a less folly to abolish liberty, which is essential to political life, because it nourishes faction, than it would be to wish the annihilation of air, which is essential to animal life, because it imparts to fire its destructive agency.

The second expedient is as impracticable, as the first would be unwise. As long as the reason of man continues fallible, and he is at liberty to exercise it, different opinions will be formed. As long as the connection subsists between his reason and his self-love, his opinions and his passions will have a reciprocal influence on each other; and the former will be objects to which the latter will attach themselves. The diversity in the faculties of men, from which the rights of property originate, is not less an insuperable obstacle to an uniformity of interests. The protection of these faculties, is the first object of government. From the protection of different and unequal faculties of acquiring property, the possession of different degrees and kinds of property immediately results; and from the influence of these on the sentiments and views of the respective proprietors, ensues a division of the society into different interests and parties.

The latent causes of faction are thus sown in the nature of man; and we see them every where brought into different degrees of activity, according to the different circumstances of civil society. A zeal for different opinions concerning religion, concerning government, and many other points, as well of speculation as of practice; an attachment to different leaders, ambitiously contending for pre-eminence and power; or to persons of other descriptions, whose fortunes have been interesting to the human passions, have, in turn, divided mankind into parties, inflamed them with mutual animosity, and rendered them much more disposed to vex and oppress each other, than to co-operate for their common good. So strong is this propensity of mankind, to fall into mutual animosities, that where no substantial occasion presents itself, the most frivolous and fanciful distinctions have been sufficient to kindle their unfriendly passions, and excite their most violent conflicts. But the most common and durable source of factions, has been the various and unequal distribution of property. Those who hold, and those who are without property, have ever formed distinct interests in society. Those who are creditors, and those who are debtors, fall under a like discrimination. A landed interest, a manufacturing interest, a mercantile interest, a monied interest, with many lesser interests, grow up of necessity in civilized nations, and divide them into different classes, actuated by different sentiments and views. The regulation of these various and interfering interests, forms the principal task of modern legislation, and involves the spirit of party and faction in the necessary and ordinary operations of government.

No man is allowed to be a judge in his own cause; because his interest would certainly bias his judgment, and, not improbably, corrupt his integrity.

With equal, nay, with greater reason, a body of men are unfit to be both judges and parties, at the same time; yet, what are many of the most important acts of legislation, but so many judicial determinations, not indeed concerning the rights of single persons, but concerning the rights of large bodies of citizens? and what are the different classes of legislators, but advocates and parties to the causes which they determine? Is a law proposed concerning private debts? It is a question to which the creditors are parties on one side, and the debtors on the other. Justice ought to hold the balance between them. Yet the parties are, and must be, themselves the judges; and the most numerous party, or, in other words, the most powerful faction, must be expected to prevail. Shall domestic manufactures be encouraged, and in what degree, by restrictions on foreign manufactures? are questions which would be differently decided by the landed and the manufacturing classes; and probably by neither with a sole regard to justice and the public good. The apportionment of taxes, on the various descriptions of property, is an act which seems to require the most exact impartiality; yet there is, perhaps, no legislative act in which greater opportunity and temptation are given to a predominant party, to trample on the rules of justice. Every shilling with which they over-burden the inferior number, is a shilling saved to their own pockets.

It is in vain to say, that enlightened statesmen will be able to adjust these clashing interests, and render them all subservient to the public good. Enlightened statesmen will not always be at the helm: nor, in many cases, can such an adjustment be made at all, without taking into view indirect and remote considerations, which will rarely prevail over the immediate interest which one party may find in disregarding the rights of another, or the good of the whole.

The inference to which we are brought, is, that the *causes* of faction cannot be removed; and that relief is only to be sought in the means of controlling its *effects*.

If a faction consists of less than a majority, relief is supplied by the republican principle, which enables the majority to defeat its sinister views, by regular vote. It may clog the administration, it may convulse the society; but it will be unable to execute and mask its violence under the forms of the constitution. When a majority is included in a faction, the form of popular government, on the other hand, enables it to sacrifice to its ruling passion or interest, both the public good and the rights of other citizens. To secure the public good, and private rights, against the danger of such a faction, and at the same time to preserve the spirit and the form of popular government, is then the great object to which our inquiries are directed. Let me add, that it is the great desideratum,[1] by which alone this form of government can be rescued from the opprobrium under which it has so long labored, and be recommended to the esteem and adoption of mankind.

By what means is this object attainable? Evidently by one of two only. Either the existence of the same passion or interest in a majority, at the same time, must be prevented; or the majority, having such co-existent passion or interest, must be rendered, by their number and local situation, unable to concert and carry into effect schemes of oppression. If the impulse and the opportunity be suffered to coincide, we well know, that neither moral nor religious motives can be relied on as an adequate control. They are not found to be such on the injustice and violence of individuals, and lose their efficacy in proportion to the number combined together; that is, in proportion as their efficacy becomes needful.

From this view of the subject, it may be concluded, that a pure democracy, by which I mean, a society consisting of a small number of citizens, who assemble and administer the government in person, can admit of no cure for the mischiefs of faction. A common passion or interest will, in almost every case, be felt by a majority of the whole; a communication and concert, results from the form of government itself; and there is nothing to check the inducements to sacrifice the weaker party, or an obnoxious individual. Hence it is, that such democracies have ever been spectacles of turbulence and contention; have ever been found incompatible with personal security, or the rights of property; and have, in general, been as short in their lives, as they have been violent in their deaths. Theoretic politicians, who have patronized this species of government, have erroneously supposed, that, by reducing mankind to a perfect equality in their political rights, they would, at the same time, be perfectly equalized and assimilated in their possessions, their opinions, and their passions.

A republic, by which I mean a government in which the scheme of representation takes place, opens a different prospect, and promises the cure for which we are seeking. Let us examine the points in which it varies from pure democracy, and we shall comprehend both the nature of the cure and the efficacy which it must derive from the union.

The two great points of difference, between a democracy and a republic, are, first, the delegation of the government, in the latter, to a small number of citizens elected by the rest; secondly, the greater number of citizens, and greater sphere of country, over which the latter may be extended.

---

[1] thing to be desired

The effect of the first difference is, on the one hand, to refine and enlarge the public views, by passing them through the medium of a chosen body of citizens, whose wisdom may best discern the true interest of their country, and whose patriotism and love of justice, will be least likely to sacrifice it to temporary or partial considerations. Under such a regulation, it may well happen, that the public voice, pronounced by the representatives of the people, will be more consonant to the public good, than if pronounced by the people themselves, convened for the purpose. On the other hand, the effect may be inverted. Men of factious tempers, of local prejudices, or of sinister designs, may by intrigue, by corruption, or by other means, first obtain the suffrages, and then betray the interests of the people. The question resulting is, whether small or extensive republics are most favorable to the election of proper guardians of the public weal; and it is clearly decided in favor of the latter by two obvious considerations.

In the first place, it is to be remarked, that however small the republic may be, the representatives must be raised to a certain number, in order to guard against the cabals of a few; and that, however large it may be, they must be limited to a certain number, in order to guard against the confusion of a multitude. Hence, the number of representatives in the two cases not being in proportion to that of the constituents, and being proportionally greatest in the small republic, it follows, that if the proportion of fit characters be not less in the large than in the small republic, the former will present a greater option, and consequently a greater probability of a fit choice.

In the next place, as each representative will be chosen by a greater number of citizens in the large than in the small republic, it will be more difficult for unworthy candidates to practice with success the vicious arts, by which elections are too often carried; and the suffrages of the people being more free, will be more likely to center in men who possess the most attractive merit, and the most diffusive and established characters.

It must be confessed, that in this, as in most other cases, there is a mean, on both sides of which inconveniences will be found to lie. By enlarging too much the number of electors, you render the representative too little acquainted with all their local circumstances and lesser interests; as by reducing it too much, you render him unduly attached to these, and too little fit to comprehend and pursue great and national objects. The federal constitution forms a happy combination in this respect; the great and aggregate interests, being referred to the national, the local and particular to the state legislatures.

The other point of difference is, the greater number of citizens, and extent of territory, which may be brought within the compass of republican, than of democratic government; and it is this circumstance principally which renders factious combinations less to be dreaded in the former, than in the latter. The smaller the society, the fewer probably will be the distinct parties and interests composing it; the fewer the distinct parties and interests, the more frequently will a majority be found of the same party; and the smaller the number of individuals composing a majority, and the smaller the compass within which they are placed, the more easily will they concert and execute their plans of oppression. Extend the sphere, and you take in a greater variety of parties and interests; you make it less probable that a majority of the whole will have a common motive to invade the rights of other citizens; or if such a common motive exists, it will be more difficult for all who feel it to discover their own strength, and to act in unison with each other. Besides other impediments, it may be remarked, that where there is a consciousness of unjust or dishonorable purposes, communication is always checked by distrust, in proportion to the number whose concurrence is necessary.

Hence it clearly appears, that the same advantage, which a republic has over a democracy, in controlling the effects of faction, is enjoyed by a large over a small republic, — is enjoyed by the union over the states composing it. Does this advantage consist in the substitution of representatives, whose enlightened views and virtuous sentiments render them superior to local prejudices, and to schemes of injustice? It will not be denied, that the representation of the union will be most likely to possess these requisite endowments. Does it consist in the greater security afforded by a greater variety of parties, against the event of any one party being able to outnumber and oppress the rest? In an equal degree does the increased variety of parties, comprised within the union, increase this security. Does it, in fine, consist in the greater obstacles opposed to the concert and accomplishment of the secret wishes of an unjust and interested majority? Here, again, the extent of the union gives it the most palpable advantage.

The influence of factious leaders may kindle a flame within their particular states, but will be unable to spread a general conflagration through the other states: a religious sect may degenerate into a political faction in a part of the confederacy; but the variety of sects dispersed over the entire face of it, must secure the national councils against any danger from that source: a rage for paper money, for an abolition of debts, for an equal division of property, or for any other improper or wicked project, will be less apt to pervade the whole body of the union, than a particular member of it; in the same proportion as such a malady is more likely to taint a particular county or district, than an entire state.

In the extent and proper structure of the union, therefore, we behold a republican remedy for the diseases most incident to republican government. And according to the degree of pleasure and pride we feel in being republicans, ought to be our zeal in cherishing the spirit, and supporting the character of federalists.

PUBLIUS

Document 21

Federalist 51

Publius (James Madison)

February 6, 1788

A number of Convention delegates who declined to sign the Constitution had voiced concerns that either the legislative or executive branch of the federal government would usurp the authority of the other. Their objections were now being voiced by Antifederalist writers. Publius (who in this essay is Madison) responds here to their concerns. It is in fact possible to contrive "the interior structure of the government as that its several constituent parts may, by their mutual relations, be the means of keeping each other in their proper places." To avoid "a gradual concentration of the several powers in the same department," one must give "to those who administer each department the necessary constitutional means and personal motives to resist encroachments of the others. . . . Ambition must be made to counteract ambition. The interests of the man must be connected with the constitutional rights of the place." To provide those means and motives, one must assign each department of government distinct and competing powers and responsibilities, while taking care that the members of one branch not appoint the members of another or specify the salaries of another, except in certain specific cases.

These precautions may not be enough. Although in Federalist *10 Publius expressed a hope that the elected representatives of the people, being drawn from a large pool of candidates in so populous a republic, might be those most motivated by public interest, now Publius admits that ambition might corrupt even the best men. Such is human nature; and "What is government itself but the greatest reflection on human nature? If men were angels, no government would be necessary."*

The right of the people to elect and recall their representatives will not in itself guarantee proper behavior of those in authority; "experience has taught mankind the necessity of auxiliary precautions." Hence one must empower each branch of government to defend itself against the encroachments of others. In a republic, the legislative branch, as most connected to the will of the people, necessarily dominates. Yet one can divide the legislative power into two branches that are constituted in different ways and thus responsible to different groupings of citizens. One can also grant veto power to the executive, while prudently refraining from making the executive veto final and absolute.

Closing his essay, Publius reiterates the argument of Federalist *10, reminding the reader first, that America is a "compound republic," rather than a "single republic": it is a federation of states, each of which are governed through individual systems of balanced powers. Second, American society will "be broken down into so many parts, interests and classes of citizens, that the rights of individuals, or the minority, will be in little danger from interested combinations of the majority." Justice is always the aim of popular government, Publius asserts, pointing out that even factious parties call for an arbitrator as soon as they feel an injustice is done to themselves. We need not seek in vain for some disinterested authority, aloof from society, to judge between competing interests. Correct judgment will arise from within society, since reasonable persons with widely varying private interests will agree only on those measures tending toward "justice and the general good."*

Source: George W. Carey and James McClellan, eds., The Federalist: The Gideon Edition *(Indianapolis: Liberty Fund, 2001), 267-272.*

To what expedient then shall we finally resort, for maintaining in practice the necessary partition of power among the several departments, as laid down in the constitution? The only answer that can be given is, that as all these exterior provisions are found to be inadequate, the defect must be supplied, by so contriving the interior structure of the government, as that its several constituent parts may, by their mutual relations, be the means of keeping each other in their proper places. Without presuming to undertake a full development of this important idea, I will hazard a few general observations, which may perhaps place it in a clearer light, and enable us to form a more correct judgment of the principles and structure of the government planned by the convention.

In order to lay a due foundation for that separate and distinct exercise of the different powers of government, which, to a certain extent, is admitted on all hands to be essential to the preservation of liberty, it is evident that each department should have a will of its own; and consequently should be so constituted, that the members of each should have as little agency as possible in the appointment of the members of the others. Were this principle rigorously adhered to, it would require that all the appointments for the supreme executive, legislative, and judiciary magistracies, should be drawn from the same fountain of authority, the people, through channels having no communication whatever with one another. Perhaps such a plan of constructing the several departments, would be less difficult in practice, than it may in contemplation appear. Some difficulties, however, and some additional expense, would attend the execution of it. Some deviations, therefore, from the principle must be admitted. In the constitution of the judiciary department in particular, it might be inexpedient to insist rigorously on the principle; first, because peculiar qualifications being essential in the members, the primary consideration ought to be to select that mode of choice which best secures these qualifications; secondly, because the permanent tenure by which the appointments are held in that department, must soon destroy all sense of dependence on the authority conferring them.

It is equally evident, that the members of each department should be as little dependent as possible on those of the others, for the emoluments annexed to their offices. Were the executive magistrate, or the judges, not independent of the legislature in this particular, their independence in every other, would be merely nominal.

But the great security against a gradual concentration of the several powers in the same department, consists in giving to those who administer each department, the necessary constitutional means, and personal motives, to resist encroachments of the others. The provision for defense must in this, as in all other cases, be made commensurate to the danger of attack. Ambition must be made to counteract ambition. The interest of the man, must be connected with the constitutional rights of the place. It may be a reflection on human nature, that such devices should be necessary to control the abuses of government. But what is government itself, but the greatest of all reflections on human nature? If men were angels, no government would be necessary. If angels were to govern men, neither external nor internal controls on government would be necessary. In framing a government which is to be administered by men over men, the great difficulty lies in this: you must first enable the government to control the governed; and in the next place oblige it to control itself. A dependence on the people is, no doubt, the primary control on the government; but experience has taught mankind the necessity of auxiliary precautions.

This policy of supplying, by opposite and rival interests, the defect of better motives, might be traced through the whole system of human affairs, private as well as public. We see it particularly displayed in all the subordinate distributions of power; where the constant aim is, to divide and arrange the several offices in such a manner as that each may be a check on the other; that the private interest of every individual may be a sentinel over the public rights. These inventions of prudence cannot be less requisite in the distribution of the supreme powers of the state.

But it is not possible to give to each department an equal power of self-defense. In republican government, the legislative authority necessarily predominates. The remedy for this inconveniency is, to divide the legislature into different branches; and to render them, by different modes of election, and different principles of action, as little connected with each other, as the nature of their common functions, and their common dependence on the society, will admit. It may even be necessary to guard against dangerous encroachments by still further precautions. As the weight of the legislative authority requires that it should be thus divided, the weakness of the executive may require, on the other hand, that it should be fortified. An absolute negative[1] on the legislature, appears, at first view, to be the natural defense with which the executive magistrate should be armed. But perhaps it would be neither altogether safe, nor alone sufficient. On ordinary occasions, it might not be exerted with the requisite firmness; and on extraordinary occasions, it might be perfidiously abused. May not this defect of an absolute negative be supplied by some qualified connection between this weaker department, and the weaker branch of the stronger department, by which the latter may be led to support the constitutional rights of the former, without being too much detached from the rights of its own department?

If the principles on which these observations are founded be just, as I persuade myself they are, and they be applied as a criterion to the several state constitutions, and to the federal constitution, it will be found, that if the latter does not perfectly correspond with them, the former are infinitely less able to bear such a test.

There are moreover two considerations particularly applicable to the federal system of America, which place that system in a very interesting point of view.

First. In a single republic, all the power surrendered by the people, is submitted to the administration of a single government; and the usurpations are guarded against, by a division of the government into distinct and separate departments. In the compound republic of America, the power surrendered by the people, is first divided between two distinct governments, and then the portion allotted to each subdivided among distinct and separate departments. Hence a double security arises to the rights of the people. The different governments will control each other; at the same time that each will be controlled by itself.

Second. It is of great importance in a republic, not only to guard the society against the oppression of its rulers; but to guard one part of the society against the injustice of the other part. Different interests necessarily exist in different

---

[1] veto

classes of citizens. If a majority be united by a common interest, the rights of the minority will be insecure. There are but two methods of providing against this evil: the one, by creating a will in the community independent of the majority, that is, of the society itself; the other, by comprehending in the society so many separate descriptions of citizens, as will render an unjust combination of a majority of the whole very improbable, if not impracticable. The first method prevails in all governments possessing an hereditary or self-appointed authority. This, at best, is but a precarious security; because a power independent of the society may as well espouse the unjust views of the major, as the rightful interests of the minor party, and may possibly be turned against both parties. The second method will be exemplified in the federal republic of the United States. Whilst all authority in it will be derived from, and dependent on the society, the society itself will be broken into so many parts, interests, and classes of citizens, that the rights of individuals, or of the minority, will be in little danger from interested combinations of the majority. In a free government, the security for civil rights must be the same as that for religious rights. It consists in the one case in the multiplicity of interests, and in the other, in the multiplicity of sects. The degree of security in both cases will depend on the number of interests and sects; and this may be presumed to depend on the extent of country and number of people comprehended under the same government.

This view of the subject must particularly recommend a proper federal system to all the sincere and considerate friends of republican government: since it shows, that in exact proportion as the territory of the union may be formed into more circumscribed confederacies, or states, oppressive combinations of a majority will be facilitated; the best security under the republican form, for the rights of every class of citizens, will be diminished; and consequently, the stability and independence of some member of the government, the only other security, must be proportionally increased. Justice is the end of government. It is the end of civil society. It ever has been, and ever will be, pursued, until it be obtained, or until liberty be lost in the pursuit. In a society, under the forms of which the stronger faction can readily unite and oppress the weaker, anarchy may as truly be said to reign, as in a state of nature, where the weaker individual is not secured against the violence of the stronger: and as, in the latter state, even the stronger individuals are prompted, by the uncertainty of their condition, to submit to a government which may protect the weak, as well as themselves: so, in the former state, will the more powerful factions or parties be gradually induced, by a like motive, to wish for a government which will protect all parties, the weaker as well as the more powerful. It can be little doubted, that if the state of Rhode Island was separated from the confederacy, and left to itself, the insecurity of rights under the popular form of government within such narrow limits, would be displayed by such reiterated oppressions of factious majorities, that some power altogether independent of the people, would soon be called for by the voice of the very factions whose misrule had proved the necessity of it. In the extended republic of the United States, and among the great variety of interests, parties, and sects, which it embraces, a coalition of a majority of the whole society could seldom take place upon any other principles, than those of justice and the general good: whilst there being thus less danger to a minor from the will of the major party, there must be less pretext also, to provide for the security of the former, by introducing into the government a will not dependent on the latter: or, in other words, a will independent of the society itself. It is no less certain than it is important, notwithstanding the contrary opinions which have been entertained, that the larger the society, provided it lie within a practicable sphere, the more duly capable it will be of self-government. And happily for the *republican cause*, the practicable sphere may be carried to a very great extent, by a judicious modification and mixture of the *federal principle.*

PUBLIUS

Document 22

Brutus XV

March 20, 1788

This essay continues an argument Brutus introduced in Brutus XIV, where he maintained "that the supreme court under this constitution would be exalted above all other power in the government, and subject to no control." Here Brutus explains this position and discusses the dangers arising from giving the judiciary its power to review and decide on the Constitutionality of the actions of the other branches. He points out that 1) "There is no power above them that can correct their errors or control their decisions," 2) "they cannot be removed from office or suffer a diminution of their salaries, for any error in judgment or want of capacity," and 3) "the power of this court is in many cases superior to that of the legislature." To prove the last point, Brutus says that "the supreme court . . . have a right, independent of the legislature, to give a construction to the constitution and every part of it, and there is no power provided in this system to correct their construction or do it away."

Brutus warns: "Men placed in this situation will generally soon feel themselves independent of heaven itself."

Some of Brutus's claims seem far-fetched — for example, that the framers designed the judiciary to advance a project "to abolish entirely the state governments, and to melt down the states into one entire government." He goes on to suggest that Congress and the Court might collude to complete this project. However, in elaborating this theory, Brutus illuminates tendencies of the court on which we might well reflect today: "Their decisions on the meaning of the constitution will commonly take place in cases which arise between individuals, with which the public will not be generally acquainted; one adjudication will form a precedent to the next, and this to a following one. These cases will immediately affect individuals only; so that a series of determinations will probably take place before even the people will be informed of them. In the mean time all the art and address of those who wish for the change will be employed to make converts to their opinion." Undoubtedly, Brutus's argument about the threat to the state governments suggests some of the reasons that, shortly after the ratification of the Constitution, Congress would include in the Bill of Rights the tenth amendment, which reserves rights to the states or the people.

Source: Herbert J. Storing, ed., The Complete Anti-Federalist, *(Chicago: The University of Chicago Press, 1981) 2:437-442.*

I said in my last number, that the supreme court under this constitution would be exalted above all other power in the government, and subject to no control. The business of this paper will be to illustrate this, and to show the danger that will result from it. I question whether the world ever saw, in any period of it, a court of justice invested with such immense powers, and yet placed in a situation so little responsible. Certain it is, that in England, and in the several states, where we have been taught to believe, the courts of law are put upon the most prudent establishment, they are on a very different footing.

The judges in England, it is true, hold their offices during their good behavior, but then their determinations are subject to correction by the house of lords; and their power is by no means so extensive as that of the proposed supreme court of the union. — I believe they in no instance assume the authority to set aside an act of parliament under the idea that it is inconsistent with their constitution.[1] They consider themselves bound to decide according to the existing laws of the land, and never undertake to control them by adjudging that they are inconsistent with the constitution — much less are they vested with the power of giving an *equitable* construction[2] to the constitution.

The judges in England are under the control of the legislature, for they are bound to determine according to the laws passed by them. But the judges under this constitution will control the legislature, for the supreme court are authorized in the last resort, to determine what is the extent of the powers of the Congress; they are to give the constitution an explanation, and there is no power above them to set aside their judgment. The framers of this constitution appear to have followed that of the British, in rendering the judges *independent*, by granting them their offices during good behavior, without following the constitution of England, in instituting a tribunal in which their errors may be corrected; and without adverting to this, that the judicial under this system

---

[1] Brutus either ignores or is unaware of the fact that Britain at that time, and even today, lacks a written constitution, that is, it has no document codifying the structure of the government and the relationship of the people to that government. The British "constitution" is nothing more than the body of accumulated law: the Acts of Parliament, prior court judgments, and conventions of law.

[2] a liberal and extensive construction, as opposed to a literal and restrictive

have a power which is above the legislative, and which indeed transcends any power before given to a judicial by any free government under heaven.

I do not object to the judges holding their commissions during good behavior. I suppose it a proper provision provided they were made properly responsible. But I say, this system has followed the English government in this, while it has departed from almost every other principle of their jurisprudence, under the idea, of rendering the judges independent — which, in the British constitution, means no more than that they hold their places during good behavior, and have fixed salaries — they have made the judges independent, in the fullest sense of the word. There is no power above them, to control any of their decisions. There is no authority that can remove them, and they cannot be controlled by the laws of the legislature. In short, they are independent of the people, of the legislature, and of every power under heaven. Men placed in this situation will generally soon feel themselves independent of heaven itself. Before I proceed to illustrate the truth of these assertions, I beg liberty to make one remark — Though in my opinion the judges ought to hold their offices during good behavior, yet I think it is clear, that the reasons in favor of this establishment of the judges in England, do by no means apply to this country.

The great reason assigned, why the judges in Britain ought to be commissioned during good behavior, is this, that they may be placed in a situation, not to be influenced by the crown, to give such decisions, as would tend to increase its powers and prerogatives. While the judges held their places at the will and pleasure of the king, on whom they depended not only for their offices, but also for their salaries, they were subject to every undue influence. If the crown wished to carry a favorite point, to accomplish which the aid of the courts of law was necessary, the pleasure of the king would be signified to the judges. And it required the spirit of a martyr, for the judges to determine contrary to the king's will. — They were absolutely dependent upon him both for their offices and livings. The king, holding his office during life, and transmitting it to his posterity as an inheritance, has much stronger inducements to increase the prerogatives of his office than those who hold their offices for stated periods, or even for life. Hence the English nation gained a great point, in favor of liberty. When they obtained the appointment of the judges, during good behavior, they got from the crown a concession, which deprived it of one of the most powerful engines with which it might enlarge the boundaries of the royal prerogative and encroach on the liberties of the people. But these reasons do not apply to this country, we have no hereditary monarch; those who appoint the judges do not hold their offices for life, nor do they descend to their children. The same arguments, therefore, which will conclude in favor of the tenor of the judge's offices for good behavior, lose a considerable part of their weight when applied to the state and condition of America. But much less can it be shown, that the nature of our government requires that the courts should be placed beyond all account more independent, so much so as to be above control.

I have said that the judges under this system will be *independent* in the strict sense of the word: To prove this I will show — That there is no power above them that can control their decisions, or correct their errors. There is no authority that can remove them from office for any errors or want of capacity, or lower their salaries, and in many cases their power is superior to that of the legislature.

1st. There is no power above them that can correct their errors or control their decisions — The adjudications of this court are final and irreversible, for there is no court above them to which appeals can lie, either in error or on the merits. — In this respect it differs from the courts in England, for there the house of lords is the highest court, to whom appeals, in error, are carried from the highest of the courts of law.

2d. They cannot be removed from office or suffer a diminution of their salaries, for any error in judgment or want of capacity.

It is expressly declared by the constitution, — "That they shall at stated times receive a compensation for their services which shall not be diminished during their continuance in office."

The only clause in the constitution which provides for the removal of the judges from office, is that which declares, that "the president, vice-president, and all civil officers of the United States, shall be removed from office, on impeachment for, and conviction of treason, bribery, or other high crimes and misdemeanors." By this paragraph, civil officers, in which the judges are included, are removable only for crimes. Treason and bribery are named, and the rest are included under the general terms of high crimes and misdemeanors. — Errors in judgment, or want of capacity to discharge the duties of the office, can never be supposed to be included in these words, *high crimes and misdemeanors*. A man may mistake a case in giving judgment, or manifest that he is incompetent to the discharge of the duties of a judge, and yet give no evidence of corruption or want of integrity. To support the charge, it will be necessary to give in evidence some facts that will show, that the judges committed the error from wicked and corrupt motives.

3d. The power of this court is in many cases superior to that of the legislature. I have showed, in a former paper, that this court will be authorized to decide upon the meaning of the constitution, and that, not only according to the natural and obvious meaning of the words, but also according to the spirit and intention of it. In the exercise of this power they will not be subordinate to, but above the legislature. For all the departments of this government will receive their powers, so far as they are expressed in the constitution, from the people immediately, who are the source of power. The legislature can only exercise such powers as are given them by the constitution, they cannot assume any of the rights annexed to the judicial, for this plain reason, that the same authority which vested the legislature with their powers, vested the judicial with theirs — both are derived from the same source, both therefore are equally valid, and the judicial hold their powers independently of the legislature, as the legislature do of the judicial. — The supreme court then have a right, independent of the legislature, to give a construction to the constitution and every part of it, and there is no power provided in this system to correct their construction or do it away. If, therefore, the legislature pass any laws, inconsistent with the sense the judges put upon the constitution, they will declare it void; and therefore in this respect their power is superior to that of the legislature. In England the judges are not only subject to have their decisions set aside by the house of lords, for error, but in cases where they give an explanation to the laws or constitution of the country, contrary to the sense of the parliament, though the parliament will not set aside the judgment of the court, yet, they have authority, by a new law, to explain a former one, and by this means to prevent a reception of such decisions. But no such power is in the legislature. The judges are supreme — and no law, explanatory of the constitution, will be binding on them.

From the preceding remarks, which have been made on the judicial powers proposed in this system, the policy of it may be fully developed.

I have, in the course of my observation on this constitution, affirmed and endeavored to show, that it was calculated to abolish entirely the state governments, and to melt down the states into one entire government, for every purpose as well internal and local, as external and national. In this opinion the opposers of the system have generally agreed — and this has been uniformly denied by its advocates in public. Some individuals, indeed, among them, will confess, that it has this tendency, and scruple not to say, it is what they wish; and I will venture to predict, without the spirit of prophecy, that if it is adopted without amendments, or some such precautions as will ensure amendments immediately after its adoption, that the same gentlemen who have employed their talents and abilities with such success to influence the public mind to adopt this plan, will employ the same to persuade the people, that it will be for their good to abolish the state governments as useless and burdensome.

Perhaps nothing could have been better conceived to facilitate the abolition of the state governments than the constitution of the judicial. They will be able to extend the limits of the general government gradually, and by insensible degrees, and to accommodate themselves to the temper of the people. Their decisions on the meaning of the constitution will commonly take place in cases which arise between individuals, with which the public will not be generally acquainted; one adjudication will form a precedent to the next, and this to a following one. These cases will immediately affect individuals only; so that a series of determinations will probably take place before even the people will be informed of them. In the mean time all the art and address of those who wish for the change will be employed to make converts to their opinion. The people will be told, that their state officers, and state legislatures are a burden and expense without affording any solid advantage, for that all the laws passed by them, might be equally well made by the general legislature. If to those who will be interested in the change, be added, those who will be under their influence, and such who will submit to almost any change of government, which they can be persuaded to believe will ease them of taxes, it is easy to see, the party who will favor the abolition of the state governments would be far from being inconsiderable. — In this situation, the general legislature, might pass one law after another, extending the general and abridging the state jurisdictions, and to sanction their proceedings would have a course of decisions of the judicial to whom the constitution has committed the power of explaining the constitution. — If the states remonstrated, the constitutional mode of deciding upon the validity of the law, is with the supreme court, and neither people, nor state legislatures, nor the general legislature can remove them or reverse their decrees.

Had the construction of the constitution been left with the legislature, they would have explained it at their peril; if they exceed their powers, or sought to find, in the spirit of the constitution, more than was expressed in the letter, the people from whom they derived their power could remove them, and do themselves right; and indeed I can see no other remedy that the people can have against their rulers for encroachments of this nature. A constitution is a compact of a people with their rulers; if the rulers break the compact, the people have a right and ought to remove them and do themselves justice; but in order to enable them to do this with the greater facility, those whom the people choose at stated periods, should have the power in the last resort to determine the sense of the compact; if they determine contrary to the understanding of the people, an appeal will lie to[3] the people at the period when the rulers are to be elected, and they will have it in their power to remedy the evil; but when this power is lodged in the hands of men independent of the people, and of their representatives, and who are not, constitutionally, accountable for their opinions, no way is left to control them but *with a high hand and an outstretched arm.*[4]

Brutus

[3] a review of their decision will be available to

[4] Brutus alludes to Biblical language used to describe the power of God; see, for example, Deuteronomy 26:8.

Document 23

Federalist 78

Publius (Alexander Hamilton)

May 28, 1788

This is the first of five essays by Publius (in this case, Hamilton) on the judiciary. The heart of this essay covers the case for the duration of judges in office. Publius points out that their lifetime appointments are guaranteed only "during good behavior." He calls the insistence on this standard "one of the most valuable of the modern improvements in the practice of government." To insure that judges maintain this standard, resisting encroachments from the legislature (to which presumably they would be vulnerable by means of bribes or threats), the Constitution gives them "permanent tenure."

Publius then makes the famous claim that the judiciary "will always be the least dangerous to the political rights of the Constitution. . . . It may truly be said to have neither FORCE nor WILL but merely judgment." As "the weakest of the three departments of power," it needs fortification.

It is the "duty" of the courts "to declare all acts contrary to the manifest tenor of the constitution void." Without an independent judiciary to fulfill this task, any rights reserved to the people by the Constitution "would amount to nothing," since the legislature cannot be relied upon to police itself. This arrangement does not render the judiciary the supreme branch of government. Rather, it ensures that the Constitution remain the supreme law of the land.

Publius's argument here recognizes the possibility that in a representative government there are competing contenders to represent the people. Those elected to Congress rightly claim to act on the people's authority; yet the Constitution, having been ratified by the people, itself represents the people's will, and will have priority over more recently elected representatives. Publius contrasts this rule with that which applies in representative governments without a written constitution. In those systems, if a law is passed which contradicts an earlier law, judges are obliged to rule that the more recently passed law invalidates the first. But in a Constitutional system, any law contradicting the Constitution will be ruled invalid.

Implicitly, Publius recognizes the fallibility of the people and their representatives. He asserts, in effect, that the proposed Constitution insures that the careful, considered judgment of the Framers — made after considerable debate and compromise — will have priority over "dangerous innovations in the government" pushed by "designing men."

He also predicts that a judicial branch with permanent tenure will discourage the appointment of incompetent or dishonest judges, while also preventing unconstitutional legislation from even being proposed.

Source: George W. Carey and James McClellan, eds., The Federalist: The Gideon Edition*, (Indianapolis: Liberty Fund, 2001), 401-408.*

We proceed now to an examination of the judiciary department of the proposed government.

In unfolding the defects of the existing Confederation, the utility and necessity of a federal judicature have been clearly pointed out. It is the less necessary to recapitulate the considerations there urged as the propriety of the institution in the abstract is not disputed; the only questions which have been raised being relative to the manner of constituting it, and to its extent. To these points, therefore, our observations shall be confined.

The manner of constituting it seems to embrace these several objects: 1st. The mode of appointing the judges. 2nd. The tenure by which they are to hold their places. 3d. The partition of the judiciary authority between different courts and their relations to each other.

First. As to the mode of appointing the judges: this is the same with that of appointing the officers of the Union in general and has been so fully discussed in the two last numbers that nothing can be said here which would not be useless repetition.

Second. As to the tenure by which the judges are to hold their places: this chiefly concerns their duration in office; the provisions for their support, and the precautions for their responsibility.

According to the plan of the convention, all the judges who may be appointed by the United States are to hold their offices *during good behavior*; which is conformable to the most approved of the State constitutions, and among the rest, to that of this State. Its propriety having been drawn into question by the adversaries of that plan is no light symptom of the rage for objection which disorders their imaginations and judgments. The standard of good behavior for the continuance in office of the judicial magistracy is certainly one of the most valuable of the modern improvements in the practice of government. In a monarchy it is an excellent barrier to the despotism of the prince; in a republic it is a no less excellent barrier to the encroachments and oppressions of the representative body. And it is the best expedient which can be devised in any government to secure a steady, upright and impartial administration of the laws.

Whoever attentively considers the different departments of power must perceive that, in a government in which they are separated from each other, the judiciary, from the nature of its functions, will always be the least dangerous to the political rights of the Constitution; because it will be least in a capacity to annoy or injure them. The executive not only dispenses the honors but holds the sword of the community. The legislature not only commands the purse but prescribes the rules by which the duties and rights of every citizen are to be regulated. The judiciary, on the contrary, has no influence over either the sword or the purse; no direction either of the strength or of the wealth of the society, and can take no active resolution whatever. It may truly be said to have neither FORCE nor WILL but merely judgment; and must ultimately depend upon the aid of the executive arm even for the efficacy of its judgments.

This simple view of the matter suggests several important consequences. It proves incontestably that the judiciary is beyond comparison the weakest of the three departments of power; that it can never attack with success either of the other two; and that all possible care is requisite to enable it to defend itself against their attacks. It equally proves that though individual oppression may now and then proceed from the courts of justice, the general liberty of the people can never be endangered from that quarter: I mean, so long as the judiciary remains truly distinct from both the legislative and executive. For I agree that "there is no liberty if the power of judging be not separated from the legislative and executive powers."[1] And it proves, in the last place, that as liberty can have nothing to fear from the judiciary alone, but would have everything to fear from its union with either of the other departments; that as all the effects of such a union must ensue from a dependence of the former on the latter, notwithstanding a nominal and apparent separation; that as, from the natural feebleness of the judiciary, it is in continual jeopardy of being overpowered, awed or influenced by its coordinate branches; and that as nothing can contribute so much to its firmness and independence as permanency in office, this quality may therefore be justly regarded as an indispensable ingredient in its constitution, and in a great measure as the citadel of the public justice and the public security.

The complete independence of the courts of justice is peculiarly essential in a limited Constitution. By a limited Constitution, I understand one which contains certain specified exceptions to the legislative authority; such, for

---

[1] Publius here quotes Montesquieu, *The Spirit of the Laws*, XI, 6.

instance, as that it shall pass no bills of attainder, no *ex post facto* laws,[2] and the like. Limitations of this kind can be preserved in practice no other way than through the medium of the courts of justice, whose duty it must be to declare all acts contrary to the manifest tenor of the Constitution void. Without this, all the reservations of particular rights or privileges would amount to nothing.

Some perplexity respecting the right of the courts to pronounce legislative acts void, because contrary to the Constitution, has arisen from an imagination that the doctrine would imply a superiority of the judiciary to the legislative power. It is urged that the authority which can declare the acts of another void must necessarily be superior to the one whose acts may be declared void. As this doctrine is of great importance in all the American constitutions, a brief discussion of the grounds on which it rests cannot be unacceptable.

There is no position which depends on clearer principles than that every act of a delegated authority, contrary to the tenor of the commission under which it is exercised, is void. No legislative act therefore contrary to the constitution can be valid. To deny this would be to affirm that the deputy is greater than his principal; that the servant is above his master; that the representatives of the people are superior to the people themselves; that men acting by virtue of powers may do not only what their powers do not authorize, but what they forbid.

If it be said that the legislative body are themselves the constitutional judges of their own powers and that the construction they put upon them is conclusive upon the other departments it may be answered that this cannot be the natural presumption where it is not to be collected from any particular provisions in the Constitution. It is not otherwise to be supposed that the Constitution could intend to enable the representatives of the people to substitute their *will* to that of their constituents. It is far more rational to suppose that the courts were designed to be an intermediate body between the people and the legislature in order, among other things, to keep the latter within the limits assigned to their authority. The interpretation of the laws is the proper and peculiar province of the courts. A constitution is in fact, and must be regarded by the judges as, a fundamental law. It therefore belongs to them to ascertain its meaning as well as the meaning of any particular act proceeding from the legislative body. If there should happen to be an

---

[2] Article I, section 9 of the Constitution states that "No Bill of Attainder or ex post facto Law shall be passed." A bill of attainder is a law declaring an individual guilty of treason or other felony without a trial; an *ex post facto* law is a law that makes citizens vulnerable to prosecution for actions they took before the law was passed.

irreconcilable variance between the two, that which has the superior obligation and validity ought, of course; to be preferred; or, in other words, the Constitution ought to be preferred to the statute, the intention of the people to the intention of their agents.

Nor does this conclusion by any means suppose a superiority of the judicial to the legislative power. It only supposes that the power of the people is superior to both, and that where the will of the legislature, declared in its statutes, stands in opposition to that of the people, declared in the Constitution, the judges ought to be governed by the latter rather than the former. They ought to regulate their decisions by the fundamental laws rather than by those which are not fundamental.

This exercise of judicial discretion in determining between two contradictory laws is exemplified in a familiar instance. It not uncommonly happens that there are two statutes existing at one time, clashing in whole or in part with each other, and neither of them containing any repealing clause or expression. In such a case, it is the province of the courts to liquidate and fix their meaning and operation. So far as they can, by any fair construction, be reconciled to each other, reason and law conspire to dictate that this should be done; where this is impracticable, it becomes a matter of necessity to give effect to one in exclusion of the other. The rule which has obtained in the courts for determining their relative validity is that the last in order of time shall be preferred to the first. But this is mere rule of construction, not derived from any positive law but from the nature and reason of the thing. It is a rule not enjoined upon the courts by legislative provision but adopted by themselves, as consonant to truth and propriety, for the direction of their conduct as interpreters of the law. They thought it reasonable that between the interfering acts of an *equal* authority that which was the last indication of its will, should have the preference.

But in regard to the interfering acts of a superior and subordinate authority of an original and derivative power, the nature and reason of the thing indicate the converse of that rule as proper to be followed. They teach us that the prior act of a superior ought to be preferred to the subsequent act of an inferior and subordinate authority; and that, accordingly, whenever a particular statute contravenes the Constitution, it will be the duty of the judicial tribunals to adhere to the latter and disregard the former.

It can be of no weight to say that the courts, on the pretense of a repugnancy, may substitute their own pleasure to the constitutional intentions of the legislature. This might as well happen in the case of two contradictory statutes; or it might as well happen in every adjudication upon any single statute. The courts must declare the sense of the law; and if they should be disposed to exercise WILL instead of JUDGMENT, the consequence would equally be the substitution of their pleasure to that of the legislative body. The observation, if it proved any thing, would prove that there ought to be no judges distinct from that body.

If, then, the courts of justice are to be considered as the bulwarks of a limited Constitution against legislative encroachments, this consideration will afford a strong argument for the permanent tenure of judicial offices, since nothing will contribute so much as this to that independent spirit in the judges which must be essential to the faithful performance of so arduous a duty.

This independence of the judges is equally requisite to guard the Constitution and the rights of individuals from the effects of those ill humors which the arts of designing men, or the influence of particular conjunctures, sometimes disseminate among the people themselves, and which, though they speedily give place to better information, and more deliberate reflection, have a tendency, in the meantime, to occasion dangerous innovations in the government, and serious oppressions of the minor party in the community. Though I trust the friends of the proposed Constitution will never concur with its enemies in questioning that fundamental principle of republican government which admits the right of the people to alter or abolish the established Constitution whenever they find it inconsistent with their happiness; yet it is not to be inferred from this principle that the representatives of the people, whenever a momentary inclination happens to lay hold of a majority of their constituents incompatible with the provisions in the existing Constitution would, on that account, be justifiable in a violation of those provisions; or that the courts would be under a greater obligation to connive at infractions in this shape than when they had proceeded wholly from the cabals of the representative body. Until the people have, by some solemn and authoritative act, annulled or changed the established form, it is binding upon themselves collectively, as well as individually; and no presumption, or even knowledge of their sentiments, can warrant their representatives in a departure from it prior to such an act. But it is easy to see that it would require an uncommon portion of fortitude in the judges to do their duty as faithful guardians of the Constitution, where legislative invasions of it had been instigated by the major voice of the community.

But it is not with a view to infractions of the Constitution only that the independence of the judges may be an essential safeguard against the effects of occasional ill humors in the society. These sometimes extend no farther than to the injury of the private rights of particular classes of citizens, by unjust and partial laws. Here also the firmness of the judicial magistracy is of vast importance in mitigating the severity and confining the operation of such laws. It not only serves to moderate the immediate mischiefs of those which may have been passed but it operates as a check upon the legislative body in passing them; who, perceiving that obstacles to the success of an iniquitous intention are to be expected from the scruples of the courts, are in a manner compelled, by the very motives of the injustice they meditate, to qualify their attempts. This is a circumstance calculated to have more influence upon the character of our governments than but few may be aware of. The benefits of the integrity and moderation of the judiciary have already been felt in more states than one; and though they may have displeased those whose sinister expectations they may have disappointed, they must have commanded the esteem and applause of all the virtuous and disinterested. Considerate men of every description ought to prize whatever will tend to beget or fortify that temper in the courts; as no man can be sure that he may not be tomorrow the victim of a spirit of injustice, by which he may be a gainer today. And every man must now feel that the inevitable tendency of such a spirit is to sap the foundations of public and private confidence and to introduce in its stead universal distrust and distress.

That inflexible and uniform adherence to the rights of the Constitution, and of individuals, which we perceive to be indispensable in the courts of justice, can certainly not be expected from judges who hold their offices by a temporary commission. Periodical appointments, however regulated, or by whomsoever made, would in some way or other, be fatal to their necessary independence. If the power of making them was committed either to the executive or legislature there would be danger of an improper complaisance to the branch which possessed it; if to both, there would be an unwillingness to hazard the displeasure of either; if to the people, or to persons chosen by them for the special purpose, there would be too great a disposition to consult popularity to justify a reliance that nothing would be consulted but the Constitution and the laws.

There is yet a further and a weighty reason for the permanency of the judicial offices which is deducible from the nature of the qualifications they require. It has been frequently remarked with great propriety that a voluminous code of laws is one of the inconveniences necessarily connected with the advantages of a free government. To avoid an arbitrary discretion in the courts, it is indispensable that they should be bound down by strict rules and precedents which serve to define and point out their duty in every particular case that comes before them; and it will readily be conceived from the variety of controversies which grow out of the folly and wickedness of mankind that the records of those precedents must unavoidably swell to a very considerable bulk and must demand long and laborious study to acquire a competent knowledge of them. Hence it is that there can be but few men in the society who will have sufficient skill in the laws to qualify them for the stations of judges. And making the proper deductions for the ordinary depravity of human nature, the number must be still smaller of those who unite the requisite integrity with the requisite knowledge. These considerations apprise us that the government can have no great option between fit characters; and that a temporary duration in office which would naturally discourage such characters from quitting a lucrative line of practice to accept a seat on the bench would have a tendency to throw the administration of justice into hands less able and less well qualified to conduct it with utility and dignity. In the present circumstances of this country and in those in which it is likely to be for a long time to come, the disadvantages on this score would be greater than they may at first sight appear; but it must be confessed that they are far inferior to those which present themselves under the other aspects of the subject.

Upon the whole, there can be no room to doubt that the convention acted wisely in copying from the models of those constitutions which have established *good behavior* as the tenure of their judicial offices, in point of duration; and that so far from being blamable on this account, their plan would have been inexcusably defective if it had wanted this important feature of good government. The experience of Great Britain affords an illustrious comment on the excellence of the institution.

PUBLIUS

Document 24

The Jefferson - Madison Exchange

December 20, 1787 to March 15, 1789

Thomas Jefferson might have been expected to play an important role in the debates at the Constitutional Convention, but at the time they took place, he was serving as Ambassador to France. He depended on Madison to keep him abreast of progress on the new frame of government.

In the first letter excerpted below, sent during the campaign for ratification, Jefferson gives his views on the proposed Constitution. He warmly compliments many features of the plan, appearing particularly pleased by the unexpected compromise achieved in the argument between small and large states over representation in Congress. But then, more importantly, he indicates what "I do not like," namely, "the omission of a bill of rights," and the absence of any provision to insure that elected officials not serve indefinitely — what today we would call "term limits."

In the second letter, Madison responds to Jefferson's challenge about the absence of a bill of rights. He states he is in favor of it primarily because others seem to think it necessary (implying that the addition of a bill of rights might help to insure ratification of the Constitution). However, he acknowledges that such an addition to the Constitution "might be of use, and if properly executed could not be of disservice." Then he notes the ways in which a bill of rights would have to be designed with particular care so as to achieve its desired purposes.

In the third letter, Jefferson provides a detailed response to Madison's comments on the possible dangers of adding a bill of rights to the Constitution. He ends the letter on an optimistic note: "I am much pleased with the prospect that a declaration of rights will be added; and hope it will be done in that way which will not endanger the whole frame of the government, or any essential part of it."

Source: Gordon Lloyd and Margie Lloyd, eds., The Essential Bill of Rights *(Lanham, Maryland: University Press of America, 1998) 320, 325-328, 329-331.*

I. Jefferson to Madison: Paris, December 20, 1787

. . . . The season admitting only of operations in the Cabinet, and these being in great measure secret, I have little to fill a letter. I will therefore make up the deficiency by adding a few words on the Constitution proposed by our Convention. I like much the general idea of framing a government which should go on itself peaceably, without needing continual recurrence to the state legislatures. I like the organization of the government into Legislative, Judiciary and Executive. I like the power given the Legislature to levy taxes and for that reason solely approve of the greater house being chosen by the people directly. For though I think a house chosen by them will be very ill qualified to legislate for the Union, for foreign nations, etc. yet this evil does not weigh against the good of preserving inviolate the fundamental principle that the people are not to be taxed but by representatives chosen immediately by themselves. I am captivated by the compromise of the opposite claims of the great and little states, of the latter to equal, and the former to proportional influence. I am much pleased too with the substitution of the method of voting by persons, instead of that voting by states: and I like the negative given to the Executive with a third of either house, though I should have liked it better had the Judiciary been associated for that purpose, or invested with a similar and separate power. There are other good things of less moment.

I will now add what I do not like.

First the omission of a bill of rights providing clearly and without the aid of sophisms for freedom of religion, freedom of the press, protection against standing armies, restriction against monopolies,[1] the eternal and unremitting force of the habeas corpus law,[2] and trials by jury in all matter of fact triable by

---

[1] Jefferson is most likely referring to commercial monopolies established by governments, as was the British East India Company, which was founded by royal charter in 1600. He may not have foreseen the possibility that business monopolies could arise independently of government sanction.

[2] The Latin term *habeas corpus* translates roughly as "You may have the body." A writ of habeas corpus is a court order commanding a government official who is holding a prisoner to bring the prisoner into a court of law, where the legality of his imprisonment can be determined. In short, the habeas corpus law forbids holding anyone prisoner without trial.

the laws of the land and not by the law of Nations.[3] To say, as Mr. Wilson does that a bill of rights was not necessary because all is reserved in the case of the general government which is not given, while in the particular ones all is given which is not reserved[,] might do for the Audience to whom it was addressed,[4] but is surely *gratis dictum*,[5] opposed by strong inferences from the body of the instrument, as well as from the omission of the clause of our present confederation which had declared that in express terms. It was a hard conclusion to say because there has been no uniformity among the states as to the cases triable by jury, because some have been so incautious as to abandon this mode of trial, therefore the more prudent states shall be reduced to the same level of calamity. It would have been much more just and wise to have concluded the other way that as most of the states had judiciously preserved this palladium,[6] those who had wandered should be brought back to it, and to have established general right instead of general wrong. Let me add that a bill of rights is what the people are entitled to against every government on earth, general or particular, and what no just government should refuse, or rest on inference.

The second feature I dislike, and greatly dislike, is the abandonment in every instance of the necessity of rotation in office, and most particularly in the case of the President. Experience concurs with reason in concluding that the first magistrate will always be re-elected if the constitution permits it. He is then an officer for life. This once observed[,] it becomes of so much consequence to certain nations to have a friend or a foe at the head of our affairs that they will interfere with money and with arms. A Gallo man or an Anglo man will be supported by the nation he befriends. If once elected, and at

---

[3] In a letter to Madison on August 28,1789, Jefferson details what he means by "cases triable . . . the Law of Nations": cases involving foreigners, court martial cases during a time of war or insurrection, and impeachments of government officials as allowed by the Constitution (*Memoirs, correspondence and private papers of Thomas Jefferson*, ed. Thomas Jefferson Randolph (London: Henry Colburn and Richard Bentley, 1829),Volume 3, p. 26 (retrieved through Google ebooks).

[4] James Wilson, a Pennsylvania delegate to the Constitutional Convention, gave a speech on October 6, 1787 in the Pennsylvania statehouse to a friendly crowd, attacking the Antifederalists and asserting that the Constitution reserves to the states all powers that are not specifically enumerated as belonging to the federal government.

[5] a saying made voluntarily that is not legally binding

[6] Jefferson uses the word "palladium" to mean "safeguard." The word referred originally to a statue of Pallas Athena erected in Troy and on which the safety of the city was believed to depend.

a second or third election outvoted by one or two votes, he will pretend false votes, foul play, hold possession of the reins of government, be supported by the states voting for him, especially if they are the central ones lying in a compact body themselves and separating their opponents; and they will be aided by one nation of Europe, while the majority are aided by another. The election of a President of America some years hence will be much more interesting to certain nations of Europe than ever the election of a king of Poland was. Reflect on all the instances in history ancient and modern, of elective monarchies, and say if they do not give foundation for my fears[:] the Roman emperors, the popes, while they were of any importance, the German emperors till they became hereditary in practice, the kings of Poland, the Deys of the Ottoman dependencies. It may be said that if elections are to be attended with these disorders, the seldomer they are renewed the better. But experience shows that the only way to prevent disorder is to render them uninteresting by frequent changes. An incapacity to be elected a second time would have been the only effectual preventative. The power of removing him every fourth year by the vote of the people is a power which will not be exercised. The king of Poland is removable every day by the Diet, yet he is never removed....

I have thus told you freely what I like and dislike: merely as a matter of curiosity for I know your own judgment has been formed on all these points after having heard every thing which could be urged on them. I own I am not a friend to a very energetic government. It is always oppressive. The late rebellion in Massachusetts[7] has given me more alarm than I think it should have done. Calculate that one rebellion in 13 states in the course of 11 years is but one for each state in a century and a half. No country should be so long without one. Nor will any degree of power in the hands of government prevent insurrections. France with all its despotism, and two or three hundred thousand men always in arms, has had three insurrections in the three years I have been here in every one of which greater numbers were engaged than in Massachusetts and a great deal more blood was spilt....

After all, it is my principle that the will of the Majority should always prevail. If they approve the proposed Convention in all its parts, I shall concur in it cheerfully, in hopes that they will amend it whenever they shall find it work wrong. I think our governments will remain virtuous for many centuries;

---

[7] Jefferson refers to Shays' rebellion, a series of armed protests by farmers who were losing their lands because they could not repay loans on them.

as long as they are chiefly agricultural; and this will be as long as there shall be vacant lands in any part of America. . . .

Above all things I hope the education of the common people will be attended to; convinced that on their good sense we may rely with the most security for the preservation of a due degree of liberty. . . .

II. Madison to Jefferson: New York, October 17, 1788

. . . . The little pamphlet herewith enclosed will give you a collective view of the alterations which have been proposed for the new Constitution. Various and numerous as they appear they certainly omit many of the true grounds of opposition. The articles relating to Treatises, to paper money, and to contracts, created more enemies than all errors in the System positive and negative put together. It is true nevertheless that not a few, particularly in Virginia have contended for the proposed alterations from the most honorable and patriotic motives; and that among the advocates for the Constitution there are some who wish for further guards to public liberty and individual rights. As far as these may consist of a constitutional declaration of the most essential rights, it is probable they will be added; though there are many who think such addition unnecessary, and not a few who think it misplaced in such a Constitution. There is scarce any point on which the party in opposition is so much divided as to its importance and its propriety.

My own opinion has always been in favor of a bill of rights; provided it be so framed as not to imply powers not meant to be included in the enumeration.[8] At the same time I have never thought the omission a material defect nor been anxious to supply it even by *subsequent* amendment, for any other reason than that it is anxiously desired by others. I have favored it because I supposed it might be of use, and if properly executed could not be of disservice.

I have not viewed it in an important light 1. Because I conceive that in a certain degree, though not in the extent argued by Mr. Wilson,[9] the rights in question are reserved by the manner in which the federal powers are granted. 2. Because there is great reason to fear that a positive declaration of some of the most essential rights could not be obtained in the requisite latitude. I am sure that the rights of conscience in particular, if submitted to the public

---

[8] By "the enumeration," Madison means the powers explicitly given to the federal government by the Constitution.

[9] James Wilson of Pennsylvania

definition[,] would be narrowed much more than they are likely ever to be by an assumed power. One of the objections in New England was that the Constitution by prohibiting religious tests opened a door for Jews, Turks and infidels. 3. Because the limited powers of the federal Government and the jealousy of the subordinate Governments, afford a security which has not existed in the case of the State Governments, and exists in no other. 4. Because experience proves the inefficacy of a bill of rights on those occasions when its control is most needed. Repeated violations of these parchment barriers have been committed by overbearing majorities in every State. In Virginia I have seen the bill of rights violated in every instance where it has been opposed to a popular current. Notwithstanding the explicit provision contained in that instrument for the rights of Conscience it is well known that a religious establishment would have taken place and on narrower ground than was then proposed, notwithstanding the additional obstacle which the law has since created. Wherever the real power in a Government lies, there is the danger of oppression.

In our Governments the real power lies in the majority of the Community, and the invasion of private rights is *chiefly* to be apprehended, not from acts of Government contrary to the sense of its constituents, but from acts in which the Government is the mere instrument of the majority of the constituents. This is a truth of great importance, but not yet sufficiently attended to: and is probably more strongly impressed on my mind by facts, and reflections suggested by them, than on yours which has contemplated abuses of power issuing from a very different quarter. Wherever there is an interest and power to do wrong, wrong will generally be done, and not less readily by a powerful and interested party than by a powerful and interested prince. The difference, so far as it relates to the superiority of republics over monarchies, lies in the less degree of probability that interest may prompt abuses of power in the former than in the latter; and in the security in the former against oppression of more than the smaller part of the Society, whereas in the former [*Madison seems to have erred, writing "former" when he meant "latter" — ie., in monarchies*] it may be extended in a manner to the whole. The difference so far as it relates to the point in question — the efficacy of a bill of rights in controlling abuses of power — lies in this: that in a monarchy the latent force of the nation is superior to that of the Sovereign, and a solemn charter of popular rights must have a great effect, as a standard for trying the validity of public acts, and a signal for rousing and uniting the superior force of the community; whereas in a popular Government, the political and physical power may be considered as vested in the same hands, that is in a majority of the people, and consequently the tyrannical will of the sovereign is not to be controlled by the dread of an appeal to any other force within the community.

What use then it may be asked can a bill of rights serve in popular Governments? I answer the two following, which, though less essential than in other Governments, sufficiently recommend the precaution. 1. The political truths declared that in solemn manner acquire by degrees the character of fundamental maxims of free Government, and as they become incorporated with the national sentiment, counteract the impulses of interest and passion. 2. Although it be generally true as above stated that the danger of oppression lies in the interested majorities of the people rather than in usurped acts of the Government, yet there may be occasions on which the evil may spring from the latter sources; and on such, a bill of rights will be a good ground for an appeal to the sense of the community. Perhaps too there may be a certain degree of danger, that a succession of artful and ambitious rulers, may by gradual and well-timed advances, finally erect an independent Government on the subversion of liberty. Should this danger exist at all, it is prudent to guard against it, especially when the precaution can do no injury. At the same time I must own that I see no tendency in our governments to danger on that side. It has been remarked that there is a tendency in all Governments to an augmentation of power at the expense of liberty. But the remark as usually understood does not appear to me well founded. Power when it has attained a certain degree of energy and independence goes on generally to further degrees. But when below that degree, the direct tendency is to further degrees of relaxation, until the abuses of liberty beget a sudden transition to an undue degree of power. With this explanation the remark may be true; and in the latter sense only is it in my opinion applicable to the Governments in America. It is a melancholy reflection that liberty should be equally exposed to danger whether the Government have too much or too little power; and that the line which divides these extremes should be so inaccurately defined by experience.

Supposing a bill of rights to be proper, the articles which ought to compose it admit of much discussion. I am inclined to think that *absolute* restrictions in cases that are doubtful, or where emergencies may overrule them, ought to be avoided. The restrictions however strongly marked on paper will never be regarded when opposed to the decided sense of the public; and after repeated violations in extraordinary cases, they will lose even their ordinary efficacy. Should a Rebellion or insurrection alarm the people as well as the Government, and a suspension of the Hab. Corp.[10] be dictated by the

---

[10] habeas corpus law

alarm, no written prohibitions on earth would prevent the measure. Should an army in time of peace be gradually established in our neighborhood by Britain or Spain, declarations on paper would have as little effect in preventing a standing force for the public safety. The best security against these evils is to remove the pretext for them.

With regard to Monopolies, they are justly classed among the greatest nuisances in Government. But is it clear that as encouragements to literary works and indigenous discoveries, they are not too valuable to be wholly renounced? Would it not suffice to reserve in all cases a right to the public to abolish the privilege at a price to be specified in the grant of it? Is there not also infinitely less danger of this abuse in our Governments than in most others? Monopolies are sacrifices of the many to the few. Where the power is in the few it is natural for them to sacrifice the many to their own partialities and corruptions. Where the power, as with us, is in the many not in the few, the danger cannot be very great that the few will be thus favored. It is much more to be dreaded that the few will be unnecessarily sacrificed to the many. . . .

III. Jefferson to Madison: Paris, March 15, 1789

. . . . Your thoughts on the subject of the declaration of rights in the letter of October the 17th, I have weighed with great satisfaction. Some of them had not occurred to me before, but were acknowledged just in the moment they were presented to my mind. In the arguments in favor of a declaration of rights, you omit one which has great weight with me; the legal check which it puts into the hands of the judiciary. This is a body, which, if rendered independent, and kept strictly to their own department, merits great confidence for their learning and integrity. In fact, what degree of confidence would be too much, for a body composed of such men as Wythe,[11] Blair,[12] and Pendleton?[13] On characters like these, the "*civium ardor prava jubentium*"[14] would make no impression. I am happy to find that, on the whole, you are a friend to this amendment. The declaration of rights is, like all other human blessings, alloyed with some inconveniences, and not accomplishing fully its object. But the good

---

[11] George Wythe of Virginia

[12] John Blair of Virginia

[13] Edmund Pendleton of Virginia

[14] Jefferson quotes Horace: "the wild fury of one's fellow citizens ordering evil measures to be pursued."

of this instance vastly overweighs the evil. I cannot refrain from making short answers to the objections which your letter states to have been raised.

1. That the rights in question are reserved by the manner in which the federal powers are granted. Answer: A constitutive act may, certainly, be so formed, as to need no declaration of rights. The act itself has the force of a declaration, as far as it goes; and if it goes to all material points, nothing more is wanting. In the draught[15] of a constitution which I had once a thought of proposing in Virginia, and printed afterwards, I endeavored to reach all the great objects of public liberty, and did not mean to add a declaration of rights. Probably the object was imperfectly executed; but the deficiencies would have been supplied by others, in the course of discussion. But in a constitutive act which leaves some precious articles unnoticed, and raises implications against others, a declaration of rights becomes necessary, by way of supplement. This is the case of our new federal Constitution. This instrument forms us into one State, as to certain objects, and gives us a legislative and executive body for these objects. It should, therefore, guard us against their abuses of power, within the field submitted to them.

2. A positive declaration of some essential rights could not be obtained in the requisite latitude. Answer: Half a loaf is better than no bread. If we cannot secure all our rights, let us secure what we can.

3. The limited powers of the federal government, and jealousy of the subordinate governments, afford a security which exists in no other instance. Answer: The first member of this seems resolvable into the first objection before stated. The jealousy of the subordinate governments is a precious reliance. But observe that those governments are only agents. They must have principles furnished them, whereon to found their opposition. The declaration of rights will be the text, whereby they will try all the acts of the federal government. In this view, it is necessary to the federal government also; as by the same text they may try the opposition of the subordinate governments.

4. Experience proves the inefficacy of a bill of rights. True. But though it is not absolutely efficacious under all circumstances, it is of great potency always, and rarely inefficacious. A brace the more will often keep up the building which would have fallen with that brace the less. There is a remarkable difference between the characters of the inconveniencies which attend a declaration of rights, and those which attend the want of it. The inconveniences of the declaration are, that it may cramp government in its useful exertions. But the evil of this is short-lived, moderate and reparable. The inconveniencies of the

---

[15] draft

want of a declaration are permanent, afflicting and irreparable. They are in constant progression from bad to worse. The executive, in our governments, is not the sole, it is scarcely the principal object of my jealousy. The tyranny of the legislatures is the most formidable dread at present, and will be for many years. That of the executive will come in its turn; but it will be at a remote period.

I know there are some among us, who would now establish a monarchy. But they are inconsiderable in number and weight of character. The rising race are all republicans. We were educated in royalism; no wonder if some of us retain that idolatry still. Our young people are educated in republicanism; an apostasy from that to royalism, is unprecedented and impossible. I am much pleased with the prospect that a declaration of rights will be added; and hope it will be done in that way which will not endanger the whole frame of the government, or any essential part of it. . . .

Document 25

First Inaugural Address

George Washington

April 30, 1789

On September 17, 1787, 39 delegates at the Constitutional Convention signed the document they had labored over for three months. Nine states needed to ratify before it went into effect. New Hampshire was the ninth state to do so, on June 21, 1788. After much debate and many close votes, the grand experiment in self-government was about to begin. (Two more states, Virginia and New York, would ratify the Constitution before Washington's inauguration. Eventually, all the states would ratify).

The first Presidential inaugural address of this new government was not delivered to a public audience, as it is today. Washington took the oath of office on a second-floor balcony of Federal Hall in New York City, where an assembled crowd could witness the historic event, but afterwards he retired to the Senate Chamber to speak before a joint session of the new Congress. Noting his Constitutional duty to advise the legislature, he offered encouragement and instruction to Congress as they embarked on an historic "experiment" in republican government, one that heaven had "entrusted to the hands of the American people" but that the entire world would note and learn from. At the same time, he spoke with characteristic humility, prefacing his speech with a denial of any ambition for the honor of the presidency and professing a feeling of inadequacy to the task before him.

After praising the work of the Constitutional Convention and giving thanks to the "invisible hand" of Providence for directing the deliberations at the convention and the ratification process that followed it, Washington signaled his desire that the First Congress complete the Convention's work, by adopting a bill of rights. Again, he referred Congress to a provision already made in the Constitution: the amendment process. Instead of speaking of particular rights needing protection, he spoke of a need to guarantee "the characteristic rights of freemen" without undermining the unity of the nation and the effectiveness of the federal government.

Source: W.B. Allen, ed., George Washington: A Collection *(Indianapolis: Liberty Classics, 1988) 460-463.*

Fellow Citizens of the Senate and of the House of Representatives.

Among the vicissitudes incident to life, no event could have filled me with greater anxieties than that of which the notification was transmitted by your order, and received on the fourteenth day of the present month. On the one hand, I was summoned by my Country, whose voice I can never hear but with veneration and love, from a retreat which I had chosen with the fondest predilection, and, in my flattering hopes, with an immutable decision, as the asylum of my declining years: a retreat which was rendered every day more necessary as well as more dear to me, by the addition of habit to inclination, and of frequent interruptions in my health to the gradual waste committed on it by time. On the other hand, the magnitude and difficulty of the trust to which the voice of my Country called me, being sufficient to awaken in the wisest and most experienced of her citizens, a distrustful scrutiny into his qualifications, could not but overwhelm with despondence, one, who, inheriting inferior endowments from nature and unpracticed in the duties of civil administration, ought to be peculiarly conscious of his own deficiencies. In this conflict of emotions, all I dare aver,[1] is, that it has been my faithful study to collect my duty from a just appreciation of every circumstance, by which it might be affected. All I dare hope, is, that, if in executing this task I have been too much swayed by a grateful remembrance of former instances, or by an affectionate sensibility to this transcendent proof, of the confidence of my fellow-citizens; and have thence too little consulted my incapacity as well as disinclination for the weighty and untried cares before me; my error will be palliated by the motives which misled me, and its consequences be judged by my Country, with some share of the partiality in which they originated.

Such being the impressions under which I have, in obedience to the public summons, repaired to the present station; it would be peculiarly improper to omit in this first official Act, my fervent supplications to that Almighty Being who rules over the Universe, who presides in the Councils of Nations, and whose providential aids can supply every human defect, that his benediction may consecrate to the liberties and happiness of the People of the United States, a Government instituted by themselves for these essential purposes: and may enable every instrument employed in its administration to execute with success, the functions allotted to his charge. In tendering this homage to the Great Author of every public and private good I assure myself that it expresses your sentiments not less than my own; nor those of my fellow-

[1] assert

citizens at large, less than either. No People can be bound to acknowledge and adore the invisible hand, which conducts the Affairs of men more than the People of the United States. Every step, by which they have advanced to the character of an independent nation, seems to have been distinguished by some token of providential agency. And in the important revolution just accomplished in the system of their United Government, the tranquil deliberations and voluntary consent of so many distinct communities, from which the event has resulted, cannot be compared with the means by which most Governments have been established, without some return of pious gratitude along with an humble anticipation of the future blessings which the past seem to presage. These reflections, arising out of the present crisis, have forced themselves too strongly on my mind to be suppressed. You will join with me I trust in thinking, that there are none under the influence of which, the proceedings of a new and free Government can more auspiciously commence.

By the article[2] establishing the Executive Department, it is made the duty of the President "to recommend to your consideration, such measures as he shall judge necessary and expedient." The circumstances under which I now meet you, will acquit me from entering into that subject, farther than to refer to the Great Constitutional Charter under which you are assembled; and which, in defining your powers, designates the objects to which your attention is to be given. It will be more consistent with those circumstances, and far more congenial with the feelings which actuate me, to substitute, in place of a recommendation of particular measures, the tribute that is due to the talents, the rectitude, and the patriotism which adorn the characters selected to devise and adopt them. In these honorable qualifications, I behold the surest pledges, that as on one side, no local prejudices, or attachments; no separate views, nor party animosities, will misdirect the comprehensive and equal eye which ought to watch over this great assemblage of communities and interests: so, on another, that the foundations of our National policy will be laid in the pure and immutable principles of private morality; and the pre-eminence of a free Government, be exemplified by all the attributes which can win the affections of its Citizens, and command the respect of the world. I dwell on this prospect with every satisfaction which an ardent love for my Country can inspire: since there is no truth more thoroughly established, than that there exists in the economy and course of nature, an indissoluble union between virtue and happiness, between duty and advantage, between the genuine maxims of an

---

[2] Article II of the Constitution

honest and magnanimous policy, and the solid rewards of public prosperity and felicity: Since we ought to be no less persuaded that the propitious smiles of Heaven, can never be expected on a nation that disregards the eternal rules of order and right, which Heaven itself has ordained: And since the preservation of the sacred fire of liberty, and the destiny of the Republican model of Government, are justly considered as *deeply*, perhaps as *finally* staked, on the experiment entrusted to the hands of the American people.

Besides the ordinary objects submitted to your care, it will remain with your judgment to decide, how far an exercise of the occasional power delegated by the Fifth article of the Constitution[3] is rendered expedient at the present juncture by the nature of objections which have been urged against the System, or by the degree of inquietude which has given birth to them. Instead of undertaking particular recommendations on this subject, in which I could be guided by no lights derived from official opportunities, I shall again give way to my entire confidence in your discernment and pursuit of the public good: For I assure myself that whilst you carefully avoid every alteration which might endanger the benefits of an United and effective Government, or which ought to await the future lessons of experience; a reverence for the characteristic rights of freemen, and a regard for the public harmony, will sufficiently influence your deliberations on the question how far the former can be more impregnably fortified, or the latter be safely and advantageously promoted.

To the preceding observations I have one to add, which will be most properly addressed to the House of Representatives. It concerns myself, and will therefore be as brief as possible. When I was first honored with a call into the Service of my Country, then on the eve of an arduous struggle for its liberties, the light in which I contemplated my duty required that I should renounce every pecuniary compensation. From this resolution I have in no instance departed. And being still under the impressions which produced it, I must decline as inapplicable to myself, any share in the personal emoluments, which may be indispensably included in a permanent provision for the Executive Department; and must accordingly pray that the pecuniary estimates for the Station in which I am placed, may, during my continuance in it, be limited to such actual expenditures as the public good may be thought to require.

Having thus imported to you my sentiments, as they have been awakened by the occasion which brings us together, I shall take my present leave; but not without resorting once more to the benign parent of the human race, in

---

[3] Article V of the Constitution outlines the amendment process.

humble supplication that since he has been pleased to favor the American people, with opportunities for deliberating in perfect tranquility, and dispositions for deciding with unparalleled unanimity on a form of Government, for the security of their Union, and the advancement of their happiness; so his divine blessing may be equally *conspicuous* in the enlarged views, the temperate consultations, and the wise measures on which the success of this Government must depend.

Document 26

James Madison Argues for Constitutional Amendments

June 8, 1789

During the months that elapsed between his letter to Jefferson in October 1788 and the opening of the first session of the new Congress in April 1789, Madison reached the conclusion that the Constitution did indeed need amendment to guarantee citizens certain rights. On June 8, 1789, Madison persuaded the Federalist majority in the House of Representatives to take this concern seriously. Some doubted that amendments were needed, while others argued that consideration be postponed. Madison insisted that Congress pay attention to the wishes of those constituents who still held reservations about whether the federal government would respect their rights. He noted that two states (North Carolina and Rhode Island) had not yet voted to ratify the Constitution, and added that significant minorities in the states that had ratified would be reassured if amendments were enacted.

He admitted the danger that worried many of his colleagues: that by considering amendments to the Constitution at this early date, Congress might open "a door . . . for a re-consideration of the whole structure of the Government — for a re-consideration of the principles and the substance of the powers given." Yet he insisted that no such wide-open reconsideration of the Constitution need happen. There were certain rights not yet guaranteed by the Constitution that a two-thirds majority of Congress would readily accept. "I will not propose a single alteration which I do not wish to see take place, as intrinsically proper in itself, or proper because it is wished for by a respectable number of my fellow-citizens; and therefore I shall not propose a single alteration but is likely to meet the concurrence required by the Constitution," he assured his fellow House members.

Madison proposed nine separate amendments which, broken down, amounted to 39 particular measures to safeguard liberties he thought potentially threatened. None aimed at altering the structure or powers of the general government. Yet Madison wanted to open up the Constitution and insert these 39 specific changes where appropriate. It was very likely this mode of amending the Constitution that made fellow House members such as Roger Sherman of Connecticut and James

Jackson of Georgia reluctant to move forward on Madison's proposals. The longest and most important of Madison's proposals, the fourth, would have added ten additional exceptions to the powers of Congress in Article I, section 9. The list in Madison's fourth amendment contains seven of the ten amendments adopted subsequently by the state legislatures.

Having meditated at length on the rights that needed to be secured, Madison now had synthesized Jefferson's arguments for a bill of rights with his own earlier arguments in their exchange of letters on the matter. In particular, he joined Jefferson's notion that "a bill of rights is what the people are entitled to against every government on earth" with his own concern that the greatest danger to liberty is at the state level. Accordingly, he challenged fellow House members to resolve that "no State shall violate the equal right of the conscience, freedom of the press, or trial by jury in criminal cases." This feature was defeated when the proposals arrived at the Senate.

Source: 1 Annals of Cong. *424-450 (1789).*

Mr. MADISON.—

I will state my reasons why I think it proper to propose amendments; and state the amendments themselves, so far as I think they ought to be proposed. If I thought I could fulfill the duty which I owe to myself and my constituents, to let the subject pass over in silence, I most certainly should not trespass upon the indulgence of this House. But I cannot do this; and am therefore compelled to beg a patient hearing to what I have to lay before you. And I do most sincerely believe, that if Congress will devote but one day to this subject, so far as to satisfy the public that we do not disregard their wishes, it will have a salutary influence on the public councils, and prepare the way for a favorable reception of our future measures.

. . . And if there are amendments desired of such a nature as will not injure the Constitution, and they can be engrafted so as to give satisfaction to the doubting part of our fellow-citizens, the friends of the Federal Government will evince that spirit of deference and concession for which they have hitherto been distinguished.

It cannot be a secret to the gentlemen in this House, that, notwithstanding the ratification of this system of Government by eleven of the thirteen United States, in some cases unanimously, in others by large majorities; yet still there is a great number of our constituents who are dissatisfied with it; among whom are many respectable for their talents and patriotism, and respectable for the jealousy they have for their liberty, which, though mistaken in its object, is laudable in its motive. . . . But perhaps there is a stronger motive than this for our going into a consideration of the subject. It is to provide those securities for liberty which are required by a part of the community; I allude in a particular manner to those two States[1] who have not thought fit to throw themselves into the bosom of the Confederacy. It is a desirable thing, on our part as well as theirs, that a re-union should take place as soon as possible. I have no doubt, if we proceed to take those steps which would be prudent and requisite at this juncture, that in a short time we should see that disposition prevailing in those States that are not come in, that we have seen prevailing in those States which have embraced the Constitution.

But I will candidly acknowledge, that, over and above all these considerations, I do conceive that the Constitution may be amended; that is to say, if all power is subject to abuse, that then it is possible the abuse of the powers of the General Government may be guarded against in a more secure manner than is now done, while no one advantage arising from the exercise of that power shall be damaged or endangered by it. We have in this way something to gain, and, if we proceed with caution, nothing to lose. And in this case it is necessary to proceed with caution; for while we feel all these inducements to go into a revisal of the Constitution, we must feel for the Constitution itself, and make that revisal a moderate one. I should be unwilling to see a door opened for a re-consideration of the whole structure of the Government — for a re-consideration of the principles and the substance of the powers given; because I doubt, if such a door were opened, we should be very likely to stop at that point which would be safe to the Government itself. But I do wish to see a door opened to consider, so far as to incorporate those provisions for the security of rights, against which I believe no serious objection has been made by any class of our constituents: such as would be likely to meet with the concurrence of two-thirds of both Houses, and the approbation of three-fourths of the State Legislatures. I will not propose a single alteration which I do not wish to see take place, as intrinsically proper in itself, or proper because it is wished for by a respectable number of my fellow-citizens; and therefore I shall not propose a single alteration but is likely to meet the concurrence required by the Constitution. There have been

---

[1] North Carolina declined to ratify the Constitution at the state's initial ratification convention. After learning that Congress had endorsed the proposal for a Bill of Rights, it called a second convention, and ratified on November 21, 1789. Rhode Island refused to call a ratifying convention until the end of the first session of Congress. It finally ratified in a close vote on May 29, 1790.

objections of various kinds made against the Constitution. . . . I believe that the great mass of the people who opposed it, disliked it because it did not contain effectual provision against the encroachments on particular rights, and those safeguards which they have been long accustomed to have interposed between them and the magistrate who exercised the sovereign power: nor ought we to consider them safe, while a great number of our fellow-citizens think these securities necessary. . . .

The amendments which have occurred to me, proper to be recommended by Congress to the State Legislatures, are these:

[Madison's first proposed amendment would have added to the Constitution a preface declaring several of the rights articulated in the Declaration, including the right of the people to amend their form of government. His second and third amendments dealt with the ratio of representatives in the House to the inhabitants they represented and the ability of Congressmen to fix their own salaries.]

. . . Fourthly. That in article 1st, section 9, between clauses 3 and 4, be inserted these clauses, to wit: The civil rights of none shall be abridged on account of religious belief or worship, nor shall any national religion be established, nor shall the full and equal rights of conscience be in any manner, or on any pretext, infringed.

The people shall not be deprived or abridged of their right to speak, to write, or to publish their sentiments; and the freedom of the press, as one of the great bulwarks of liberty, shall be inviolable.

The people shall not be restrained from peaceably assembling and consulting for their common good; nor from applying to the legislature by petitions, or remonstrances for redress of their grievances.

The right of the people to keep and bear arms shall not be infringed; a well armed and well regulated militia being the best security of a free country: but no person religiously scrupulous of bearing arms shall be compelled to render military service in person.

No soldier shall in time of peace be quartered in any house without the consent of the owner; nor at any time, but in a manner warranted by law.

No person shall be subject, except in cases of impeachment, to more than one punishment, or one trial for the same offence; nor shall be compelled to be a witness against himself; nor be deprived of life, liberty, or property, without due process of law; nor be obliged to relinquish his property, where it may be necessary for public use, without a just compensation.

Excessive bail shall not be required, nor excessive fines imposed, nor cruel and unusual punishments inflicted.

The rights of the people to be secured in their persons, their houses, their papers, and their other property, from all unreasonable searches and seizures, shall not be violated by warrants issued without probable cause, supported by oath or affirmation, or not particularly describing the places to be searched, or the persons or things to be seized.

In all criminal prosecutions, the accused shall enjoy the right to a speedy and public trial, to be informed of the cause and nature of the accusation, to be confronted with his accusers, and the witnesses against him; to have a compulsory process for obtaining witnesses in his favor; and to have the assistance of counsel for his defense.

The exceptions here or elsewhere in the Constitution, made in favor of particular rights, shall not be so construed as to diminish the just importance of other rights retained by the people, or as to enlarge the powers delegated by the Constitution; but either as actual limitations of such powers, or as inserted merely for greater caution.

Fifthly. That in article 1st, section 10, between clauses 1 and 2, be inserted this clause, to wit:

No State shall violate the equal rights of conscience, or the freedom of the press, or the trial by jury in criminal cases.

Sixthly. That, in article 3d, section 2, be annexed to the end of clause 2d, these words, to wit:

But no appeal to such court shall be allowed where the value in controversy shall not amount to _____ dollars: nor shall any fact triable by jury, according to the course of common law, be otherwise re-examinable than may consist with the principles of common law.

Seventhly. That in article 3d, section 2, the third clause be struck out, and in its place be inserted the clauses following, to wit:

The trial of all crimes (except in cases of impeachments, and cases arising in the land or naval forces, or the militia when on actual service, in time of war or public danger) shall be by an impartial jury of freeholders of the vicinage,[2] with the requisite of unanimity for conviction, of the right of challenge, and other accustomed requisites; and in all crimes punishable with loss of life or member, presentment or indictment by a grand jury shall be an essential preliminary, provided that in cases of crimes committed within any county which may be in possession of an enemy, or in which a general insurrection may prevail, the trial may by law be authorized in some other county of the same State, as near as may be to the seat of the offence.

---

[2] area near about (where the crime took place)

In cases of crimes committed not within any county, the trial may by law be in such county as the laws shall have prescribed. In suits at common law, between man and man, the trial by jury, as one of the best securities to the rights of the people, ought to remain inviolate.

Eighthly. That immediately after article 6th, be inserted, as article 7th, the clauses following, to wit:

The powers delegated by this Constitution are appropriated to the departments to which they are respectively distributed: so that the Legislative Department shall never exercise the powers vested in the Executive or Judicial, nor the Executive exercise the powers vested in the Legislative or Judicial, nor the Judicial exercise the powers vested in the Legislative or Executive Departments.

The powers not delegated by this Constitution, nor prohibited by it to the states, are reserved to the States respectively.

Ninthly. That article 7th, be numbered as article 8th.

The first of these amendments, relates to what may be called a bill of rights. I will own that I never considered this provision so essential to the Federal Constitution as to make it improper to ratify it, until such an amendment was added; at the same time, I always conceived, that in a certain form, and to a certain extent, such a provision was neither improper nor altogether useless. I am aware that a great number of the most respectable friends to the Government, and champions for republican liberty, have thought such a provision not only unnecessary, but even improper, nay, I believe some have gone so far as to think it even dangerous. . . .

. . . The people of many States, have thought it necessary to raise barriers against power in all forms and departments of Government, and I am inclined to believe, if once bills of rights are established in all the States as well as the Federal Constitution, we shall find, that, although some of them are rather unimportant, yet, upon the whole, they will have a salutary tendency. It may be said, in some instances, they do no more than state the perfect equality of mankind. This, to be sure, is an absolute truth, yet it is not absolutely necessary to be inserted at the head of a Constitution. . . .

In our Government it is, perhaps, less necessary to guard against the abuse in the Executive Department than any other; because it is not the stronger branch of the system, but the weaker. It therefore must be leveled against the Legislative, for it is the most powerful, and most likely to be abused, because it is under the least control. Hence, so far as a declaration of rights can tend to prevent the exercise of undue power, it cannot be doubted but such declaration is proper. But I confess that I do conceive, that in a Government modified like this of the United States, the great danger lies rather in the abuse of the community than in the Legislative body. The prescriptions in favor of liberty ought to be leveled against that quarter where the greatest danger lies, namely, that which possesses the highest prerogative of power. But this is not found in either the Executive or Legislative departments of Government, but in the body of the people, operating by the majority against the minority.

It may be thought all paper barriers against the power of the community are too weak to be worthy of attention. I am sensible they are not so strong as to satisfy gentlemen of every description who have seen and examined thoroughly the texture of such a defense; yet, as they have a tendency to impress some degree of respect for them, to establish the public opinion in their favor, and rouse the attention of the whole community, it may be one means to control the majority from those acts to which they might be otherwise inclined.

It has been said, by way of objection to a bill of rights, by many respectable gentlemen out of doors, and I find opposition on the same principles likely to be made by gentlemen on this floor, that they are unnecessary articles of a Republican Government, upon the presumption that the people have those rights in their own hands, and that is the proper place for them to rest. It would be a sufficient answer to say, that this objection lies against such provisions under the State Government, as well as under the General Government; and there are, I believe, but few gentlemen who are inclined to push their theory so far as to say that a declaration of rights in those cases is either ineffectual or improper. It has been said, that in the Federal Government they are unnecessary, because the powers are enumerated, and it follows, that all that are not granted by the Constitution are retained; that the Constitution is a bill of powers, the great residuum[3] being the rights of the people; and, therefore, a bill of rights cannot be so necessary as if the residuum was thrown into the hands of the Government. I admit that these arguments are not entirely without foundation; but they are not conclusive to the extent which has been supposed. It is true, the powers of the General Government are circumscribed, they are directed to particular objects; but even if Government keeps within those limits, it has certain discretionary powers with respect to the means, which may admit of abuse to a certain extent, in the same manner as the powers of the State Governments under their constitutions may to an indefinite extent; because in the Constitution of the United States, there is a clause granting to Congress the power to make all laws which shall be

[3] thing that is left behind

necessary and proper for carrying into execution all the powers vested in the Government of the United States, or in any department or officer thereof; this enables them to fulfill every purpose for which the Government was established. Now, may not laws be considered necessary and proper by Congress, (for it is them who are to judge of the necessity and propriety to accomplish those special purposes which they may have in contemplation,) which laws in themselves are neither necessary or proper; as well as improper laws could be enacted by the State Legislatures, for fulfilling the more extended objects of those Governments? I will state an instance, which I think in point, and proves that this might be the case. The General Government has a right to pass all laws which shall be necessary to collect its revenue; the means for enforcing the collection are within the direction of the Legislature: may not general warrants be considered necessary for this purpose, as well as for some purposes which it was supposed at the framing of their constitutions the State Governments had in view? If there was reason for restraining the State Governments from exercising this power, there is like reason for restraining the Federal Government.

It may be said, indeed it has been said, that a bill of rights is not necessary, because the establishment of this Government has not repealed those declarations of rights which are added to the several State constitutions; that those rights of the people which had been established by the most solemn act, could not be annihilated by a subsequent act of that people, who meant and declared at the head of the instrument, that they ordained and established a new system, for the express purpose of securing to themselves and posterity the liberties they had gained by an arduous conflict.

I admit the force of this observation, but I do not look upon it to be conclusive. In the first place, it is too uncertain ground to leave this provision upon, if a provision is at all necessary to secure rights so important as many of those I have mentioned are conceived to be, by the public in general, as well as those in particular who opposed the adoption of this Constitution. Beside some States have no bills of rights, there are others provided with very defective ones, and there are others whose bills of rights are not only defective, but absolutely improper; instead of securing some in the full extent which republican principles would require, they limit them too much to agree with the common ideas of liberty.[4]

It has been objected also against a bill of rights, that, by enumerating particular exceptions to the grant of power, it would disparage those rights which were not placed in that enumeration; and it might follow by implication, that those rights which were not singled out, were intended to be assigned into the hands of the General Government, and were consequently insecure. This is one of the most plausible arguments I have ever heard urged against the admission of a bill of rights into this system; but, I conceive, that may be guarded against. I have attempted it, as gentlemen may see by turning to the last clause of the fourth resolution.

It has been said that it is unnecessary to load the Constitution with this provision, because it was not found effectual in the constitution of the particular States. It is true, there are a few particular States in which some of the most valuable articles have not, at one time or other, been violated; but does it not follow but they may have, to a certain degree, a salutary effect against the abuse of power. If they are incorporated into the Constitution, independent tribunals of justice will consider themselves in a peculiar manner the guardians of those rights; they will be an impenetrable bulwark against every assumption of power in the Legislative or Executive; they will be naturally led to resist every encroachment upon rights expressly stipulated for in the Constitution by the declaration of rights. Besides this security, there is a great probability that such a declaration in the federal system would be enforced; because the State Legislatures will jealously and closely watch the operations of this Government, and be able to resist with more effect every assumption of power, than any other power on earth can do; and the greatest opponents to a Federal Government admit the State Legislatures to be sure guardians of the people's liberty. I conclude, from this view of the subject, that it will be proper in itself, and highly politic, for the tranquility of the public mind, and the stability of the Government, that we should offer something, in the form I have proposed, to be incorporated in the system of Government, as a declaration of the rights of the people. . . .

I wish, also, in revising the Constitution, we may throw into that section, which interdicts the abuse of certain powers in the State Legislatures, some

---

[4] See Madison's letter to Jefferson (Document 24), in which he writes, "I am sure that the rights of conscience in particular, if submitted to the public definition[,] would be narrowed much more than they are likely ever to be by an assumed power. One of the objections in New England was that the Constitution by prohibiting religious tests opened a door for Jews, Turks and infidels."

other provisions of equal if not greater importance than those already made. The words, "No state shall pass any bill of attainder, ex post facto law," &c., were wise and proper restrictions in the Constitution. I think there is more danger of those powers being abused by the State Governments than by the Government of the United States. The same may be said of other powers which they possess, if not controlled by the general principle, that laws are unconstitutional which infringe the rights of the community. I should, therefore, wish to extend this interdiction, and add, as I have stated in the 5th resolution, that no State shall violate the equal right of conscience, freedom of the press, or trial by jury in criminal cases; because it is proper that every Government should be disarmed of powers which trench upon those particular rights. I know, in some of the State constitutions, the power of the Government is controlled by such a declaration; but [in] others [it is] not. I cannot see any reason against obtaining even a double security on those points; and nothing can give a more sincere proof of the attachment of those who opposed this Constitution to these great and important rights, than to see them join in obtaining the security I have now proposed; because it must be admitted, on all hands, that the State Governments are as liable to attack these invaluable privileges as the General Government is, and therefore ought to be as cautiously guarded against. . . .

I find, from looking into the amendments proposed by the State conventions, that several are particularly anxious that it should be declared in the Constitution, that the powers not therein delegated, should be reserved to the several States. Perhaps words which may define this more precisely than the whole of the instrument now does, may be considered as superfluous. I admit they may be deemed unnecessary; but there can be no harm in making such a declaration, if gentlemen will allow that the fact is as stated. I am sure I understand it so, and do therefore propose it.

These are the points on which I wish to see a revision of the Constitution take place. How far they will accord with the sense of this body, I cannot take upon me absolutely to determine; but I believe every gentleman will readily admit that nothing is in contemplation, so far as I have mentioned, that can endanger the beauty of the Government in any one important feature, even in the eyes of its most sanguine admirers. I have proposed nothing that does not appear to me as proper in itself, or eligible as patronized by a respectable number of our fellow-citizens; and if we can make the Constitution better in the opinion of those who are opposed to it, without weakening its frame, or abridging its usefulness in the judgment of those who are attached to it, we act the part of wise and liberal men to make such alterations as shall produce that effect.

Having done what I conceived was my duty, in bringing before this House the subject of amendments, and also stated such as I wish for and approve, and offered the reasons which occurred to me in their support, I shall content myself, for the present, with moving "that a committee be appointed to consider of and report such amendments as ought to be proposed by Congress to the Legislatures of the States, to become, if ratified by three fourths thereof, part of the Constitution of the United States." By agreeing to this motion, the subject may be going on in the committee, while other important business is proceeding to a conclusion in the House. I should advocate greater dispatch in the business of amendments, if I was not convinced of the absolute necessity there is of pursuing the organization of the Government; because I think we should obtain the confidence of our fellow-citizens, in proportion as we fortify the rights of the people against the encroachments of the Government.

[*James Jackson of Georgia, Elbridge Gerry of Massachusetts, Samuel Livermore of New Hampshire, Roger Sherman of Connecticut, Thomas Sumter of South Carolina, and John Vining of Delaware debated the merits of sending Madison's proposals to a select committee.*]

Mr. MADISON found himself unfortunate in not satisfying gentlemen with respect to the mode of introducing the business; he thought, from the dignity and the peculiarity of the subject, that it ought to be referred to a Committee of the Whole. He accordingly made that motion first, but finding himself not likely to succeed in that way, he had changed his ground. Fearing again to be discomfited, he would change his mode, and move the propositions he had stated before, and the House might do what they thought proper with them. He accordingly moved the propositions by way of resolutions to be adopted by the House.

[*After a brief discussion,*] "Mr. MADISON'S propositions were ordered to be referred to a Committee of the Whole on the State of the Union."

Appendices

Appendix A:
Thematic Table of Contents

I. A NEW COURSE

II. THE CONSTITUTIONAL CONVENTION (MAY 28, 1787 - SEPTEMBER 17, 1787)

A. The Three Alternative Plans

B. The Connecticut Compromise

C. Bicameralism and the Separation of Powers

Appendix B: The Three Plans from Which the Constitution Grew

The Constitutional Convention met from May 25 to September 17, 1787. Two different plans of government, and one plan compromising between them, shaped the Convention's deliberations.

On May 29, Edmund Randolph introduced "The Virginia Plan" (Document 5), which reflected the shift of sovereignty from the States to the Federal Government that Madison had recommended in his "Vices of the Political System of the United States" (Document 4). It stripped the states *qua* states of the pre-eminence they held under the Articles of Confederation (Document 3). In particular, according to the Virginia Plan, the states would no longer have the right either to equal representation in the federal structure or to elect representatives to the Congress. The states fared no better in the area of powers: Congress was granted the right "to legislate in all cases to which the separate States were incompetent . . . [and] . . . to negative all laws passed by the several States, contravening in the opinion of the national legislature the articles of Union." The Virginia Plan also introduced bicameralism and the separation of powers to the federal structure.

By contrast, the New Jersey Plan, introduced by William Patterson on June 15 (Document 7), did not reduce the power of the states. It retained the structural features of the Articles of Confederation and focused instead on enhancing the power of a unicameral Congress in which each state was equally represented. The plan acknowledged the defects in the Articles, but these "vices" were due solely to the want of power. It authorized Congress "to pass acts for raising a revenue . . . [and] . . . for the regulation of trade & commerce as well with foreign nations as with each other."

On July 16th the delegates adopted, by a narrow margin, the "Connecticut Compromise" (Documents 9 and 10) which retained the bicameral legislature of the Virginia Plan but gave equal representation to the people in the House and equal representation to each State in the Senate. The compromise also restricted the Senate from altering money bills introduced by the House, a feature that would be absent in the final Constitution.

The Committee of Detail Report (Document 12), which was to fill in some of the details of the working plan, was presented to the Convention on August 6th. Among other things, the Report abandoned an earlier feature of the Virginia Plan: Congress was no longer authorized to "legislate in all cases to which the separate States are incompetent." Instead of this broad grant of power, Congress was given enumerated, that is specified, powers.

Appendix C: Free and Slave Populations by State

According to the 1790 Census

State	Free Whites	Other Free Persons	Slaves	% Slave	Total
Vermont	85,268	255	16	0.01	85,539
N. Hampshire	141,097	630	158	0.1	141,885
Maine	96,002	538	none	0	96,540
Massachusetts	373,324	5,463	none	0	378,787
Rhode Island	64,470	3,407	948	1	68,825
Connecticut	232,374	2,808	2,764	1	237,946
New York	314,142	4,654	21,324	6	340,120
Pennsylvania	424,099	6,537	3,737	0.8	434,373
Delaware	46,310	3,899	8,887	15	59,096
Maryland	208,649	8,043	103,036	32	319,728
Virginia	442,117	12,866	292,627	39	747,610
Kentucky	61,133	114	12,430	17	73,677
N. Carolina	288,204	4,975	100,572	25	393,751
S. Carolina	140,178	1,801	107,094	43	249,073
Georgia	52,886	398	29,264	35	82,548

Appendix D: Declaration of Independence

In CONGRESS, July 4, 1776

The unanimous Declaration of the thirteen united States of America,

When in the Course of human events, it becomes necessary for one people to dissolve the political bands which have connected them with another, and to assume among the powers of the earth, the separate and equal station to which the Laws of Nature and of Nature's God entitle them, a decent respect to the opinions of mankind requires that they should declare the causes which impel them to the separation.

We hold these truths to be self-evident, that all men are created equal, that they are endowed by their Creator with certain unalienable Rights, that among these are Life, Liberty and the pursuit of Happiness. — That to secure these rights, Governments are instituted among Men, deriving their just powers from the consent of the governed, — that whenever any Form of Government becomes destructive of these ends, it is the Right of the People to alter or to abolish it, and to institute new Government, laying its foundation on such principles and organizing its powers in such form, as to them shall seem most likely to effect their Safety and Happiness. Prudence, indeed, will dictate that Governments long established should not be changed for light and transient causes; and accordingly all experience hath shewn, that mankind are more disposed to suffer, while evils are sufferable, than to right themselves by abolishing the forms to which they are accustomed. But when a long train of abuses and usurpations, pursuing invariably the same Object evinces a design to reduce them under absolute Despotism, it is their right, it is their duty, to throw off such Government, and to provide new Guards for their future security. — Such has been the patient sufferance of these Colonies; and such is now the necessity which constrains them to alter their former Systems of Government. The history of the present King of Great Britain is a history of repeated injuries and usurpations, all having in direct object the establishment of an absolute Tyranny over these States. To prove this, let Facts be submitted to a candid world.

He has refused his Assent to Laws, the most wholesome and necessary for the public good.

He has forbidden his Governors to pass Laws of immediate and pressing importance, unless suspended in their operation till his Assent should be obtained; and when so suspended, he has utterly neglected to attend to them.

He has refused to pass other Laws for the accommodation of large districts of people, unless those people would relinquish the right of Representation in the Legislature, a right inestimable to them and formidable to tyrants only.

He has called together legislative bodies at places unusual, uncomfortable, and distant from the depository of their public Records, for the sole purpose of fatiguing them into compliance with his measures.

He has dissolved Representative Houses repeatedly, for opposing with manly firmness his invasions on the rights of the people.

He has refused for a long time, after such dissolutions, to cause others to be elected; whereby the Legislative powers, incapable of Annihilation, have returned to the People at large for their exercise; the State remaining in the mean time exposed to all the dangers of invasion from without, and convulsions within.

He has endeavoured to prevent the population of these States; for that purpose obstructing the Laws for Naturalization of Foreigners; refusing to pass others to encourage their migrations hither, and raising the conditions of new Appropriations of Lands.

He has obstructed the Administration of Justice, by refusing his Assent to Laws for establishing Judiciary powers.

He has made Judges dependent on his Will alone, for the tenure of their offices, and the amount and payment of their salaries.

He has erected a multitude of New Offices, and sent hither swarms of Officers to harrass our people, and eat out their substance.

He has kept among us, in times of peace, Standing Armies without the Consent of our legislatures.

He has affected to render the Military independent of and superior to the Civil power.

He has combined with others to subject us to a jurisdiction foreign to our constitution, and unacknowledged by our laws; giving his Assent to their Acts of pretended Legislation:

For Quartering large bodies of armed troops among us:

For protecting them, by a mock Trial, from punishment for any Murders which they should commit on the Inhabitants of these States:

For cutting off our Trade with all parts of the world:

For imposing Taxes on us without our Consent:

For depriving us in many cases, of the benefits of Trial by Jury:

For transporting us beyond Seas to be tried for pretended offences:

For abolishing the free System of English Laws in a neighbouring Province, establishing therein an Arbitrary government, and enlarging its Boundaries so as to render it at once an example and fit instrument for introducing the same absolute rule into these Colonies:

For taking away our Charters, abolishing our most valuable Laws, and altering fundamentally the Forms of our Governments:

For suspending our own Legislatures, and declaring themselves invested with power to legislate for us in all cases whatsoever.

He has abdicated Government here, by declaring us out of his Protection and waging War against us.

He has plundered our seas, ravaged our Coasts, burnt our towns, and destroyed the lives of our people.

He is at this time transporting large Armies of foreign Mercenaries to compleat the works of death, desolation and tyranny, already begun with circumstances of Cruelty & perfidy scarcely paralleled in the most barbarous ages, and totally unworthy the Head of a civilized nation.

He has constrained our fellow Citizens taken Captive on the high Seas to bear Arms against their Country, to become the executioners of their friends and Brethren, or to fall themselves by their Hands.

He has excited domestic insurrections amongst us, and has endeavoured to bring on the inhabitants of our frontiers, the merciless Indian Savages, whose known rule of warfare, is an undistinguished destruction of all ages, sexes and conditions.

In every stage of these Oppressions We have Petitioned for Redress in the most humble terms: Our repeated Petitions have been answered only by repeated injury. A Prince whose character is thus marked by every act which may define a Tyrant, is unfit to be the ruler of a free people.

Nor have We been wanting in attentions to our British brethren. We have warned them from time to time of attempts by their legislature to extend an unwarrantable jurisdiction over us. We have reminded them of the circumstances of our emigration and settlement here. We have appealed to their native justice and magnanimity, and we have conjured them by the ties of our common kindred to disavow these usurpations, which, would inevitably interrupt our connections and correspondence. They too have been deaf to the voice of justice and of consanguinity. We must, therefore, acquiesce in the necessity, which denounces our Separation, and hold them, as we hold the rest of mankind, Enemies in War, in Peace Friends.

We, THEREFORE, the Representatives of the UNITED STATES OF AMERICA, in General Congress, Assembled, appealing to the Supreme Judge of the world for the rectitude of our intentions, do, in the Name, and by Authority of the good People of these Colonies, solemnly publish and declare, That these United Colonies are, and of Right ought to be FREE AND INDEPENDENT STATES; that they are Absolved from all Allegiance to the British Crown, and that all political connection between them and the State of Great Britain, is and ought to be totally dissolved; and that as Free and Independent States, they have full Power to levy War, conclude Peace, contract Alliances, establish Commerce, and to do all other Acts and Things which Independent States may of right do. And for the support of this Declaration, with a firm reliance on the protection of divine Providence, we mutually pledge to each other our Lives, our Fortunes and our sacred Honor.

[Georgia:]
Button Gwinnett
Lyman Hall
George Walton

[North Carolina:]
William Hooper
Joseph Hewes
John Penn

[South Carolina:]
Edward Rutledge
Thomas Heyward, Jr.
Thomas Lynch, Jr.
Arthur Middleton

[Maryland:]
Samuel Chase
William Paca
Thomas Stone
Charles Carroll of Carrollton

[Virginia:]
George Wythe
Richard Henry Lee
Thomas Jefferson
Benjamin Harrison
Thomas Nelson, Jr.
Francis Lightfoot Lee
Carter Braxton

[Pennsylvania:]
Robert Morris
Benjamin Rush
Benjamin Franklin
John Morton
George Clymer
James Smith
George Taylor
James Wilson
George Ross

[Delaware:]
Caesar Rodney
George Read
Thomas McKean

[New York:]
William Floyd
Philip Livingston
Francis Lewis
Lewis Morris

[New Jersey:]
Richard Stockton
John Witherspoon
Francis Hopkinson
John Hart
Abraham Clark

[New Hampshire:]
Josiah Bartlett
William Whipple
Matthew Thornton

[Massachusetts:]
John Hancock
Samuel Adams
John Adams
Robert Treat Paine
Elbridge Gerry

[Rhode Island:]
Stephen Hopkins
William Ellery

[Connecticut:]
Roger Sherman
Samuel Huntington
William Williams
Oliver Wolcott

Appendix E: Constitution of the United States of America

September 17, 1787

[Editors' note: Bracketed sections in the text of the Constitution have been superceded or modified by Constitutional amendments.]

We the People of the United States, in Order to form a more perfect Union, establish Justice, insure domestic Tranquility, provide for the common defence, promote the general Welfare, and secure the Blessings of Liberty to ourselves and our Posterity, do ordain and establish this Constitution for the United States of America.

Article. I.

Section. 1. All legislative Powers herein granted shall be vested in a Congress of the United States, which shall consist of a Senate and House of Representatives.

Section. 2. The House of Representatives shall be composed of Members chosen every second Year by the People of the several States, and the Electors in each State shall have the Qualifications requisite for Electors of the most numerous Branch of the State Legislature.

No Person shall be a Representative who shall not have attained to the Age of twenty five Years, and been seven Years a Citizen of the United States, and who shall not, when elected, be an Inhabitant of that State in which he shall be chosen.

[Representatives and direct Taxes shall be apportioned among the several States which may be included within this Union, according to their respective Numbers, which shall be determined by adding to the whole Number of free Persons, including those bound to Service for a Term of Years, and excluding Indians not taxed, three fifths of all other Persons.][1] The actual Enumeration shall be made within three Years after the first Meeting of the Congress of the United States, and within every subsequent Term of ten Years, in such Manner as they shall by Law direct. The Number of Representatives shall not exceed one for every thirty Thousand, but each State shall have at Least one

---

[1] modified by Section 2 of the Fourteenth Amendment

Representative; and until such enumeration shall be made, the State of New Hampshire shall be entitled to chuse three, Massachusetts eight, Rhode-Island and Providence Plantations one, Connecticut five, New-York six, New Jersey four, Pennsylvania eight, Delaware one, Maryland six, Virginia ten, North Carolina five, South Carolina five, and Georgia three.

When vacancies happen in the Representation from any State, the Executive Authority thereof shall issue Writs of Election to fill such Vacancies.

The House of Representatives shall chuse their Speaker and other Officers; and shall have the sole Power of Impeachment.

Section. 3. The Senate of the United States shall be composed of two Senators from each State, [chosen by the Legislature thereof,][2] for six Years; and each Senator shall have one Vote.

Immediately after they shall be assembled in Consequence of the first Election, they shall be divided as equally as may be into three Classes. The Seats of the Senators of the first Class shall be vacated at the Expiration of the second Year, of the second Class at the Expiration of the fourth Year, and of the third Class at the Expiration of the sixth Year, so that one third may be chosen every second Year; [and if Vacancies happen by Resignation, or otherwise, during the Recess of the Legislature of any State, the Executive thereof may make temporary Appointments until the next Meeting of the Legislature, which shall then fill such Vacancies.][3]

No Person shall be a Senator who shall not have attained to the Age of thirty Years, and been nine Years a Citizen of the United States, and who shall not, when elected, be an Inhabitant of that State for which he shall be chosen.

The Vice President of the United States shall be President of the Senate, but shall have no Vote, unless they be equally divided.

The Senate shall chuse their other Officers, and also a President pro tempore, in the Absence of the Vice President, or when he shall exercise the Office of President of the United States.

The Senate shall have the sole Power to try all Impeachments. When sitting for that Purpose, they shall be on Oath or Affirmation. When the President of the United States is tried, the Chief Justice shall preside: And no Person shall be convicted without the Concurrence of two thirds of the Members present.

Judgment in Cases of Impeachment shall not extend further than to removal from Office, and disqualification to hold and enjoy any Office of

---

[2] superseded by the Seventeenth Amendment

[3] modified by the Seventeenth Amendment

honor, Trust or Profit under the United States: but the Party convicted shall nevertheless be liable and subject to Indictment, Trial, Judgment and Punishment, according to Law.

Section. 4. The Times, Places and Manner of holding Elections for Senators and Representatives, shall be prescribed in each State by the Legislature thereof; but the Congress may at any time by Law make or alter such Regulations, except as to the Places of chusing Senators.

The Congress shall assemble at least once in every Year, and such Meeting shall be [on the first Monday in December,][4] unless they shall by Law appoint a different Day.

Section. 5. Each House shall be the Judge of the Elections, Returns and Qualifications of its own Members, and a Majority of each shall constitute a Quorum to do Business; but a smaller Number may adjourn from day to day, and may be authorized to compel the Attendance of absent Members, in such Manner, and under such Penalties as each House may provide.

Each House may determine the Rules of its Proceedings, punish its Members for disorderly Behaviour, and, with the Concurrence of two thirds, expel a Member.

Each House shall keep a Journal of its Proceedings, and from time to time publish the same, excepting such Parts as may in their Judgment require Secrecy; and the Yeas and Nays of the Members of either House on any question shall, at the Desire of one fifth of those Present, be entered on the Journal.

Neither House, during the Session of Congress, shall, without the Consent of the other, adjourn for more than three days, nor to any other Place than that in which the two Houses shall be sitting.

Section. 6. The Senators and Representatives shall receive a Compensation for their Services, to be ascertained by Law, and paid out of the Treasury of the United States. They shall in all Cases, except Treason, Felony and Breach of the Peace, be privileged from Arrest during their Attendance at the Session of their respective Houses, and in going to and returning from the same; and for any Speech or Debate in either House, they shall not be questioned in any other Place.

No Senator or Representative shall, during the Time for which he was elected, be appointed to any civil Office under the Authority of the United States, which shall have been created, or the Emoluments whereof shall have been encreased during such time; and no Person holding any Office under the

---

[4] modified by Section 2 of the Twentieth Amendment

United States, shall be a Member of either House during his Continuance in Office.

Section. 7. All Bills for raising Revenue shall originate in the House of Representatives; but the Senate may propose or concur with Amendments as on other Bills.

Every Bill which shall have passed the House of Representatives and the Senate, shall, before it become a Law, be presented to the President of the United States; If he approve he shall sign it, but if not he shall return it, with his Objections to that House in which it shall have originated, who shall enter the Objections at large on their Journal, and proceed to reconsider it. If after such Reconsideration two thirds of that House shall agree to pass the Bill, it shall be sent, together with the Objections, to the other House, by which it shall likewise be reconsidered, and if approved by two thirds of that House, it shall become a Law. But in all such Cases the Votes of both Houses shall be determined by yeas and Nays, and the Names of the Persons voting for and against the Bill shall be entered on the Journal of each House respectively. If any Bill shall not be returned by the President within ten Days (Sundays excepted) after it shall have been presented to him, the Same shall be a Law, in like Manner as if he had signed it, unless the Congress by their Adjournment prevent its Return, in which Case it shall not be a Law.

Every Order, Resolution, or Vote to which the Concurrence of the Senate and House of Representatives may be necessary (except on a question of Adjournment) shall be presented to the President of the United States; and before the Same shall take Effect, shall be approved by him, or being disapproved by him, shall be repassed by two thirds of the Senate and House of Representatives, according to the Rules and Limitations prescribed in the Case of a Bill.

Section. 8. The Congress shall have Power To lay and collect Taxes, Duties, Imposts and Excises, to pay the Debts and provide for the common Defence and general Welfare of the United States; but all Duties, Imposts and Excises shall be uniform throughout the United States;

To borrow Money on the credit of the United States;

To regulate Commerce with foreign Nations, and among the several States, and with the Indian Tribes;

To establish an uniform Rule of Naturalization, and uniform Laws on the subject of Bankruptcies throughout the United States;

To coin Money, regulate the Value thereof, and of foreign Coin, and fix the Standard of Weights and Measures;

To provide for the Punishment of counterfeiting the Securities and current Coin of the United States;

To establish Post Offices and post Roads;

To promote the Progress of Science and useful Arts, by securing for limited Times to Authors and Inventors the exclusive Right to their respective Writings and Discoveries;

To constitute Tribunals inferior to the supreme Court;

To define and punish Piracies and Felonies committed on the high Seas, and Offenses against the Law of Nations;

To declare War, grant Letters of Marque and Reprisal, and make Rules concerning Captures on Land and Water;

To raise and support Armies, but no Appropriation of Money to that Use shall be for a longer Term than two Years;

To provide and maintain a Navy;

To make Rules for the Government and Regulation of the land and naval Forces;

To provide for calling forth the Militia to execute the Laws of the Union, suppress Insurrections and repel Invasions;

To provide for organizing, arming, and disciplining, the Militia, and for governing such Part of them as may be employed in the Service of the United States, reserving to the States respectively, the Appointment of the Officers, and the Authority of training the Militia according to the discipline prescribed by Congress;

To exercise exclusive Legislation in all Cases whatsoever, over such District (not exceeding ten Miles square) as may, by Cession of particular States, and the Acceptance of Congress, become the Seat of the Government of the United States, and to exercise like Authority over all Places purchased by the Consent of the Legislature of the State in which the Same shall be, for the Erection of Forts, Magazines, Arsenals, dock-Yards, and other needful Buildings; —And

To make all Laws which shall be necessary and proper for carrying into Execution the foregoing Powers, and all other Powers vested by this Constitution in the Government of the United States, or in any Department or Officer thereof.

Section. 9. The Migration or Importation of such Persons as any of the States now existing shall think proper to admit, shall not be prohibited by the Congress prior to the Year one thousand eight hundred and eight, but a Tax or duty may be imposed on such Importation, not exceeding ten dollars for each Person.

The Privilege of the Writ of Habeas Corpus shall not be suspended, unless when in Cases of Rebellion or Invasion the public Safety may require it.

No Bill of Attainder or ex post facto Law shall be passed.

No Capitation, or other direct, Tax shall be laid, unless in Proportion to the Census or Enumeration herein before directed to be taken.[5]

No Tax or Duty shall be laid on Articles exported from any State.

No Preference shall be given by any Regulation of Commerce or Revenue to the Ports of one State over those of another: nor shall Vessels bound to, or from, one State, be obliged to enter, clear, or pay Duties in another.

No Money shall be drawn from the Treasury, but in Consequence of Appropriations made by Law; and a regular Statement and Account of the Receipts and Expenditures of all public Money shall be published from time to time.

No Title of Nobility shall be granted by the United States: And no Person holding any Office of Profit or Trust under them, shall, without the Consent of the Congress, accept of any present, Emolument, Office, or Title, of any kind whatever, from any King, Prince, or foreign State.

Section. 10. No State shall enter into any Treaty, Alliance, or Confederation; grant Letters of Marque and Reprisal; coin Money; emit Bills of Credit; make any Thing but gold and silver Coin a Tender in Payment of Debts; pass any Bill of Attainder, ex post facto Law, or Law impairing the Obligation of Contracts, or grant any Title of Nobility.

No State shall, without the Consent of the Congress, lay any Imposts or Duties on Imports or Exports, except what may be absolutely necessary for executing it's inspection Laws: and the net Produce of all Duties and Imposts, laid by any State on Imports or Exports, shall be for the Use of the Treasury of the United States; and all such Laws shall be subject to the Revision and Controul of the Congress.

No State shall, without the Consent of Congress, lay any Duty of Tonnage, keep Troops, or Ships of War in time of Peace, enter into any Agreement or Compact with another State, or with a foreign Power, or engage in War, unless actually invaded, or in such imminent Danger as will not admit of delay.

---

[5] modified by the Sixteenth Amendment

Article. II.

Section. 1. The executive Power shall be vested in a President of the United States of America. He shall hold his Office during the Term of four Years, and, together with the Vice President, chosen for the same Term, be elected, as follows:

Each State shall appoint, in such Manner as the Legislature thereof may direct, a Number of Electors, equal to the whole Number of Senators and Representatives to which the State may be entitled in the Congress: but no Senator or Representative, or Person holding an Office of Trust or Profit under the United States, shall be appointed an Elector.

[The Electors shall meet in their respective States, and vote by Ballot for two Persons, of whom one at least shall not be an Inhabitant of the same State with themselves. And they shall make a List of all the Persons voted for, and of the Number of Votes for each; which List they shall sign and certify, and transmit sealed to the Seat of the Government of the United States, directed to the President of the Senate. The President of the Senate shall, in the Presence of the Senate and House of Representatives, open all the Certificates, and the Votes shall then be counted. The Person having the greatest Number of Votes shall be the President, if such Number be a Majority of the whole Number of Electors appointed; and if there be more than one who have such Majority, and have an equal Number of Votes, then the House of Representatives shall immediately chuse by Ballot one of them for President; and if no Person have a Majority, then from the five highest on the List the said House shall in like Manner chuse the President. But in chusing the President, the Votes shall be taken by States, the Representation from each State having one Vote; A quorum for this purpose shall consist of a Member or Members from two thirds of the States, and a Majority of all the States shall be necessary to a Choice. In every Case, after the Choice of the President, the Person having the greatest Number of Votes of the Electors shall be the Vice President. But if there should remain two or more who have equal Votes, the Senate shall chuse from them by Ballot the Vice President.][6]

The Congress may determine the Time of chusing the Electors, and the Day on which they shall give their Votes; which Day shall be the same throughout the United States.

No Persons except a natural born Citizen, or a Citizen of the United States, at the time of the Adoption of this Constitution, shall be eligible to the Office of President; neither shall any Person be eligible to that Office who shall

---

[6] modifed by the Twelfth Amendment

not have attained to the Age of thirty five Years, and been fourteen Years a Resident within the United States.

[In Case of the Removal of the President from Office, or of his Death, Resignation, or Inability to discharge the Powers and Duties of the said Office, the Same shall devolve on the Vice President, and the Congress may by Law provide for the Case of Removal, Death, Resignation or Inability, both of the President and Vice President, declaring what Officer shall then act as President, and such Officer shall act accordingly, until the Disability be removed, or a President shall be elected.][7]

The President shall, at stated Times, receive for his Services, a Compensation, which shall neither be increased nor diminished during the Period for which he shall have been elected, and he shall not receive within that Period any other Emolument from the United States, or any of them.

Before he enter on the Execution of his Office, he shall take the following Oath or Affirmation:— "I do solemnly swear (or affirm) that I will faithfully execute the Office of President of the United States, and will to the best of my Ability, preserve, protect and defend the Constitution of the United States."

Section. 2. The President shall be Commander in Chief of the Army and Navy of the United States, and of the Militia of the several States, when called into the actual Service of the United States; he may require the Opinion, in writing, of the principal Officer in each of the executive Departments, upon any Subject relating to the Duties of their respective Offices, and he shall have Power to grant Reprieves and Pardons for Offences against the United States, except in Cases of Impeachment.

He shall have Power, by and with the Advice and Consent of the Senate, to make Treaties, provided two thirds of the Senators present concur; and he shall nominate, and by and with the Advice and Consent of the Senate, shall appoint Ambassadors, other public Ministers and Consuls, Judges of the supreme Court, and all other Officers of the United States, whose Appointments are not herein otherwise provided for, and which shall be established by Law: but the Congress may by Law vest the Appointment of such inferior Officers, as they think proper, in the President alone, in the Courts of Law, or in the Heads of Departments.

The President shall have Power to fill up all Vacancies that may happen during the Recess of the Senate, by granting Commissions which shall expire at the End of their next Session.

---

[7] modified by the Twenty-Fifth Amendment

Section. 3. He shall from time to time give to the Congress Information of the State of the Union, and recommend to their Consideration such Measures as he shall judge necessary and expedient; he may, on extraordinary Occasions, convene both Houses, or either of them, and in Case of Disagreement between them, with Respect to the Time of Adjournment, he may adjourn them to such Time as he shall think proper; he shall receive Ambassadors and other public Ministers; he shall take Care that the Laws be faithfully executed, and shall Commission all the Officers of the United States.

Section. 4. The President, Vice President and all civil Officers of the United States, shall be removed from Office on Impeachment for, and Conviction of, Treason, Bribery, or other high Crimes and Misdemeanors.

Article. III.

Section. 1. The judicial Power of the United States, shall be vested in one supreme Court, and in such inferior Courts as the Congress may from time to time ordain and establish. The Judges, both of the supreme and inferior Courts, shall hold their Offices during good Behaviour, and shall, at stated Times, receive for their Services, a Compensation, which shall not be diminished during their Continuance in Office.

Section. 2. The judicial Power shall extend to all Cases, in Law and Equity, arising under this Constitution, the Laws of the United States, and Treaties made, or which shall be made, under their Authority;—to all Cases affecting Ambassadors, other public Ministers and Consuls;—to all Cases of admiralty and maritime Jurisdiction;—to Controversies to which the United States shall be a Party;—to Controversies between two or more States;—[between a State and Citizens of another State;—][8] between Citizens of different States;—between Citizens of the same State claiming Lands under Grants of different States, [and between a State, or the Citizens thereof, and foreign States, Citizens or Subjects.][9]

In all Cases affecting Ambassadors, other public Ministers and Consuls, and those in which a State shall be Party, the supreme Court shall have original Jurisdiction. In all the other Cases before mentioned, the supreme Court shall have appellate Jurisdiction, both as to Law and Fact, with such Exceptions, and under such Regulations as the Congress shall make.

The Trial of all Crimes, except in Cases of Impeachment, shall be by Jury; and such Trial shall be held in the State where the said Crimes shall have been

---

[8] superseded by the Eleventh Amendment

[9] superseded by the Eleventh Amendment

committed; but when not committed within any State, the Trial shall be at such Place or Places as the Congress may by Law have directed.

Section. 3. Treason against the United States, shall consist only in levying War against them, or in adhering to their Enemies, giving them Aid and Comfort. No Person shall be convicted of Treason unless on the Testimony of two Witnesses to the same overt Act, or on Confession in open Court.

The Congress shall have Power to declare the Punishment of Treason, but no Attainder of Treason shall work Corruption of Blood, or Forfeiture except during the Life of the Person attained.

Article. IV.

Section. 1. Full Faith and Credit shall be given in each State to the public Acts, Records, and judicial Proceedings of every other State. And the Congress may by general Laws prescribe the Manner in which such Acts, Records and Proceedings shall be proved, and the Effect thereof.

Section. 2. The Citizens of each State shall be entitled to all Privileges and Immunities of Citizens in the several States.

A Person charged in any State with Treason, Felony, or other Crime, who shall flee from Justice, and be found in another State, shall on Demand of the executive Authority of the State from which he fled, be delivered up, to be removed to the State having Jurisdiction of the Crime.

[No Person held to Service or Labour in one State, under the Laws thereof, escaping into another, shall, in Consequence of any Law or Regulation therein, be discharged from such Service or Labour, but shall be delivered up on Claim of the Party to whom such Service or Labour may be due.][10]

Section. 3. New States may be admitted by the Congress into this Union; but no new State shall be formed or erected within the Jurisdiction of any other State; nor any State be formed by the Junction of two or more States, or Parts of States, without the Consent of the Legislatures of the States concerned as well as of the Congress.

The Congress shall have Power to dispose of and make all needful Rules and Regulations respecting the Territory or other Property belonging to the United States; and nothing in this Constitution shall be so construed as to Prejudice any Claims of the United States, or of any particular State.

Section. 4. The United States shall guarantee to every State in this Union a Republican Form of Government, and shall protect each of them against

[10] superseded by the Thirteenth Amendment

Invasion; and on Application of the Legislature, or of the Executive (when the Legislature cannot be convened) against domestic Violence.

Article. V.

The Congress, whenever two thirds of both Houses shall deem it necessary, shall propose Amendments to this Constitution, or, on the Application of the Legislatures of two thirds of the several States, shall call a Convention for proposing Amendments, which, in either Case, shall be valid to all Intents and Purposes, as Part of this Constitution, when ratified by the Legislatures of three fourths of the several States, or by Conventions in three fourths thereof, as the one or the other Mode of Ratification may be proposed by the Congress; Provided that no Amendment which may be made prior to the Year One thousand eight hundred and eight shall in any Manner affect the first and fourth Clauses in the Ninth Section of the first Article; and that no State, without its Consent, shall be deprived of its equal Suffrage in the Senate.

Article. VI.

All Debts contracted and Engagements entered into, before the Adoption of this Constitution, shall be as valid against the United States under this Constitution, as under the Confederation.

This Constitution, and the Laws of the United States which shall be made in Pursuance thereof; and all Treaties made, or which shall be made, under the Authority of the United States, shall be the supreme Law of the Land; and the Judges in every State shall be bound thereby, any Thing in the Constitution or Laws of any State to the Contrary notwithstanding.

The Senators and Representatives before mentioned, and the Members of the several State Legislatures, and all executive and judicial Officers, both of the United States and of the several States, shall be bound by Oath or Affirmation, to support this Constitution; but no religious Test shall ever be required as a Qualification to any Office or public Trust under the United States.

Article. VII.

The Ratification of the Conventions of nine States, shall be sufficient for the Establishment of this Constitution between the States so ratifying the Same.

Done in Convention by the Unanimous Consent of the States present the Seventeenth Day of September in the Year of our Lord one thousand seven hundred and Eighty seven and of the Independence of the United States of

America the Twelfth In Witness whereof We have hereunto subscribed our Names,

Go. Washington—
Presidt. and deputy from Virginia

New Hampshire
John Langdon
Nicholas Gilman

Massachusetts
Nathaniel Gorham
Rufus King

Connecticut
Wm. Saml. Johnson
Roger Sherman

New York
Alexander Hamilton

New Jersey
Wil: Livingston
David Brearley
Wm. Paterson
Jona: Dayton

Pennsylvania
B Franklin
Thomas Mifflin
Robt. Morris
Geo. Clymer
Thos. FitzSimons
Jared Ingersoll
James Wilson
Gouv Morris

Delaware
Geo: Read
Gunning Bedford jun
John Dickinson
Richard Bassett
Jaco: Broom

Maryland
James McHenry
Dan of St Thos. Jenifer
Danl. Carroll

Virginia
John Blair—
James Madison Jr.

North Carolina
Wm. Blount
Richd. Dobbs Spaight
Hu Williamson

South Carolina
J. Rutledge
Charles Cotesworth Pinckney
Charles Pinckney
Pierce Butler

Georgia
William Few
Abr Baldwin

Attest William Jackson Secretary

AMENDMENTS TO THE CONSTITUTION OF THE UNITED STATES OF AMERICA

Amendment I.

Ratified December 15, 1791

Congress shall make no law respecting an establishment of religion, or prohibiting the free exercise thereof; or abridging the freedom of speech, or of the press; or the right of the people peaceably to assemble, and to petition the Government for a redress of grievances.

Amendment II.

Ratified December 15, 1791

A well regulated Militia, being necessary to the security of a free State, the right of the people to keep and bear Arms, shall not be infringed.

Amendment III.

Ratified December 15, 1791

No Soldier shall, in time of peace be quartered in any house, without the consent of the Owner, nor in time of war, but in a manner to be prescribed by law.

Amendment IV.

Ratified December 15, 1791

The right of the people to be secure in their persons, houses, papers, and effects, against unreasonable searches and seizures, shall not be violated, and no Warrants shall issue, but upon probable cause, supported by Oath or affirmation, and particularly describing the place to be searched, and the persons or things to be seized.

Amendment V.

Ratified December 15, 1791

No person shall be held to answer for a capital, or otherwise infamous crime, unless on a presentment or indictment of a Grand Jury, except in cases arising in the land or naval forces, or in the Militia, when in actual service in time of War or public danger; nor shall any person be subject for the same offence to be twice put in jeopardy of life or limb, nor shall be compelled in any criminal case to be a witness against himself, nor be deprived of life, liberty, or property, without due process of law; nor shall private property be taken for public use, without just compensation.

Amendment VI.

Ratified December 15, 1791

In all criminal prosecutions, the accused shall enjoy the right to a speedy and public trial, by an impartial jury of the State and district wherein the crime shall have been committed, which district shall have been previously ascertained by law, and to be informed of the nature and cause of the accusation; to be confronted with the witnesses against him; to have compulsory process for obtaining witnesses in his favor, and to have the assistance of counsel for his defence.

Amendment VII.

Ratified December 15, 1791

In Suits at common law, where the value in controversy shall exceed twenty dollars, the right of trial by jury shall be preserved, and no fact tried by a jury, shall be otherwise reexamined in any Court of the United States, than according to the rules of the common law.

Amendment VIII.

Ratified December 15, 1791

Excessive bail shall not be required, nor excessive fines imposed, nor cruel and unusual punishments inflicted.

Amendment IX.

Ratified December 15, 1791

The enumeration in the Constitution, of certain rights, shall not be construed to deny or disparage others retained by the people.

Amendment X.

Ratified December 15, 1791

The powers not delegated to the United States by the Constitution, nor prohibited by it to the States, are reserved to the States respectively, or to the people.

Appendix F: Study Questions

For each of the Documents in this collection, we suggest below in section A questions relevant for that document alone and in Section B questions that require comparison between documents.

1. Virginia Declaration of Rights and Constitution (June 12 and 29, 1776)

A. Does it seem curious that a) the Virginia Declaration and the Virginia Constitution were written two weeks apart and that b) both preceded the passage of the Declaration of Independence? According to these two documents, what is the purpose of government? What is the role of the legislature, executive, and judiciary in the newly adopted Virginia Constitution? What sort of "republicanism" do these two documents express? Is it surprising that the Virginia Bill of Rights precedes the Virginia Constitution?

B. By what authority was the Virginia Declaration of Rights and Constitution initiated and adopted? Compare and contrast the Virginia authorization with other authorizations during the Founding period. See Documents 2, 3, 5, 12, and Appendices D and E.

2. Jefferson's Draft of The Declaration of Independence (July 2 – 4, 1776)

A. Does Jefferson's original draft of the Declaration convey a substantially different meaning from that of the document the Continental Congress signed? Would the less moderate tone of the draft have communicated a different message to the audience outside of America? To American loyalists and those uncertain whether to join the revolution? Is it likely that the explicit condemnation of slavery would have changed the conversation about slavery at the Founding or during the next eighty years?

B. Who or what is the authorization for the Declaration? Is there a parallel between the complaints listed in the Declaration and the rights to be secured by the Virginia Declaration of Rights? See Documents 1 and 3; also consider Madison's comments in Document 4.

3. Articles of Confederation (1781)

A. Is there a central contradiction at the heart of the Articles, given that the union is supposed to be perpetual, "a firm league of friendship," yet the powers of the union are "expressly delegated?" Is there a separation of powers under the Articles? Why is it significant that the delegates sign the document?

B. What is the status of the states under the Articles? How is the union to operate under the Articles? What is the difference between a confederation/federation and a national government with respect to: a) the structure of the institutions and b) the powers of the union? Compare the Articles to the Virginia Plan (Document 6), the New Jersey Plan (Document 8), and the solution proposed by Oliver Ellsworth in Document 9.

4. "Vices of the Political System of the United States" (April 1787)

A. Why does Madison argue that the very structure of the Articles of Confederation needs to be altered? What is Madison's case against the traditional small republic and how does that argument assist in his critique of the inadequacies of the Confederation?

B. Madison's critique of the Articles does not assume that republican government will necessarily be supported by the virtue of the governed. How does this critique anticipate the Virginia Plan (Document 5) and the Hamilton Plan (Document 8)? How does it anticipate his argument in Federalist 10?

5. The Virginia Plan

A. Do the states have any significant role under the Virginia Plan? The Virginia Plan on the one hand seems to place principle responsibility for governing in the national legislature; but at the same time, the proposed Council of Revision seems to tilt the balance of power toward the executive and the judiciary. Is there a tension at the heart of the Virginia Plan?

B. In what way is the Virginia Plan a radical departure from the Articles of Confederation? How is its vision of republicanism similar to, or different from, earlier and later statements of representative government? Compare it to the Virginia Declaration of Rights and Constitution (Document 1), the New Jersey Plan (Document 7), the Hamilton Plan (Document 8) and Madison's account of representative government in Federalist 10 (Document 20).

6. Introducing a Fateful Compromise: A Debate on Property and the Revised Virginia Plan (June 11th and 13th, 1787)

A. Is the South Carolina delegates' argument that "property" should be represented in republican government supported by real concerns about the financial challenges facing the new republic? What are the weaknesses in the South Carolina delegates' argument? Why does Madison record the vote in favor of the three-fifths compromise without comment?

B. Is the Revised Virginia Plan pretty much the same as the original Virginia Plan? See Document 5. Is there support in other founding documents for the representation of "property" in republican government? See Document 2 and Appendix D.

7. Return to Starting Point: New Jersey Plan (June 15, 1787)

A. How are we to interpret Dickinson's remark that it was Madison's unwillingness to compromise that brought about this breakdown in negotiations?

B. Is the New Jersey Plan pretty much the same as the Articles of Confederation? See Document 3. Where does the three-fifths clause fit into the New Jersey Plan and the revised Virginia plan (Document 6)? Can we say that these two documents make it clear that the key debate is between the small states and the large states?

8. The Hamilton Plan (June 18, 1787)

A. Hamilton suggests that his plan is still within the proper sphere of both republicanism and federalism rather than a reformulation of monarchy and nationalism. Does his plan support his claim? Do the states have any role under his plan? Has he elevated the Presidency to a position of more importance than the Governors of the States?

B. Compare and contrast Hamilton's position on the separation of powers with that found in the Virginia Plan, the New Jersey Plan, and the Committee of Detail Report. See Documents 5, 7, and 12.

9. Partly National, Partly Federal (June 29 and 30, 1787)

A. When Ellsworth argues here on behalf of equal representation of the States in the Senate, is he offering a principled compromise? Is Madison's argument that the great divide in American politics is the issue of slavery persuasive? How does the three-fifths clause become part of the discussion of representation? What role did Madison and Sherman play in response to the introduction of the three-fifths clause?

B. How is this discussion over the "partly national, partly federal" character of the union similar to and different from earlier and later discussions of the issue of federal representation? When Sherman argued earlier (in Document 6) on behalf of equal representation of the States in the Senate, was he arguing from principle? How does the debate on June 29 and 30 influence the later discussion of the three-fifths clause? See Documents 3, 5 - 8, 11, and 12.

10. The Gerry Committee Report (July 2 and 5, 1787)

A. Students of the American Founding are usually introduced to the partly national/partly federal nature of the Constitution through reading Federalist 39. In that essay, it is not completely clear where Madison (writing as Publius) stands on the five tests of federalism and nationalism to which he subjects the Constitution. At the Convention, Madison argues that the partly national/partly federal solution is unprincipled; what is his argument? Who at the Constitutional Convention understood the partly national/partly federal solution to rise to the level of principle, albeit a newly discovered principle? What kind of compromise is a 5-4-1 vote with 3 absent?

B. Reflect on the "dynamics" of the Convention between May 28 and the Report of the Gerry Committee. Who has "won," and who has "lost" – or has everyone actually won by the time we get to July 16? See Documents 5 - 9 and 11.

11. The Three-Fifths Clause Revisited (July 11, 12, 13, 14 and 16, 1787)

A. Is it surprising that the South Carolina delegates want to count slaves as "five-fifths" of a person? Do they offer any logical grounds for this position? Why is the three-fifths clause embedded in a discussion about the "scheme of representation" appropriate for a federal republic?

B. Do the arguments between July 11 and 16 on the representation of people, states, and wealth mirror and flesh out the discussions on June 11, June 29, and June 30, or do they break new ground? See Documents 6 and 9.

12. The Committee of Detail Report (July 23, 24, and August 6, 1787)

A. From which states were the five delegates chosen? Does this matter? What strikes you as novel, and what as traditional, in this draft of the Constitution? Were there any changes made to the Connecticut Compromise that settled the structural or representative question? How does the Committee of Detail propose that the Constitution be adopted and altered?

B. Compare and contrast the powers of Congress listed in the Committee of Detail Report with the powers of Congress found in the Articles of Confederation (Document 3), the Virginia Plan (Document 5), the Revised Virginia Plan (Document 6), the New Jersey Plan (Document 7), and the final Constitution (Appendix D).

13. The Slave Trade Clause (August 21, 22, 24, and 25, 1787)

A. In what way did the Committee of Eleven alter the Report of the Committee of Detail concerning the slave trade? Who was on that Committee who wasn't on the Committee of Detail? Did the delegates who voted against the 1808 compromise want a date of "never" or of 1800?

B. Why did it take until the end of August to consider the slave trade clause? Does this clause resolve issues raised by Sections 4, 5 and 6 of Article VII of the Committee of Detail Report (Document 12)? How does the Fugitive Slave Clause (Document 14) temper our understanding of the Founders' expectation that the institution of slavery would end?

14. The Fugitive Slave Clause (July 14, August 6, 28, 29, September 12, 15, and 17, 1787)

A. What is the significance of the change in language from "justly" to "legally" to "under the laws thereof"? Why is the Fugitive Slave Clause located right under the Extradition Clause in the Constitution? Is there a significant difference between the language of the Fugitive Slave Clause and the Extradition Clause?

B. Do the fugitive slave clause and the three-fifths clause (Document 11) contradict the claim in the Declaration of Independence that all men are created equal? How do the discussions of these provisions in the Constitutional Convention address that question? What do the inclusion of these clauses and the inclusion of the ban on the slave trade (Document 13) tell us about the relationship between the Declaration and the Constitution?

15. Gerry, Mason, and Randolph Decline to Sign the Constitution (September 10, 12, 15, and 17, 1787)

A. Do Randolph, Gerry, and Mason have similar reasons for declining to sign the Constitution? Do they share a central concern about the Constitution? Other delegates had reservations, yet they still signed; do Randolph, Gerry and Mason expect a kind of perfection that would have been impossible? Or does their dissent demonstrate an admirable feature of the American experiment?

B. Prior to this point, other delegates have dissented to decisions made during the 88 days of the Constitutional Convention. See, for example, Patterson's introduction of the New Jersey Plan (Document 7), Sherman's objection to the Virginia plan for representation in the Senate (Document 6), Hamilton's introduction of his own plan (Document 8), and Madison's refusal to vote for the Connecticut Compromise (Documents 9 and 10). Does it strike you as a bit odd that Randolph, who introduced and defended the Virginia Plan, objected to signing the Constitution? What is so different about these three dissents from other objections? Compare, also, Jefferson's objections to the new Constitution (Document 24) to those of Gerry, Mason, and Randolph.

16. Centinel I (October 5, 1787)

A. What is it about the new Constitution that leads Centinel to argue that it contains the potentiality for a "permanent aristocracy"? Does he suggest a solution to this great difficulty?

B. Compare the remarks of Centinel with those made by Brutus (Document 17) and Publius (Documents 19 and 20) concerning the principles of the Constitution. How does Centinel's argument about the need for virtue in a republican people contrast with Madison's argument in *Federalist* 51 (Document 21)?

17. Brutus I (October 18, 1787)

A. Does Brutus make a strong case for the momentousness of the choice facing Americans? For example, is the appeal to the wisdom of Montesquieu and the experience of history persuasive? With which powers of the new government is Brutus here especially concerned? Why does Brutus believe that a republic as large as the one proposed by the Constitution will lead to tyranny?

B. Compare and contrast Brutus' arguments with those of Publius concerning 1) what is at stake in Federalist 1 (Document 18), 2) the status of Montesquieu – in Federalist 9 (Document 19), and 3) the case for the extended republic in Federalist 10 (Document 20).

18. Federalist 1 (October 27, 1787)

A. Publius opens Federalist 1 by raising the momentousness of the choice that lay before New Yorkers and the American people as a whole. What is it about "deliberation and choice" that Hamilton urges Americans to take seriously? Why is it critically important for Americans to ratify the Constitution? If Americans fail to choose well in the ratification process, what will they have proven to the world and their posterity? Why does Hamilton expect strong opposition to the Constitution from some Americans?

B. Do Brutus and Publius adequately summarize the choice facing the American people? What do each need to expand on or express more fully in the coming months of debate? Do you agree that the Antifederalists are in favor of disunion? See Documents 17, 19, and 20.

19. Federalist 9 (November 21, 1787)

A. Which parts of the improved science of politics were wholly unknown to the ancients and which were inadequately understood? Is Montesquieu part of the ancient world as far as Publius is concerned?

B. Is Publius saying that the interpretation of Montesquieu by the Antifederalists is: a) wrong or b) irrelevant? Compare Federalist 9 with Centinel I (Document16) and Brutus I (Document 17).

20. Federalist 10 (November 22, 1787)

A. What does Madison mean by "faction"? What are the causes of faction? What is wrong with eliminating the causes of faction? Why is so little time spent on minority faction in Federalist 10? How does Publius define a republic? Why is an extended territory such an important element in Madison's coverage of faction?

B. How does Publius' argument in Federalist 10 compare and contrast with that of Brutus I (Document 17)?

21. Federalist 51 (February 6, 1788)

A. According to Publius, what is the best way, in practice, to keep the powers of government properly separated among the branches? Why is framing a good government made difficult by human nature? What are the two possible sources of oppression and what remedies does Madison propose to prevent them?

B. Compare the argument in Federalist 51 about the great difficulty of founding a government with the argument of Brutus I (Document 17) and the arguments of Publius in Federalist 9 and 10 (Documents 19 and 20).

22. Brutus XV (March 20, 1788)

A. Why does Brutus think that the Supreme Court is the most dangerous branch?

B. Compare and contrast the case made by Brutus that the Supreme Court is the most dangerous branch with the case made by Publius in Federalist 78 (Document 23) that the Supreme Court is the least dangerous branch.

23. Federalist 78 (May 28, 1788)

A. Why does Publius think that the judiciary is the least dangerous branch? Does he make the case for what we today would call judicial review? According to Publius, why is it safe to grant life tenure to federal judges?

B. Compare Publius' defense of the Judiciary with the critique presented in Brutus XV (Document 22).

24. The Jefferson-Madison Exchange (December 20, 1787 - March 15, 1789)

A. Did either Madison or Jefferson change his mind about a bill of rights as a result of this exchange? Do they approach the question with the same or with different priorities in mind? In the end, do they agree or disagree on the centrality of a bill of rights to securing republican liberty?

B. Between his exchange of letters with Jefferson and his June 8 speech to Congress (Document 26), how did Madison's views on the need for a bill of rights develop? Compare the Jefferson-Madison exchange over the inclusion of a bill of rights that is consistent with the Constitution drafted by the Framers with Madison's June 8 speech to Congress and Washington's First Inaugural Address. See Documents 24 and 25.

25. George Washington's First Inaugural Address (April 30, 1789)

A. What is the "conflict in emotions" to which Washington refers? Beyond expressing his personal feelings at this moment, does this portion of the speech serve any public purpose? Why does Washington refer to "the invisible hand," "providential agency" and "the propitious smiles of Heaven" at the beginning of his presidency? Does this language serve a public purpose?

B. Compare Washington's comment on the "preservation of the sacred fire of liberty" to the opening paragraph of Federalist 1 (Document 19). Compare this speech also with Madison's June 8, 1789 speech to the First Congress. See Document 25.

26. James Madison Argues for Constitutional Amendments (June 8, 1789)

A. What is Madison's case for the adoption of a bill of rights? Why does he prefer to insert these rights into the text of the new Constitution?

B. Compare Madison's case here for a bill of rights with his exchange with Jefferson. Are there any surprises in his list of 39 rights? How does his list of rights compare to those enumerated in the Virginia Declaration of Rights (Document 1)? To what extent do the 39 amendments he proposes answer the objections of Gerry, Mason, and Randolph, the three delegates to the convention who refused to sign the Constitution (Document 15)? To what extent does Madison's list of rights answer the objections of Centinel I (Document 16)?

Appendix G: Suggestions For Further Reading

Allen, W. B., ed. *George Washington: A Collection.* Indianapolis: Liberty Classics, 1988.

Banning, Lance. *Jefferson and Madison.* Madison, WI: Madison House, 1995.

Beeman, Richard. *Plain, Honest Men: The Making of the American Constitution.* New York: Random House, 2009.

Bloom, Sol. *History of the Formation of the Union Under the Constitution.* Washington, DC: Government Printing Office. 1937.

Bowen, Catherine Drinker. *Miracle at Philadelphia.* New York: Little, Brown and Company, 1966.

Brant, Irving. *James Madison: Father of the Constitution, 1787-1800.* Indianapolis: Bobbs-Merrill Company, 1950.

Cogan, Neil H., ed. *The Complete Bill of Rights: The Drafts, Debates, Sources, and Origins.* Oxford: Oxford University Press, 1997.

Commager, Henry Steele, ed. *Documents of American History.* New York: Appleton-Century-Crofts, 1968.

Conley, Patrick T., and John P. Kaminski, eds. *The Constitution and the States: The Role of the Original Thirteen in the Framing and Adoption of the Constitution.* Madison, WI: Madison House, 1988.

Conley, Patrick T, and John P. Kaminski, eds. *The Bill of Rights and the States: The Colonial and Revolutionary Origins of American Liberties.* Madison: Madison House, 1992.

Elliot, Jonathan, ed. *The Debates in the Several State Conventions on the Adoption of the Federal Constitution.* 5 vols. Philadelphia: J.B. Lippencott Company, 1836.

Ferris, Robert, ed. *Signers of the Constitution.* Washington, DC: National Park Service, 1976.

Ford, Paul Leicester, ed. *Pamphlets on the Constitution of the United States.* New York: Da Capo Press, 1968.

Ford, W. C., ed. *Journals of the Continental Congress: 1774-1789.* Washington, DC: Government Printing Office, 1904.

Gales, Joseph, Sr., ed. *Annals of Congress.* Washington, DC: Government Printing Office, 1834.

Hening, W. W., ed. *Statutes at Large.* Richmond: George Cochran, 1823.

Hunt, Gaillard, ed. *The Writings of James Madison.* New York: G.P. Putman's Sons, 1900-1910.

Hutchinson, William T., et al, eds. *The Papers of James Madison.* 17 vols. Chicago: University of Chicago Press; Charlottesville: University of Virginia Press, 1962-91.

Hyneman, Charles S., and Donald S. Lutz, eds. *American Political Writings During the Founding Era.* 2 vols. Indianapolis: Liberty Press, 1985.

Kurland, Philip B., and Ralph Lerner, eds. *The Founders' Constitution.* 5 vols. Chicago: University of Chicago Press, 1987.

Jensen, Merrill, ed. *Documentary History of the Ratification of the Constitution.* Madison: State Historical Society of Wisconsin, 1976.

Lloyd, Gordon and Margie Lloyd, eds. *The Essential Bill of Rights.* Lanham, Maryland: University Press of America, 1998.

Lloyd, Gordon, ed. *Debates in the Federal Convention of 1787 by James Madison, a Member.* Ashland, Ohio: Ashbrook Center, 2014.

Labunski, Richard. *James Madison and the Struggle for the Bill of Rights.* Oxford: Oxford University Press, 2006.

Maier, Pauline. *Ratification: The People Debate the Constitution, 1787-1788.* New York: Simon and Schuster, 2010.

Main, Jackson Turner. *The Antifederalists: Critics of the Constitution, 1781-1788.* Chicago: Quadrangle Books, 1961.

McDonald, Forrest. *E Pluribus Unum: The Formation of the American Republic, 1776-1790.* Indianapolis: Liberty Fund: 1979.

McMaster, John B., and Frederick Stone, eds. *Pennsylvania and the Federal Constitution, 1787-1788.* Lancaster, PA: The Historical Society of Pennsylvania, 1888.

Morris, Richard B. *Witness at the Creation.* New York: New American Library, 1985.

Rossiter, Clinton. *1787: The Grand Convention.* New York: The New American Library, 1966.

Rutland, Robert Allen, et al, eds. *The Papers of James Madison.* Chicago: University of Chicago Press, 1975.

Rutland, Robert Allen. *The Ordeal of the Constitution: The Antifederalists and the Ratification Struggle of 1787-1788.* Boston: Northeastern University Press, 1983.

Rutland, Robert Allen. *The Birth of the Bill of Rights, 1776-1791.* Boston: Northeastern University Press, 1983.

Schechter, Stephen L. and Richard Bernstein, eds. *The Contexts of the Bill of Rights.* Albany, New York: New York State Commission on the Bicentennial of the Constitution, 1990.

Stewart, David O. *The Men Who Invented the Constitution.* New York: Simon and Schuster, 2007.

Storing, Herbert, ed. *The Complete Anti-Federalist.* 7 vols. Chicago: University of Chicago Press, 1981.

Stryett, Harold and Jacob Cooke, eds. *The Papers of Alexander Hamilton.* 27 vols. New York: Columbia University Press, 1961-1987.

Swindler, William F., ed. *Sources and Documents of United States Constitutions.* Dobbs Ferry, NY: Oceana Publications, 1973.

Tansill, Charles. *Documents Illustrative of the Formation of the Union of the United States.* Washington, DC: Government Printing Office, 1927.

Thorpe, F.N., ed. *The Federal and State Constitutions.* 7 vols. Washington, DC: Government Printing Office, 1909.

Van Doren, Charles. *The Great Rehearsal.* New York: Penguin Books, 1986.

Veit, Helen, Kenneth Bowling, and Charles Bangs Bickford, eds. *Creating the Bill of Rights: The Documentary Record of the First Federal Congress.* Baltimore: The Johns Hopkins Press, 1991.

Vile, John R. *The Writing and Ratification of the U.S. Constitution.* Lanham, Maryland: Rowman and Littlefield, 2012.

Vile, John R. *The Men Who Made The Constitution.* Lanham, Maryland: Scarecrow Press, 2013.

Wood, Gordon S. *The Creation of the American Republic, 1776-1787.* Williamsburg, VA: Institute of Early American History and Culture, 1969.